Oral and Written
African Poetry and Poetics
AFRICAN LITERATURE TODAY 42

Editor Ernest N. Emenyonu

🔘 JAMES CURREY

GUIDELINES FOR SUBMISSIONS

The Editor invites submission of articles on the announced themes of forthcoming issues. Submissions will be acknowledged promptly and decisions communicated within six months of the receipt of the paper. Your name and institutional affiliation (with full mailing address and email) should appear on a separate sheet, plus a brief biographical profile of not more than six lines. The editor cannot undertake to return materials submitted, and contributors are advised to keep a copy of any material sent. Articles should be submitted in the English Language. Articles are reviewed blindly, so do not insert your name, institutional affiliation and contact information on the article itself. Instead, provide such information on a separate page.

Please avoid footnotes or endnotes.

Do not quote directly from the Internet without properly citing the source as you would when quoting from a book. Use substantive sources for obtaining your information and depend less on general references.

If your article is accepted for publication, we will require a short (max 50-word) biography for the Notes on Contributors at the front of the volume.

Length: Articles should not exceed 5,000 words.

Format: Articles should be double-spaced, and should use 12pt Times New Roman.

Citations: Limit your sources to the most recent, or the most important books and journals, in English. Cite works in foreign languages only when no English-language books are available. Cite websites only if they are relatively permanent and if they add important information unavailable elsewhere: give both a publication date, and an access date.

Style: UK or US spellings are acceptable, but must be used consistently. Direct quotations should retain the spellings used in the original source. Check the accuracy of citations and always give the author's surname and page number in the text, and a full reference in the Works Cited list at the end of the article. Use single inverted commas throughout except for quotes within quotes which are double. Avoid subtitles or sub-section headings within the text.

Italicize titles of books, plays and journals. Put in single quotes titles of short stories, journal articles and titles of poems.

Please follow the ALT Guideline for Submissions and Style Guide: https://boydelland brewer.com/james-currey-current-authors/.

Copyright: It is the responsibility of contributors to clear permissions for both text and any illustrations used, which should be b/w only. Please note, however, that ALT does not republish chapters or articles that were previously published elsewhere.

All articles should be sent to the editor, Ernest N. Emenyonu, as an e-mail attachment (Word): eernest@umich.edu,
African Literature Today,
Department of Africana Studies,
University of Michigan-Flint,
303 East Kearsley Street,
Flint MI 48502, USA.

Books for review to be sent to the Reviews Editor:
Obi Nwakanma, University of Central Florida,
English Department,
Colburn Hall,
12790 Aquarius Agora Drive,
Orlando, FL 32816, USA
Obi.Nwakanma@ucf.edu

AFRICAN LITERATURE TODAY

For details of all previous volumes please go to www.boydellandbrewer.com.

ALT 26 War in African Literature Today
ALT 27 New Novels in African Literature Today
ALT 28 Film in African Literature Today
ALT 29 Teaching African Literature Today
ALT 30 Reflections & Retrospectives in African Literature Today
ALT 31 Writing Africa in the Short Story
ALT 32 Politics & Social Justice
ALT 33 Children's Literature & Story-telling
ALT 34 Diaspora & Returns in Fiction
ALT 35 Focus on Egypt
ALT 36 Queer Theory in Film & Fiction
ALT 37
ALT 38 Environmental Transformations
ALT 39 Speculative & Science Fiction
ALT 40 African Literature Comes of Age
ALT 41 African Literature in African Languages

Oral and Written African Poetry and Poetics

AFRICAN LITERATURE TODAY 42

EDITORIAL BOARD

Editor: *Ernest Emenyonu*
University of Michigan-Flint

Deputy Editor: *Isidore Diala*
Imo State University

Assistant Editor: *Patricia T. Emenyonu*
University of Michigan-Flint

Associate Editors: *Adélékè Adéẹ̀kọ́*
Ohio State University

Ernest Cole
Hope College, Holland, Michigan

Pauline Dodgson-Katiyo
Anglia Ruskin University

Louisa Uchum Egbunike
Durham University

Akachi Ezeigbo
Alex Ekwueme Federal University, Abakiliki

Cajetan Iheka
Yale University

Susan Kiguli
Makerere University, Uganda

Madhu Krishnan
University of Bristol

Grace Musila
University of the Witwatersrand, South Africa

Stephanie Newell
Yale University

Iniobong I. Uko
University of Uyo

Reviews Editor: *Obi Nwakanma*
University of Central Florida

© Contributors 2024

All Rights Reserved. Except as permitted under current legislation
no part of this work may be photocopied, stored in a retrieval system,
published, performed in public, adapted, broadcast, transmitted,
recorded or reproduced in any form or by any means, without the
prior permission of the copyright owner

First published 2024

James Currey
James Currey is an imprint of Boydell & Brewer Ltd
PO Box 9, Woodbridge, Suffolk IP12 3DF, UK
www.jamescurrey.com
and of Boydell & Brewer Inc.
668 Mt Hope Avenue, Rochester, NY 14620-2731, USA
www.boydellandbrewer.com

ISBN 978-1-84701-391-0

A CIP catalogue record for this book is available from the British Library

The publisher has no responsibility for the continued existence or accuracy of URLs
for external or third-party internet websites referred to in this book, and does not
guarantee that any content on such websites is, or will remain, accurate or appropriate.

Contents

Notes on Contributors   xi

EDITORIAL ARTICLE

Oral and Written African Poetry and Poetics   2
ERNEST EMENYONU

ARTICLES

A New Frontier for African Heroic Saga:
The Sahara Testaments by Tade Ipadeola   8
KOFI ANYIDOHO

Nigeria's Instapoetry: Cultivating Inward, Ideological Activism,
Revitalizing African Orality and Re-defining the Art of Poetry   21
OLUWAFUMILAYO AKINPELU

A New Direction in Contemporary Nigerian Poetry:
The Pandemic Poems of Tanure Ojaide and Kola Eke   37
OGAGA OKUYADE & EDAFE MUKORO

History and the Call of Water in Romeo Oriogun's 'Nomad'   50
IQUO DIANAABASI

Voice, Identity, Tradition in Postcolonial Modernism: T. S. Eliot
and Kofi Anyidoho from the Perspectives of Posthumanism and
Post-Deconstruction   59
MILENA VLADIĆ JOVANOV

Personal Reflections on Niyi Osundare, Oríkì Praise Tradition,
and the Journey Motif in *If Only the Road Could Talk*   75
ADETAYO ALABI

Lost and Gained in Translation: Navigating the Contours
of Kofi Anyidoho's Bilingual Poetry   89
MAWULI ADJEI

viii *Contents*

Poetry and Performance: The Spoken Word Poetry as a
Reincarnation of African Oral literary Tradition 106
PARAMITA ROUTH ROY

INTERVIEWS

ALT Interview with Prof. Kofi Anyidoho – Scholar, Critic, and
Award-Winning Poet 118
ERNEST EMENYONU, CHIJI AKOMA, AKACHI EZEIGBO,
OBI NWAKANMA, ROSE SACKEYFIO, CHINYERE EZEKWESILI,
AND IQUO DIANA ABASI

Interview With Kwame Dawes 128
KADIJA GEORGE

(Re)Echoing a Collective Trauma in Nigerian Poetry:
An Interview with Kehinde Akano 139
ADEWUYI AREMU AYODEJI

TRIBUTES

Ama Ata Aidoo: Ghana's Literary Treasure:
A Tribute to Ama Ata Aidoo (23 March 1940 – 31 May 2023) 148
ROSE A. SACKEYFIO

I Mourn Ama Ata Aidoo, the Author of 'A Woman must
be Foolish for a Marriage to Work, though a bad Marriage
Destroys the Soul'. A Tribute to Ama Ata Aidoo (23 March
1940 – 31 May 2023) 154
ALEXANDER OPICHO

LITERARY SUPPLEMENT

THREE POEMS

'A Memorial for KAMAU BRATHWAITE': 'An Africa –
Africa Diaspora Dialogue' 160
'For Willie Keorapetse Kgositsile' 162
'A Song for Nyidevu' 164
KOFI ANYIDOHO

'From Freedom to Free Doom' (Poem) 165
ADEMOLA ADESOLA

Contents **ix**

'To The Memory Of Aunty Toriomo' (Poem) 166
RACHEL OLUWAFISAYO ALUKO

'I Swallow Fufu' (Poem) 169
JEROME MASAMAKA

TWO POEMS

'No Door, No Roof' 171
'Bowls for Alms' 171
MARINUS YONG

TWO POEMS

'No peace' 173
'thE bEst tEachEr' 173
VICTOR TEMITOPE ALABI

'As I Watched Her Dying' (Poem) 174
ERNEST EMENYONU

SHORT STORIES

'The Mysterious Examination Paper' 176
IFEOMA OKOYE

'The Ignored' 182
MATRIDA PHIRI

REVIEWS

Salami–Agunloye (ed), *Retelling History: Restaging African
Women in Drama and Film* 196
CAROLYN NUR WISTRAND

Chika Unigwe, *The Middle Daughter* 200
ROSE SACKEYFIO

Ọmófọ́lábọ̀, Àjàyí Ṣóyinká and Naana Banyiwa Horne (eds.),
IMMIGRANT VOICES IN SHORT STORIES: 204
Health and Wellbeing of African Immigrants
in Transnational and Transformative Encounters & Spaces
ELIZABETH ONOGWU

x *Contents*

Yaw Agawu-kakraba, *The Restless Crucible*   209
NONYE AHUMIBE

Kofi Anyidoho, *SeedTIME*   211
MAWULI ADJEI

Isidore Diala, *The Truce*   214
IRENE ISOKEN AGUNLOYE

Irene Isoken Agunloye, *Disposable Womb*   217
INIOBONG UKO

Iquo Diana-Abasi, *Coming Undone as Stiches Tighten*   221
INIOBONG UKO

Notes on Contributors

Iquo Diana Abasi writes prose, poetry, and nonfiction. Her interests include the intersection of the environment, womanhood, and African cosmology. Her poetry collections, *Symphony of Becoming* (2013), and *Coming Undone as Stitches Tighten* (2022) have been nominated for the NLNG Nigeria prize for literature and other prizes. She is the author of *Ẹ̀fọ́ Rírò and Other Stories* (2020). Iquo edits the African speculative fiction magazine, omenana.com, and is presently a graduate student at The University of Alabama.

Ademola Adesola is an Assistant Professor at the Department of English, Languages, and Cultures, Mount Royal University, Canada. He completed his PhD at the University of Manitoba, Canada; and his MA and BA are from Obafemi Awolowo University, Nigeria. Ademola's research and teaching interests are postcolonial literatures, African/Black diaspora literatures, child soldier narratives, popular culture, and human rights issues. Ademola has published essays and book chapters on African literature and socio-political issues. His poems have appeared in different publications.

Mawuli Adjei is currently a post-retirement Senior Lecturer in Creative Writing, African and Postcolonial Literatures, Oral Literature, Poetry, and Popular Genres at the Department of English, University of Ghana, Legon. He is the author of *Testament of the Seasons* (poetry, 2011), *The Jewel of Kabibi* (novel, 2012), *The Witch of Lagbati* (novel, 2014), *Filaments* (poetry, 2019), *Bakudi's Ghost* (novel, 2019), and *Guilty as Charged* (short stories, 2019). His works have won him several awards, including the VALCO Trust Literary Award (poetry, 1996), GAW Atukwei Okai Poetry Prize (2018, 2019), GAW Ayi Kwei Armah Novel Prize (2019), and GAW Ama Ata Aidoo Short Story Prize (2019).

Oluwafumilayo Akinpelu is a PhD student of English Literature at the University of Alabama, a writer, and a collaborative interactive arts enthusiast with a self-published novel titled *Half Lives*. She earned her Master's Degree in Comparative (Literary) History at Central European University, and she obtained a BA in Literature-in-English from

xii Notes on Contributors

Obafemi Awolowo University. Her research interests include Nigerian contemporary literary history, futurisms, and feminisms, digital storytelling, as well as gendered visual, material, and (East Asian) popular cultures.

Adetayo Alabi is a Professor of English at the University of Mississippi. He teaches and researches literary theories, world literatures, and cultures, particularly postcolonial African, African American, and African Caribbean cultures. He is the author of numerous publications, including books titled *Oral Forms of Nigerian Autobiography and Life Stories* published by Routledge in 2022 and *Telling Our Stories: Continuities and Divergences in Black Autobiographies* published by Palgrave in 2005.

Victor Temitope Alabi obtained his PhD in African Linguistics from Indiana University. He is a Visiting Lecturer at the Center for Language Studies in the Department of World Languages and Cultures at Brown University. He is also a Faculty Affiliate of the Watson Institute for International and Public Affairs as well as the Linguistic Program at Brown University.

Rachel Oluwafisayo Aluko is a Lecturer at Lead City University Ibadan, Nigeria. She gained her PhD in European literature from the University of Ibadan, Nigeria, where she earlier obtained a Master's degree with focus on African literature in 2008. Her areas of interest include Comparative Literature, Gender Studies, Ecocriticism, and Literature and Sustainability, among others. She has published in different journals; *End of Service Year* is her short story published under the 2020 KANAC Digital Anthology Series. Her love for creative writing is mostly expressed in poetry.

Kofi Anyidoho, bilingual poet, literary scholar, educator, and cultural activist, has been Professor of Literature; Director of the CODESRIA African Humanities Institute Program; First Occupant of the Kwame Nkrumah Chair in African Studies; Ag. Director, School of Performing Arts, and Head of the English Department at the University of Ghana, Legon. He has lectured and performed his poetry in English and Ewe globally, published several books of poetry, journal articles, and book chapters, and edited major books on African literature and the humanities. He was President of the US-based African Literature Association (ALA); Fellow and past Vice President (Arts), Ghana Academy of Arts and Sciences (FGA); and Corresponding Fellow, Royal Society of Edinburgh (FRSE).

Notes on Contributors **xiii**

Adewuyi Aremu holds a BA (Ed.) in English and an MA in Literature-in-English, both from the University of Ilorin, Nigeria. He works at present with the Schools and Colleges Division, Kwara State Teaching Service Commission, Ilorin. He is a PhD student at the University of Ilorin. His research interests include Oral Literature, Contemporary Nigerian Drama and Poetry, Creative Writing, and Literary Trauma Criticism.

Kadija George is an independent researcher. She received her doctorate from Brighton University on Black British Publishers and Pan-Africanism (to be published by AWP) and an ECR fellowship from SAS in Inclusion, Participation. and Engagement. She is the cofounder of Mboka Festival of Arts Culture and the International Black Speculative Writing Festival. She has published her poetry collection *Irki* and is developing an app on African poetry, AfriPoeTree.

Jerome Masamaka is an academic and a poet, of Ghanaian origin, who now lives in Perth, Western Australia. He holds a PhD in Creative Writing. His collection of poems, *Under the Tattered Roof* (2023), laments recent incidents of climate change and celebrates those intriguing aspects of nature that humans can only standby and appreciate. His research interests include Environmental Literature and Postcolonial Literature.

Edafe Mukoro holds a PhD in English and Literature from the University of Benin, Nigeria. He lectures in English at JUPEB Foundation School, University of Benin, Nigeria.

Ifeoma Okoye is a veteran, versatile, and prolific writer, a novelist, short story writer, and writer of children's books. Author of several award winning novels, her *Behind the Clouds* (1983) and *Men Without Ears* (1984) distinguished her as one of the most incisive pioneer feminist authors in Nigeria. *Men Without Ears* won the Association of Nigerian Authors' (ANA) Best Fiction of the Year Award in 1984. It is widely read in schools and Colleges in Nigeria and beyond. *Behind the Clouds* won, in 1983, the Nigerian Festival of Arts' Fiction Prize and has since been translated into Amharic. Her other novels include, *Chimere* (1992) and *The Fourth World* (2013). Her Short Stories have been published in numerous international anthologies with highly acclaimed reviews. Her children's books have been popular and famous on both sides of the Atlantic. They include, *The Village Boy* (1978), winner of MacMillan's Children's Literature Prize in 1978, and *Chika's House* (1995), which has been translated into Kiswahili, Ndebele, and Shona.

xiv *Notes on Contributors*

Ogaga Okuyade is Professor of English and Dean, Faculty of Arts, Niger Delta University, Nigeria. He is widely published and teaches African Literature and Culture, Popular/Folk Culture, African-American and African Diaspora Studies, as well as the English Novel. He is the editor of the seminal book entitled *Eco-critical Literature: Regreening African Landscapes*.

Alexander Opicho is a poet, essayist, and literary critic, as well as a short story writer, from Kenya.

Matrida Phiri is a poet and short story writer based in Lusaka, Zambia, who was born in 1963. She holds a Bachelor's Degree in Biblical Studies and a Diploma in Creative Writing. Matrida works for an international NGO for children and has three adult daughters and a grandson. Two of her poems, *IMPOSED NUPTIALS* and *PEVERT* have been published in the November 2023 and February 2024 Editions of the Writers Space Africa magazine, respectively, and the International Human Rights Art Movement have accepted, for publication in their June edition, her poem *TRADITION*. In 2017 she self-published a memoir, *FROTH: My Battle with Low Self-Esteem*, which is available on Amazon in paperback form and as a Kindle e-book. In her spare time, she likes to read, write, and watch soccer with her family.

Paramita Routh Roy is an M.Phil. Research scholar at Jadavpur University, and is pursuing research on African Literature with special emphasis on Black Masculinity Studies. She is currently working as a faculty member in the Department of English at Sister Nivedita University, New Town. After completing her post-graduation from University of Calcutta, Ms Roy cleared the UGC-NET examination in 2019. She has specialized in Gender Studies, Harold Pinter's works, and Modern European Classics. Many of her research articles have been published in journals of national and international repute. Her contributions to Black Masculinity Studies have been recognized by the African Literature Association, and she is looking forward to her future collaborations with them. Her research interests include African Literature, Afro-American Literature, Urdu Literature, and Queer Studies.

Rose A. Sackeyfio teaches in the Department of Liberal Studies at Winston Salem State University. She is the author of *African Women Narrating Identity: Local and Global Journeys of the Self* (Routledge 2023) and *West African Women in the Diaspora: Narratives of Other Spaces, Other Selves* (Routledge, 2021). She is editor of a volume of critical essays, *Women Writing Diaspora in the 21st Century* (Lexington Books, 2021) and co-editor of *Emerging Perspectives on Akachi Adimora Ezeigbo* (Lexington Books, 2017).

Milena Vladić Jovanov is an Associate Professor of Philology in the Department of Comparative Literature and Literary Theory at the Faculty of Philology, University of Belgrade. Her research interests encompass contemporary literary theory, the relationship between philosophy and literature, interdisciplinary studies of film, media, and literature, avant-garde movements, Anglo-American poetry and prose, nineteenth-century prose, Humanism and the Renaissance, Modernism, and Poscolonialism. She explores the intersections of political thought, identity, and exile in various forms of narrative and poetry.

Marinus Yong is an Associate Professor of Translation and Literary Studies. He has over 60 publications to his credit. His interest in poetry has yielded fruit in the publication of two collections of poems in English, *Thirsty Land* (2011) and *Thorny Crown: Corona virus poems* (2020). Some of his poems have appeared in anthologies. He is a member of the University French Teachers' Association of Nigeria (UFTAN) and is the Secretary of the Board of Trustees of Alliance française, Enugu, Enugu State, Nigeria.

Editorial Article

Oral and Written African Poetry and Poetics

ERNEST EMENYONU

We are a nation of dancers, musicians, and poets. Thus every great event such as triumphant return from battle or other cause of public rejoicing is celebrated in public dances which are accompanied with songs and music suited to the occasion.

(Olaudah Equiano, *The Interesting Narrative…* (1789). Quoted by Isidore Okpewho, 1989:18)

This issue of *African Literature Today* (ALT 42) seeks to appraise crucial developments in the broad field of African poetry (written and oral) and poetics since the publication of its first and second special issues on poetry, ALT 6 (1973) and ALT 16 (1989), respectively. Titled *Poetry in Africa,* ALT 6 explored some of the prevailing subjects and debates of the period: primarily the resistance to Western cultural hegemony, the African poet's authentic sources of inspiration and poetics, the utilitarian purpose of poetry, and the tradition in which the work of an African poet ought to be anchored. The attention paid in the volume to both written and oral poetry makes a categorical statement of purpose, just as the representative body of poetry discussed virtually established the hegemonic faction of African poetry at that time, with the expected focus on the offerings of Leopold Sedar Senghor, Christopher Okigbo, Wole Soyinka, and Dennis Brutus. Sixteen years later, ALT 16, with the theme 'Oral and Written Poetry in African Literature Today', extended the frontiers of several critical issues raised in ALT 6, especially the kinship between African oral and written literatures, questions on poetics, and the social relevance of poetry. Moreover, Soyinka and Okigbo continue to dominate critical attention, and though Niyi Osundare and Isidore Okpewho appear in the volume, they do so as critics. In his lead article in the volume, 'African Poetry: The Modern Writer and the Oral Tradition', Okpewho framed precisely the focus, expectations, and challenges for modern African poets:

2

Oral and Written African Poetry and Poetics **3**

The one solid thing that has occurred with the colonial experience is the emergence of a different breed of poets who, having usurped from the traditional poet his time-honored role of giving both delight and education to the society, have found themselves locked within a medium and a context of ideas which lack much of that immediacy that ensured a bond between the traditional poet and his people. Some of the effort in contemporary (written) African poetry is geared toward recovering that traditional image of the poet. But there are severe problems and stresses… (1989:13)

Almost half a century after ALT 6 and thirty-three years after ALT 16, the question is what has changed and what is still focalized in African poetry and poetics? There is a compelling need to examine the field in considerable detail, with a view to highlighting major developments and continuities in the practice of the art of poetry in the continent. Are there national or even regional imperatives? Are there global movements that reverberate in the praxis of African poets? Are there continuities in the tradition(s) established by Africa's pioneer poets and the work of the younger generations, and between the oral indigenous traditions and contemporary written poetry? Who are currently Africa's foremost poets? Are there crucial innovations in the arts? Are the forces responsible for the increasing attention to eco-poetry and the like and the practice of the so-called 'spoken word poetry' internal or external? What nexus (if any) is there between Africa's oral poetic heritage and written poetry? Are there new themes in African written poetry? Are there innovations in African orality? What are the impacts of important literary prizes such as the 'Nigeria Literature Prize' (NLNG) on the development of African poetry? In a nutshell, what is the state of poetry and poetics in Africa today? These and many more questions could be raised about the trajectory of a field as broad as African poetry and poetics over the past several decades. Eight critical articles address these issues and questions from a variety of perspectives.

The lead article, 'A New Frontier for African Heroic Saga: *The Sahara Testaments* by Tade Ipadeola' (Winner of the 2013 Nigeria Prize for Literature) is by Kofi Anyidoho. He is a prominent literary scholar, celebrated poet, and authoritative veteran witness who straddles the field of African Poetry in both the twentieth and twenty-first centuries. He starts with an introduction that is illuminating and startling. He puts it this way:

…The epic grandeur we encounter in *The Sahara Testaments* is not limited to any one African nation or empire. It is anchored in a pan-

4 *Ernest Emenyonu*

African vision, from the dawn of history into the far future, with Africa herself as the epic heroic figure at the centre of the narrative. As readers, we may be challenged by the breathtaking expanse of the world and knowledge covered by *The Sahara Testaments*...

Anyidoho navigates African history and its precarious contours over time and concludes with a sublime message of hope despite humbling impediments: 'The Sahara Testaments is a work of rare creative genius, written to a competent technical polish, profound in its articulation of a bold vision for the African continent and for humanity at large.'

In 'Nigeria's Instapoetry: Cultivating Inward, Ideological Activism, Revitalizing African Orality and Re-defining the Art of Poetry', Oluwafumilayo Akinpelu engages unarguably uncharted areas, forms, and productions in contemporary Nigerian poetry. The opening statement is unequivocal – 'It is the twenty-first century, and poetry as we know it is changing. Poetry is going digital, and, due to its digitality, the rhetoric of orality, which, for a long time, seems to have been supplanted by verse and rhythm, is now being re-asserted as a core element of poetry.' This article adds an important dimension to discussions of Nigerian (and African) performance poetry and could have considerable impact on debates about orality as well as discussions about social media/digital genres in relation to histories of poetic 'literary activism' on the African continent.

In 'A New Direction in Contemporary Nigerian Poetry: The Pandemic Poems of Tanure Ojaide and Kola Eke', Ogaga Okuyade and Edafe Mukoro focus on the theme of the recent major pandemic in the works of two important and innovative Nigerian poets. The article is a refreshing and significant addition to African poetry and its criticism. The authors demonstrate a wealth of understanding of the imaginative and innovative creativity of Ojaide and Eke in their respective works.

Iquo Diana Abasi's 'History and the Call of Water in Romeo Oriogun's *Nomad*' situates Oriogun within a lineage of Nigerian poets who utilize water imagery in their works, particularly Christopher Okigbo and Gabriel Okara, and highlights their collective significance and influence on Oriogun.

In a different tone, and with different particularities and emphasis, Milena Vladic Jovanov demonstrates in 'Voice, Identity, Tradition in Postcolonial Modernism: T.S. Eliot and Kofi Anyidoho from the perspectives of Posthumanism and Post-Deconstruction', an interesting and incisive comparison of the practice of two poets across global geo-temporal axes.

Adetayo Alabi's 'Personal Reflections on Niyi Osundare, Oriki Praise Tradition and the Journey Motif in *If Only the Road Could Talk*', is rich with reflections on the author's travels with Osundare. The close reading of Osundare's poem 'Eko' is exquisite.

'Lost and Gained in Translation: Navigating the Contours of Kofi Anyidoho's Bilingual Poetry' is an important piece by Mawuli Adjei on the translation of poetry from Ewe language into English. He locates the act of translation as a culturally determined form of labour.

In the last of the articles, 'Poetry and Performance: The Spoken Word Poetry as a Reincarnation of African Oral Literary Tradition', Paramita Routh Roy demonstrates a good understanding of the historical process of the development of oral African poetry. The critical perspectives cited in support of the process are quite illuminating.

In addition to the articles, the volume has interviews with three poets: Kofi Anyidoho (by the ALT team), Kwame Dawes (by Kadija George), and Kehinde Akano (by Adewuyi Aremu). There are also two tributes by Rose Sackeyfio and Alexander Opicho, respectively, in memory of Ama Ata Aidoo. Besides these, there is a Literary Supplement consisting of poems by Kofi Anyidoho, Ademola Adesola, Rachel Oluwafisayo Aluko, Jerome Masamaka, Victor Temitope Alabi, and Ernest Emenyonu, as well as two short stories by Ifeoma Okoye and Matrida Phiri, respectively. Finally, the volume contains book reviews by Rose Sackeyfio, Elizabeth Onogwu, Nonye Ahumibe, Mawuli Adjei, Petrollina Kpanah, Irene Isoken Agunloye, and Iniobong Uko.

WORK CITED

Okpewho Isidore: 'African Poetry: The Modern Writer and the Oral Tradition' in *Oral and Written Poetry in African Literature Today* (eds.) Eldred Durosimi Jones, Eustace Palmer, and Marjorie Jones, James Currey, London / Africa World Press, Trenton, New Jersey, 1989.

Articles

A New Frontier for African Heroic Saga

The Sahara Testaments by Tade Ipadeola

KOFI ANYIDOHO

To fully appreciate the significance of Tade Ipadeola's *The Sahara Testaments* as a text that takes us to a new frontier for African Heroic Saga, it is important that we establish a brief update for studies on African epic traditions and various core epic texts that came into prominence prior to the publication of Ipadeola's work. Perhaps a good place to start is Ruth Finnegan's statement in *Oral Literature in Africa* (1970) expressing doubt about the existence of the epic in Africa. The statement came as a surprise to scholars and students of African oral literature, especially when we note that Finnegan's work is such a major scholarly work, widely praised as one of the most important books on oral literature in Africa, based on several years of fieldwork and archival research. It is however important to note that Finnegan's statement was based on the fact that, although she was aware of the existence of various texts referred to as epic, almost all of them failed to meet the most basic defining feature of epic. An epic is first and foremost poetry, whether orally performed or composed as a written text. The most readily available text of the Sundiata narrative, *Sundiata: An Epic of Old Mali*, published by historian D. T. Niane in French (1960) and translated into English (1965) by G. D. Pickett, was presented as a prose narrative. We could say the same thing about anthropologist Daniel Biebuyck's presentation of the Mwindo epic (See Okpewho 1980). Fortunately, it did not take too long for researchers with competence and interest in the technical and aesthetic dimensions of these oral texts to reveal the poetic nature of, say, the Sundiata and other epics in performance, especially with attention to the interface between the bard's narration and the defining regulative function of the musical accompaniment:

> Ultimately, the expected definitive comparative work will have to wait for many more reliable studies of individual traditions. A few of these are already available, among them *The Songs of Seydou Camara Vol 1:*

A New Frontier for African Heroic Saga   **9**

The Kambili (Bird et al. 1974) and *Sunjara: Three Mandinka Versions* (Innes 1974). (Anyidoho 1985, 157).

Charles Bird, as linguist and literary scholar with extensive field research experience on the epic tradition among the Mande, was especially helpful in his analysis of the complex role of the musical timeline of the accompanying instrument in establishing the complex poetic nature of the Kambili epic text in performance. There was also much to learn from Bird's review of *Sunjara: Three Mandinkan Versions* (1974) and from John William Johnson's published text in English translation of *The Epic of Son-Jara* (Johnson 1986). It is of special significance that Bird, Innes and Johnson all give due credit and acknowledgement to well-known individual bards as the real oral poet-composers and authors of the texts they collected and translated. Unfortunately, we may not say the same thing for D. T. Niane, whose name appears on the cover and title page of 'his version' of *Sundiata: An Epic of Old Mali*. This, in spite of the fact that the text opens with an emphatic declaration of the true identity of the griot whose work he so efficiently presents:

> I am a griot. It is I, Djeli Mamoudou Kouyate, son of Bintou Kouyate and Djeli Kedian Kouyate, master in the art of eloquence. Since time immemorial, the Kouyates have been in the service of the Keita princes of Mali; we are vessels of speech, we are the repositories which harbor secrets many centuries old. The art of eloquence has no secrets for us; without us the names of kings would vanish into oblivion, we are the memory of mankind; by the spoken word we bring to life the deeds and exploits of kings for younger generations. (1).

Beyond this opening statement, the whole of the first page, and half of the second, reads and sounds as a certified curriculum vitae of the griot Mamoudou Kouyate, author of the original text. Indeed, we note that Niane's Preface to the French Edition, republished in the English Edition, acknowledges this fact of original authorship:

> This book is primarily the work of an obscure griot from the village of Djelibu Koro in the circumscription of Siguiri in Guinea. I owe everything to him. My acquaintance with Mandingo country has allowed me greatly to appreciate the knowledge and talent of Mandingo griots in matters of history. (vii)

Despite this acknowledgement, however, the published text as we have it credits D. T. Niane as the *author*, rather than *translator*, of *Sundiata: An Epic of Old Mali*, and he appears as such in almost all bibliographic listings, such as we find in the following:

10   *Kofi Anyidoho*

The Sunjata epic – You Tube (www.youtube.com): African Storytelling: **SUNDIATA** (An epic of old Mali) Part 1. Book by Guinea's Djibril Tamsir Niane. YouTube·British Library·2016 E-O 18.

One other point of special significance in the development of African poetics we need to consider is transformations in written African poetry as extensions of primary oral traditions:

> Kunene (1980), for instance, laments how the 'modern' African writer has lost the epic dimension typical of major traditional poetic compositions celebrating long-term national and social goals. To make amends for this loss, he has provided us with two major written epics, *Emperor Shaka the Great* and *Anthem of the Decades* (Anyidoho 1985, 158).

As far as I am aware, Mazisi Kunene's challenge to the 'modern' African writer has remained largely unanswered since the publication of his two great written epics. It is against this background that we must measure the unique achievement of Tade Ipadeola's *The Sahara Testaments*. The epic dimension Kunene talks about is not only fully established in Ipadeola's text but goes beyond 'a celebration of long-term national and social goals'. The epic grandeur we encounter in *The Sahara Testaments* is not limited to any one African nation or empire. It is anchored in a pan-African global vision, from the dawn of history into the far future, with Africa herself as the epic heroic figure at the centre of the narrative. As readers, we may be challenged by the breathtaking expanse of the world and knowledge covered by the 'Testaments'. Perhaps, we can take inspiration from Mamoudou Kouyate in his teasing closing statements in his version of the Sundiata epic:

> Men of today, how small you are besides your ancestors, and small in mind too, for you have trouble in grasping the meaning of my words… To acquire my knowledge, I have journeyed all around Mali. At Kita, I saw the mountain where the lake of holy water sleeps; at Segu, I learnt the history of the kings of Do and Kri; at Fadama in Hamana, I heard the Konde griot relate how the Keitas, Kondes and Kamaras conquered Wouroula. At Keyla, the village of the great masters, I learnt the origins of Mali and the art of speaking. Everywhere I was able to see and understand what my masters were teaching me, but between their hands, I took an oath to teach only what is to be taught and to conceal what is to be kept concealed. (84).

The knowledge contained in the Sundiata is indeed encyclopaedic, a key defining feature of an epic. It is knowledge that can only be

A New Frontier for African Heroic Saga **11**

acquired through an extended period of careful education. This is the impression we get as we read *The Sahara Testaments* also. But what about the griot's oath to keep some of that knowledge concealed? What about his warning not to even go seeking to acquire some of such knowledge, especially in matters of the ancestral spirits: 'Do not ever go and disturb the spirits in their eternal rest. Do not ever go into the dead cities to question the past, for the spirits never forgive. Do not seek to know what is not to be known.' (154)?

This is where the poet behind *The Sahara Testaments* parts company with the lessons of the ancestral griots. Any knowledge, however sacred, that carries the seeds of hope and is of value for the reconstruction of our fragmented history must not only be sought, but made accessible to guide us into a fruitful future. This is the primary motivation of the poet as he leads us into and through the long trail of *The Sahara Testaments* and invites us to ponder over the last three quatrains of his epic narration:

> Lengthy work, if it yields nothing beyond sand, let it be
> Far from me. Likewise meditation, aspiration and prayer
> If they beget but barrenness, let them not tent near me
> But if these sprout within a desert but an oasis, let me dare
>
> Let me hope, wielding weary hands and iron pick
> To strike spring in a rite of renewal amidst thorn bush,
> Arid seasons, dearth. Let me find water and quick
> Surcease from floundering in the harsh sun of Kush-
>
> Find me songlines, the ancient paths, the word spoken.
> Find me gardeners, keepers, planters who sing and tend,
> Nurturers made sensitive to spirit and the unspoken.
> And afterwards, let the grace begin that never end. (180).

Tade Ipadeola has proven to be one of the last flag bearers of the old guard who still insist on keeping poetry as an art for only the strong-hearted. Those are the very few who know what it is to wait upon the Muse to drop on their souls words that merge into phrases and grow into lines and stanzas until they read like chants by the oracles of Delphi. With The Sahara Testaments […] Tade Ipadeola […] has in no small way renewed the faith of many who had contemplated giving up on poetry since after the band of cavaliers broke through the gates and hijacked the stage. (Ekweremadu, 2015)

I have chosen this concluding paragraph of a short review of *The Sahara Testaments* as my entry point into my reading and assessment of

12 Kofi Anyidoho

Tade Ipadeola's epic, despite Ekweremadu's bold confession that 'Even as I write this review, I still have not been able to read the book from front page to back page not minding that I have had it for over two years now.' I would agree with this reviewer's view that 'The Sahara Testament is not the type of book that is come by every day.'

The Sahara Testaments divides into three parts or movements: FIRST BREATH, INFINITE LONGINGS and REMNANT MUSIC. The first two movements, separated by a brief section titled 'The Atlantic Interval', carry the main narrative – *Testaments*, a heroic saga of the lands and the peoples of the Sahara, from the dawn of creation and of human history through a turbulent but still hopeful present into a visionary future reclaimed from the travails of history and geography.

Tade Ipadeola's *The Sahara Testaments* is cast in the true tradition of epic poetry, collapsing large chunks and landmarks of history into a narrative flow of grandeur and lofty imaginings. Myth, legend and history blend into a complex, multilayered narrative carefully located in time. Time itself is anchored in a geography of shifting and lost landmarks and in imagination's boundless stretch over the universe.

The reader, even an intelligent reader, is likely to experience an initial difficulty with the narration. As the poem opens, we encounter too many high-sounding words, too many cryptic expressions, too many special terms calling for privileged initiation into the clarity of full comprehension. Perhaps, this is only a symbolic rumbling of poetry's supersonic jet engines as they try to shake the mind free, to break away from gravity's reluctant release, through the turbulence of dense clouds into the reassuring embrace of an endless sky, so the imagination can soar into a universe of new possibilities. Throughout the rest of this grand narrative, we cannot say that we are always in close step with the poet. He has been privy to too many sacred rituals, too many ancient systems of knowledge, too many coded thoughts, visited too many places beyond our known world. Every now and again, complete understanding of his words eludes us, his song's hidden meaning leaves us a few steps behind. But he always pauses for us to catch up, he turns round to guide our minds back or forward into familiar landscapes of geography, history, contemporary experience, even into daring leaps across time into the far future.

Movement One, FIRST BREATH, the longest, runs to five chapters, each chapter made up of several sections. The opening section recalls primeval times when today's Sahara Desert was a busy fertile land with 'echoes from the Amazon Rainforest… Habitat of Thermidor, feast-prawn of Avalon', where all manner of 'Flora breathed the nascent

Levan air'. The gradual, sometimes rapid degradation of this original paradise into a desert of pitiless aridity is the main burden of the rest of this first movement and indeed of much of the second movement as well. The process of degradation, we discover, comes through a series of catastrophic encounters designed by hostile nature and by devious human engineering.

We follow the poet as he traverses the expansive stretch of the Sahara, stopping in various countries, cities and landmarks of geography and history, bearing personal witness to Africa's often tormented, occasionally glorious experience. There is an early stop-over in Senegal, Senghor's symbolic woman, 'immortal in her blackness... a land made for poetry, the perfect/turn of every phrase'. There is a hurried flight across geography, with snapshots across lands of the Nile into Sudan, where current unfolding tragedies feed into a history as ancient as our rivers and mountains: 'And there is this Sudan.../Where janjaweed repaints memory in blood clots/Of innocents, where crude-fed militias kill in jest'. A pattern is established here that is played back again and again throughout the rest of the poem: healing images of beauty and joy alternating with indelible portraits of horror and pain, of stretches of fertile land dissolving into arid wastelands. And always, the agency of fellow humans is there, sometimes in the background, sometimes on boastful parade.

The poet's voice is always there, reminding us of a time when 'The desert relived a verdant age of creators', invoking poets of mythical fame, Kairos and Chronos, 'Their flight-path of song' spreading 'from Luxor through Bubastis into the Baltic', telling a forgetful and ungrateful world of how 'Africa touched the world before the world /touched Africa'. Often, the descriptive power of the poet's words is amazing, unforgettable:

> It was the age of flame trees, their implacable beauty
> Claiming more surface than the sand. Lavish sunlight
> Daubed each petal with pigment from stars. A fruity
> Blanket perfumed Sudan, made a galaxy of delight. (p.10)

The use of beautiful rhetoric to mislead a gullible world into devious action provides occasion for deadly satirical comment as the poet takes a side swipe at Tony Blair, at Africa's blood diamonds and at Nigeria's chronic inflation. The winds bring back 'Mansa Musa/And his caravan of gold.../The one man-hurricane that shook a peninsula/To its liquid foundations with solid wealth'. In the true traditions of epic, this poem encompasses vast stores of knowledge in an impressive encyclopaedia of memories and imagined scenarios.

14 *Kofi Anyidoho*

In contrast with Chapter I, which opens with a powerfully evocative portrait of a world in its pristine beauty clothed in floral splendour, Chapter II opens with a portrait of the desert as a wasteland devastated by heat and the terrors of slave-raiding wars, leaving the women in perpetual sorrow, singing endless laments for their lost sons, daughters and husbands. Despite their great tragedy, these are no ordinary women to be overwhelmed by the whirlwind. Like their men, planted on a hostile landscape, they are 'a people like baobabs/Like cactus, gypsum-grown in their stalwart roots… sandstone women/Singing shuttle songs with Time the weaver'.

In Mauritania, Nouakchott in particular, the poet unveils for us abundant evidence of 'Wider architectures amidst the ruins of Arab industry', three centuries of pillage and profit from human misery, presided over by a mock-parliament under whose decree 'slavers were paid/compensated for villainy'. Against this portrait of pain, we find some comfort: 'But the Negro, he is strong;/And she bears her children with faces set as flint'. Such comfort is not, cannot be, enough. So in a sequence of quatrains, the poet speaks of how 'memory suffers seizures with the script/written in blood of infants' and looks forward to a near future in which deep rooted crimes committed over centuries of pillage shall see redress and retributive justice. In the meantime, though, while we await that day of reckoning, we must serenade Africa's suppressed history in song, in symphonies of small departures into the 'Nile's polyphonies/from loud Rwanda to hushed Sudan'. Our songs must strip naked endless seasons of 'hurt's perfection/Where citizens drink gun powder tea for fuel', and young boys are schooled by zealots to accept the necessity to bottle their testicles and bury it in the sand, in the name of religious duty.

For the sake of a fuller and deeper knowledge and understanding, the poet takes it upon himself to lead us from country to country, city to city, so we can bear personal witness and testament to Africa's history buried under the rolling sands of the Sahara. Each city, each country, comes with its own basket of tales, occasionally pleasant, sometimes sad, often harrowing narratives of terror, treachery, death. Everywhere we pause, there are important lessons to learn, for instance about the myth of racial superiority-inferiority, reminding us that 'Hate's shifting colour feeds the error/Of final solutions'; and the hardest lesson of all: that 'nothing… Defeats the earth' and 'Man shall not live by dread/Alone'. There are no sacred cows in history's museum of memories, history's hall of fame and shame. Even the 'Pharaohs and their reign of labour/Their cities of death' must eventually succumb to earth's final

A New Frontier for African Heroic Saga   **15**

judgement and consignment of their glory to desert dust. The men who hunger for fame, ready to 'risk all, life and limb... /For a warrior's burial', have often lived and died forgotten, 'Genies of thwarted dreams in the sands/Waiting for the wind'.

The poet reminds us of the often underestimated horrors of the Trans-Saharan slave trade, compared to the more frequently storied Trans-Atlantic slave trade: 'There were routes to slavery's hell/Apart from ship holds... agony in every cell/From thirst and scorpions'. The agony is magnified by time as we multiply the tears and groans across the desert by two thousand seasons multiplied again by two: 'And time itself could not be tomb enough for rage'.

There are details here that, almost inevitably, remind us of Ayi Kwei Armah's portraits of the Sahara Desert and its slave trading Arab overlords in *Two Thousand Seasons*:

> Springwater flowing to the desert, where you flow there is no regeneration. The desert takes. The desert knows no giving. To the giving water of your flowing, it is not in the nature of the desert to return anything but destruction. Springwater flowing to the desert, your future is extinction (1973, ix).

Remarkably, this bleak opening of Armah's novel is counterbalanced by a visionary future as positive as the closing lines of Ipadeola's epic:

> Against this what a vision of creation yet unknown, higher, much more profound than all erstwhile creation. What a hearing of the confluence of all the waters of life overflowing to overwhelm the ashen desert's blight! What an utterance of the coming together of all the people of our way, the coming together of all people of the way (321).

And by 'our way, the way', Ayi Kwei Armah means the most fundamental principle of life-reciprocity, a principle that is alien to the nature of the desert, the nature of the predators who make much of the desert their home.

The final sections of Chapter II take the poetic voice to some of its most memorable levels of expression, poetry at its loftiest imagining, its most sublime articulation, at its most disciplined versification, most vivid image-making magic. Resistance to enslavement gives birth to a generation of warriors with the attacking skill of scorpions, gliding over desert sands like wind or smoke, 'surprising lizards/The way death surprises men'. In a concluding footnote, we are reminded of what became of the glory that once was Egypt, pride of the Nile. The lofty songs of the Pharaohs are reduced to puzzling whispers, murmurings across Time's primeval reach into eternity.

16 *Kofi Anyidoho*

Chapter III takes off from Marrakech like 'a hummingbird standing still in the sun'. We fly over Casablanca with its unfurling dreams, to legendary Fez and Jelloun's country: 'There is poetry here, of neat sculptured quatrains/And jagged, as of the edges of the distant Pyrenees'. To demonstrate how abundantly poetry flows in this land, the poet captures for us the superb flight of young eagles in exquisite and polished poetic lines, one of his finest quatrains:

The swagger of young eagles soaring in the sun
Oblivious to the weight of light resting
On outstretched wings, their trajectory of fun
Wide as Sahara, swooping low and cresting...

Soon enough, we return to the ancient tale of how Egypt lost her famed glory: 'Egypt bled from Thebes to Luxor... Civilization changed pilots, survivors wore sack/As vultures settled to feast...'. Brutal facts of history understated in cryptic poetic and proverbial lines. All civilizations, once declared Wilson Harris, are built on a series of thefts. We turn our backs on Egypt, pause for a second look at Marrakech, take note of piles of slain Almoravids, once the fearsome warriors who spread their religion with pitiless fury. In Section XI, we are offered a brief, tantalizing vision of a united Africa, unified 'across passports and boundaries', bringing solace to 'The outcast, prodigal mother of every race'. As the phantom lighthouse of Libya sinks into the sea in the emblematic city of Sirte, we notice that 'A nightingale links/Asia to Europe through Africa', a secret long known to daring 'boat people'. History as recent as Tripoli/Libya's descent into manipulated chaos is played back to us. Some argue it could have been avoided, that the signs were all so clear, but it is in the nature of tyranny to grow disdainful of the approaching storm on the horizon. The poet reminds us that 'Even saints/Cannot secure reprieve for a rat in a cat's paw'. The final section of this chapter recalls the repeated cycle of violence that continues to torment the African continent, such as in Mali, where 'Mari Djata's peace, unperturbed by the ages/Knows nothing about the troubles of Timbuktu/Today'.

Chapter IV opens with a celebration of speech, poetry and song, where, in Eritrea, the Sahara touches down, and the people, like coral, grow into the land and sea and scatter like cotton seed. We listen to a mystery woman sing in praise of the brave and we wonder 'who on earth/Presumes to know the many forms of treasons/Perpetrated against her people'. As we work our way towards the end of this chapter, we pause briefly over the ultimately fruitless industry of tomb-raiders, knowing that 'There is never enough in the coffers of thieves' even though 'greed conjures daydreams of golden-rings/Lapis lazuli, diamonds, the crown jewel of Thebes'. We are once more reminded that the Sahara was once a floral garden. But today, 'The desert is a diary of pain'. We hurry away, pursued by startling pictorial images of death: Death 'from a bullet in the eye,/Shrapnel in the guts, gas in the lungs./Death from pellets, from a shattered thigh/Crude deaths and clean, death with prongs', all designed by merchants of pain and misery, for profit.

After the horrors and putrid smells of war, we breathe a sigh of relief as Chapter V welcomes us with the fragrance of Leila's psalms, Leila, mystery woman, symbol of beauty and love. We could listen to Leila forever, but soon, too soon, our joy is interrupted by The Atlantic Interval. It is brief, and poignant, bursting with memories of dreadful images of the Trans-Atlantic Slave Trade and of the turbulent Middle Passage, 'Where the fittest marched in chains to merge/With futures alien as the skin of shipmasters'. By the strategic brevity of The Atlantic Interval, the poet seems to emphasize the fact that three hundred years of horror across the Atlantic may not, cannot, compare favourably with two thousand years of misery across the Sahara.

Movement II, INFINITE LONGINGS, is introduced with a memorable quote from 'Negus', Kamau Brathwaite's quintessential poem of hope:

I
must be given words to shape my name
to the syllables of trees

(I
must be given words to refashion futures
like a healer's hands…)

The Movement brings us to a significant departure from the endless cycle of horror and misery recorded in Movement I, despite occasional moments and memories of life lived in harmony with nature and our own human possibilities. Here is a more confident walk into the dawning of a new age of promise and hope for a life lived in relative freedom from the constant menace of predators, whether man or beast, or even a hostile geography. Reminders of past horrors and the threat of their recurrence are still around us, but our skills and strategies of resistance and resilience are much better developed. The art of survival is no longer beyond the reach of the populace at large:

18 *Kofi Anyidoho*

Millions watch the skeletons of terrors past
They drink their water quietly and eat couscous
Assured that terrors end however long they last
And meekness wins, and nothing different does.

The invading forces of Phoenicia and Assyria may still come to restage their wars of pillage. Timbuktu may come under a new wave of savage attack. And Sudan may begin to bleed all over again. But the invaders, this time round, are in for a surprise. They will find Sudan battle-ready in the hopes of the young and courageous, as recorded by the poet in a salute to the heroic defence by the youth, determined to fight genocide to the death, and resurrection of hope beyond despair. Some hard, accusing questions are raised, insinuating the complicity of nations driven by greed to reduce the earth to rubble and wasteland, the sea to a stagnant pool. But a new and determined Africa has the capacity to strategize and bring into being the birth of a new age, restoring to the Sahara its long lost capacity for fruitfulness: 'That day will come when humankind/Will reclaim the Sahara again as home'.

In a sense, the poem, so far, has played a dizzying see-saw with our thoughts and emotions, from deeply depressive dives through moments of stability and balance, up to the loftiest heights, then down and up again and again before cruising into a stable flow in which the Sahara reclaims its long lost fertility. Perhaps the *Testaments* could and should have ended here. But this is a long tale with a long tail. So we must listen to the poet's concluding reflections in a final movement titled REMNANT MUSIC. Significantly, it opens with an invocation of the spirit of one of Africa's most revered ancestors, Cheikh Anta Diop, 'High Priest of Knowledge/Sun that'll never set'. The invocation is closely followed by a serenade for a model ancestral poet. The poets are always there, to bring us relief in moments of agony, to put our minds and spirits at rest when life offers us reasons to embrace joy after seasons of sorrow and pain.

The ultimate lesson of *The Sahara Testaments* is that Africa's recurrent misery is as much a result of terror unleashed by invading forces as it is the result of a knowledge and spiritual deficit. The poet, I suggest, is urging us to rediscover who we once were, how rich our land once was and still is, at least in parts. There is need to 'remind the child of those ancestors/Stalwart in the defence of the city of Jos/Whose last words in the claws of captors/Echoed a truth from the foundations of earth/That the world never ever ends. It evolves/Like a proscenium stage through abundance or death/Memory and willed amnesia…'. It is significant that, in the final Movement, Sundiata's mortal moment is

A New Frontier for African Heroic Saga   19

incarnated in the birth of a Thomas Sankara, that the ancestral poetic narrators resurrect in the voice and vision of the incomparable Chinua Achebe, 'who wrote the monuments with alphabets of magic'. Writing in *Anthills of the Savannah* about his views of struggle, Achebe once told us: 'The story is our escort; without it we are blind'. Our final hope is in the mouth of the storytellers as poets. It is they who must keep reminding us 'That Africa will never end…', that at century's end in the year 2099, a prodigal history could and will turn the table around, with Africa seated at its head.

The Sahara Testaments is a work of rare creative genius, written to a competent technical polish, profound in its articulation of a bold vision for the African continent and for humanity at large. The use of quatrains throughout the entire poem is a brave undertaking, and even though the rhyme scheme doesn't quite work in some instances, there is more than reasonable compensation in the poet's amazing command of poetic diction, the power of imagery and vivid narrative detail. The work sets a new and exciting departure into the future of African poetics in general, the heroic saga in particular.

WORKS CITED

Anyidoho, Kofi. 1985. 'The Present State of African Oral Literature Studies'. In *The Present State of African Literature Studies: The Present State/L'Etat Present.* Stephen Arnold (ed). Washington DC: Three Continents Press.

Armah, Ayi Kwei. *Two Thousand Seasons.* Nairobi: East African Publishing House, 1973.

Bird, Charles S. *Sunjata: Three Mandinka Versions.* Gordon Innes 1974. *Research in African Literatures* 8.3: 353–369.

Bird, Charles et al. *The Songs of Seydou Camara Vol 1): Kambili.* Bloomington. The African Studies Program, Indiana University, 1974.

Ekweremadu, Uchenna. 2015 (Dec 31). 'A Review of Tade Ipadeola's *The Sahara Testaments'.* ITCHY QUILL: a Nigerian's blog, accessed 2 February 2024.

Finnegan, Ruth. *Oral Literature in Africa.* London and New York: Oxford University Press, 1970.

Innes, Gordon. *Sunjara: Three Mandinka Versions.* London: School of Oriental and African Studies, 1974.

Johnson, John William. *The Epic of Son-Jara: a West African tradition. Analytical study and translation by John William Johnson. Text by Fa- Digi Sisoko.* xii, 242 pp. Bloomington, Indiana: Indiana University Press, 1986.

Kunene, Mazisi. 1980. 'The Relevance of African Cosmological Systems to African Literature Today'. *African Literature Today* 11: 190–205.

20   Kofi Anyidoho

Niane, D.T.. *Sundiata: An Epic of Old Mali.* Translated from French by G. D. Pickett. London. Longmans, Green and Co. Ltd, 1965.

Okpewho, Isidore. *The Epic in Africa.* New York: Columbia University Press, 1979.

———1980. 'The Anthropologist Looks at Epic.' *Research in African Literatures.* 11.4: 429–448.

Tade Ipadeola. *The Sahara Testaments.* Ibadan. Khalam Editions, 2012.

Nigeria's Instapoetry: Cultivating Inward, Ideological Activism, Revitalizing African Orality and Re-defining the Art of Poetry

OLUWAFUMILAYO AKINPELU

It is the twenty-first century and poetry as we know it is changing. Poetry is going digital, and, due to its digitality, the rhetoric of orality, which, for a long time, seems to have been supplanted by verse and rhythm, is now being re-asserted as a core element of poetry. Nigerian poetry in particular is leveraging the digitization of poetic arts to enact elements of orality that have been relegated by colonial forces to the 'primitive past' (Barnes and Carmichael). Beyond having rhetorical and oratorical potency, digital poetry is also socially exigent; it speaks to the flows and fragments of ideologies within a society, thus having the power to voice different forms of injustices that affect a local setting. As Edgar Lee Masters posits, the digital poetry that captures the zeitgeist of this epoch is one that 'comes from the rhythmical vibration of the soul' (308). This kind of poetry does not take language seriously, yet it prides itself on evoking emotions greater than what a storm can stir. This poetry 'is the orientation of the soul to conditions in life, and like great waters, it may murmur or ripple or roar' (306).

The generative practice of literary activism within the realm of digitized poetry challenges the hastily generalized argument that literary activism in Nigerian literature is losing steam or becoming dysfunctional (Nomu). Given that Nigeria's literary landscape burst out of a wave of political activism fuelled by anticolonial sentiments and demands for independence, its literary scene is often considered to be an anger cauldron spilling over to generate sublime yet salacious aesthetics. The politically enthused literary activism that started with the independence fighters intensified post-1960 due to the nation's postcolonial struggles and the socio-political frustrations of citizens (Nwagbara; Williams). It is believed that, since the 2010s, the political disillusionment of Nigerian writers and their enthusiastic immigration to the Global North has calcified into apathy, thus stifling the voice of activism in the nation's literature (Feldner). However, as works of digital poetry will reveal, literary activism in Nigeria is still going strong; it has only taken on new shapes that reflect the multilayered,

22 *Oluwafumilayo Akinpelu*

ever-dynamic oppression that people in Nigeria and of Nigeria now face. In advocating for matters related to national, international, racial, and gender politics, Nigerians are diversifying storytelling traditions and rendering social media and the internet into literary platforms. This has ignited a trend of digital storytelling in Nigeria's literary space.

A fruitful exercise in digital storytelling and online poetic aesthetics has been Instapoetry, a generic practice that mainly deals with rendering poetry using Instagram as a medium. The rest of the chapter will focus on conceptualizing the fast-rising embrace of Instapoetry by Nigerian storytellers as well as dissecting the manifestations, commercial dimensions, and global significance of this phenomenon. In addition, points will be made about how Instapoetry is shaping up to be a formidable player in the tenuous occupation of defending rights, seeking social justice, and channelling inward activism to ensure empowerment against oppressive ideologies and systems in rather inventive ways. The primary case studies for this chapter are Hafsat Abdullahi (@_havfy), with the viral 'To the English Girl in Class' poem, and Wayne Samuel (@waynesamuelle), who mixes spoken poetry and AI-generated motion pictures to create a surreal voice of advocacy.

Instapoetry owes its emergence and widespread manifestations to the globally connective operations of social media. The complete dependence of this brand of poetry on nodes of online platforms, whose multimodal affordances allow for a host of services that extend beyond the literary, has caused the significance of Instapoetry to be muddied up and undermined within the context of global literary appreciation. For one, there is an overarching narrative of youthful exuberance associated with social media, and this has spilled over into the scholarly considerations accorded to literatures situated within social media. For this reason, Instapoetry has mostly been studied within the realm of technological and pedagogical innovations. Kate Kovalik and Jen Curwood, for instance, positioned Instagram poetry within a transliteracies framework, underlining how students across the globe are gaining an appreciation for poetry by channelling their creativity into social media artistic productions.

While the discussion of Instapoetry from a transliteracies viewpoint is necessary and productive for creating new models for English composition curricula, it does little to establish the quintessentiality of Instapoetry and acknowledge the dynamic poetic heritage that started taking shape at the turn of the century. The literary valence of Instapoetry needs to be undeniably established and set in stone by academic scholarship. A remarkable effort on Curwood and Kovalik's part is using their exegetic discourse of Instapoetry as an affirmative testament to the once-up-for-debate dictum that #poetryisnotdead (185). Through their work, they not only pointed attention to the proliferation of poetic works on social media but also foregrounded the ability of these works to truly engender activism.

Apart from the conceptual limitations that have affected the definition of Instapoetry, there is also a restrictiveness in what qualifies as Instapoetry. Often, scholars tag Instapoetry as poetry written to be posted on Instagram. As Kathi Inman Berens puts it, 'Instapoetry is simplistic, little more taxing than reading a meme. It is almost always inspirational or emotional' (1). However, I would like to claim that Instapoetry is a metonymic shorthand for describing any kind of poetic activity that takes place on social media in general. This is mostly because of the fluidity that comes with sharing works on social media; a similar work of art that goes on Instagram can be simultaneously uploaded to TikTok, YouTube, Twitter, Facebook, and Tumblr. However, Instapoetry has established itself as the hermeneutic concept upon which to build all other discussions of social media poetry, hence its viability as a signatory shorthand.

Furthermore, Berens approaches the discussion of Instapoetry through a techno-economic lens, discussing how the huge commercial sales of the printed version of poems already uploaded on Instagram fit into the metrics of third-generation electronic literature and offsets a new understanding of the relationship between literature and physical, playable, interactive, manipulable spaces. It is within the context of her argument that she mentions Lang Leav, Atticus, Nikita Gill, and Rupi Kaur as thriving superstars of Instapoetry and third-generation electronic literature. She regards Kaur's work as possessing a ludo-semiotic essence that underscores the playfulness of works produced in 'dynamic event spaces like Instagram' yet fraught with the affliction of 'tactical media and surveillance capitalism' (11).

The presentation of Kaur's work as a shining example of Instapoetry is seconded by other scholars like Lili Paquet, JuEunhae Knox, and Alyson Miller. The latter presents Kaur's work as an example of emotional ekphrastic poetry that has transmediatic affinity with all forms of visual art, including photography and tattoo art (Paquet: 296). Paquet goes on to laud Rupi Kaur as the pioneer of Instapoetry whose 'footsteps are being followed' (311)! It is appreciable that these scholars recognize Kaur and others as true literary poets whose 'curating of an online human brand has allowed them to gain the momentum to bypass the traditional publishing industry and communicate directly to their readers' (311). However, besides claims of plagiarism levied

24 *Oluwafumilayo Akinpelu*

against Kaur, the fact that she and other predecessors like Lang Leav are regarded as the epitome, the zenith of Instapoetry stems from the prioritization of Western ontology in all categories of existence and the failure of scholars to radicalize their examples through decolonial approaches (Belcher). Since its inception in 2010, Instagram has always been populated with works that echo the simplistic, digestible, emotional caption-like feeling of Kaur's works. From anonymous accounts that present emotive words on post-it notes to sentimental advice about relationships and romance doled out in the form of soft-core poetry, Instapoetry preceded Leav, Kaur, and all others who have now become famous for it.

From a geopolitical standpoint, Instapoetry's politics of reception are as influenced by pseudo-globalization as it is by algorithmic bias (Akinpelu). From the Nigerian side of things, Tolu Akinyemi (@poetolu) is an example of a Nigerian Instapoet whose poetry is stylistically and thematically shaped the same way as Kaur's poetry. Just as Kaur accompanies her short poems with visual sketches, he also includes sketchy digital illustrations and AI-generated photos in his Instapoems. He has also published three book collections – his latest being 'Her Head Was a Spider's Nest' – which are very much appreciated and patronized by his fans and followers ('Tolu Akinyemi'). Thus, the ontological prominence accorded to the likes of Leav and Kaur is misplaced and calls for a re-evaluation of the historiography of Insta poetry.

Although I consider Instapoetry to just be a nominal signature for social media poetry in general, the transmediatic extension of digitized Instapoetry to the realm of printing and materiality calls for a dialectic discourse. Commonsensically, it is a misnomer to call printed book collections Instapoetry once they have left the playable, dynamic space of Instagram. Even Berens admits this when she says, 'Stripped of liveness, printed Instapoetry ends up looking banal. Its treacly insights, absent the warm glow emanating from fans inside the app, hardens into branding' (9). To define Instapoetry as written poems simply uploaded to Instagram, poems that can be directly lifted from the digital and transposed onto a book without the need for any form of remixing and repurposing whatsoever is very limiting and misleading at the same time. On this note, as much as the quality of textuality is associated with Instapoetry, there needs to be other transcending qualities that distinguish a work of art as generically belonging to Instapoetry. Digitality and orality are key constituents that I conceive of as distinctive markers of Instapoetry. Digitality in this context can range from textuality and visuality to any other semiotic features that the techno-literate space of social media allows for. Orality, which denotes any form of self-constitutive aural 'language combined with the performativity of the body', is, of course, not exclusive to Instapoetry (Gunner). And yes, Instapoetry need not be oral but the quality of orality in an Instapoem foregrounds its inalterability as Instapoetry.

It is in light of my distinct inclination about the meaning of Instapoetry that I present @_havfy and @waynesamuelle as case studies in this paper. @_havfy is the Instagram name of Hafsat Abdullahi, a well-acclaimed spoken word artist who has won awards for her performances in different poetry festivals and came into the limelight when the video 'To the Girl in English Class', in which she performed a poem of hers, went viral. The video's virality has caused her poetic brand to be well sought after and has established her voice as a symbol of resilient Nigerian identity in diplomatic, educational, and corporate spaces. Before the exposure that came with 'To the Girl in English Class', Abdullahi's artistry had consistently connected the divide between orality and digitality. She is known for primarily performing live to an audience interested in the rhythmical flow of her words and the powerful lyricism they bear.

When reciting her poetry live, she performs with the same cadence that spoken poets are often known for. She enters each line with force, the last words of each rhyming line are often dragged, and dramatic pauses are inserted after lines she is most confident will catch people's attention. She moves between whispers and screams, silences meant to be heard and amplified sounds that are supposed to be unheard. Her guttural sounds are often spoken with a throaty gut and her fricatives filter forcefully from her lips. She hisses her s's and hammers down on her h's. With her powerful voice and confident gait coupled with the stylish attires in which she presents and performs, she is the quintessential Nigerian spoken poet.

Her performance at the first round of the LIPFEST22 Poetry Slam is a testament to this fact. She came in forcefully with simple yet resonant punchlines: 'I grew up on these streets/And here on these streets, education is key/But what good a key when there are no doors for the poor' (*Orange Poetry*). These lines stir a spirit of resonance in listeners; by identifying as part of the population she is talking about, she is able to appeal to the imaginations of her listeners such that by the time she starts heaping rhymes and pentameters onto these

26 Oluwafumilayo Akinpelu

uncomplicated lines, she does not lose their attention. More so, Abdullahi engages in transmedia art. Not only does she perform on the stage of large corporate events, but her poems are also on Spotify and other streaming platforms. She also performs at events organized by and flooded with popular Nigerian celebrities.

Besides her live performances, Abdullahi is very intentional about digitizing her poems, and the intentionality behind her digital output earmarks her art as Instapoetry. For instance, the same poem she rendered at LIPFEST22 was her entry for the World Bank's #YouthActOnEDU spoken word competition for which she won first place ('World Bank'). It is impossible not to notice the changes Abdullahi makes to the reading of the poem in its digital format.

Knowing that she is facing a virtual congregation whose attention span and tangible participation she cannot gauge or count on, Abdullahi becomes more assertive in her body language. She gesticulates with her hands and raises her eyebrow in a way that suggests that her remarks are aimed at interrogating and castigating the educational system and stakeholders in Nigeria. Also, she does not accentuate her words or so much as engage in the rise-and-fall cadence that comes with reading on a live stage. Her tone is near-even, and her words are spoken fast. She knows to rely on the element of textuality that digital videos afford. The captioning of her words on the screen of the video works to augment the punctuational mishaps that come with reciting the poem at high speed.

Rather than focus on wording her statements in such specific ways, what becomes the high point of focus is the visuals. In addition to her assertive facial expression, Abdullahi presents herself as a model Nigerian youth through her look; her bright yellow Ankara blouse is styled with blue jeans and the scarf wrapped around her head is tied in a way that screams Gen-Z aesthetics. What's more, in the video, transitions are made from her image to frames of her writing on a notebook. The transition between her self-fashioning as the modern educated Nigerian woman to the introspective writer who is contemplatively presenting words on a page is fitting for the educational theme of the poem. It also gives off an aura of intellectualism thus commanding attention to herself and her words.

The influence of digitality on her oral persona is remarkably evident in her viral video 'To the Girl in English Class' (@_havfy). Despite being on different platforms from Twitter to Tik-Tok to YouTube, 'To the Girl' can rightly be called an Instapoem because it took flight mostly on Instagram and has garnered a huge level of engagement on this platform. In this poem, she uses the figurative device of apostrophe to address a cross-section of the Western population that gets a kick out of accent shaming and linguistic racism while at the same time schooling Africans who are neck-deep in internalized racism against themselves and people around them. The fact that she chooses to use the figurative device of apostrophe, which invokes the presence of a second pronoun 'you', strips them of anonymity, and holds them accountable for actions that are individually or collectively perpetuated, is very intentional. It models the method of conversationality imbued in some poetic forms of the Yoruboid dialect (Nnodim).

Furthermore, given that this poem also focuses on demystifying a stereotypical orientation about education, Abdullahi goes for an aesthetical setting that shows the influence of the West on the ideals of education promoted in Nigeria. In the background of the video, there is a vintage television model and a vase with a plant in it that gives off an autumn vibe. She wears a brown Ankara blouse that fits the background and adorns her hair and jeans, thus reflecting the Nigerian Gen-Z outlook again. The vintage TV speaks to Nigeria's colonial past, in which people strived to get a British education, speak in a British accent, and deck their homes with interior decorations that reflected the climate of the colonial masters. To be educated at the time (and even now) was to have a TV like that in the sitting room and mementos that represented the weather-y state of existence present in European spaces. The aspiration to be Western in linguistic posturing as well as the doctrine of accentual assimilation normalized in the current day are what Abdullahi goes on to attack in her words.

Having semiotically established her line of criticism about the apostrophic 'girl' and her Nigerian audience using visual inferences, Abdullahi draws semantically from African orality to evoke sentiments against neo-colonial assaults against the African identity. The use of rhetorical questions all through the poem, right from the first two lines, is where she begins to expend an arsenal of oral contrivances. 'To the girl in English class', she says, 'What is funny?/What is hilarious about my painful attempt to communicate in a language that is not even my own?' (@_havfy). Rhetorical questions take on more meaningful connotations in oral circumstances, and they are deeply embedded in the constitution of the orality of Nigerian ethnic groups. As if answering her questions, Abdullahi goes on to call attention to the underlying history behind her accent and the poetic heritage it upholds. She says: 'See, this accent/Tells a story of survival/Tells how my mother tongue endures to this day/So I expect/You treat my mother tongue with some respect' (@_havfy).

28   *Oluwafumilayo Akinpelu*

The attempt to create a rhyming sequence with her words is obvious enough, but it is not consistent; it is not forceful. While 'accent', 'expect', and 'respect' rhyme, when put into the larger context of the poem, they do not exactly break the mould of the free-versed nature of the poem. This tinkering with rhyme, the almost-iambic-pentameters, and alternate rhymes reveals Abdullahi's prioritization of the oral quality of rhythm over the written quality of rhyme. The alternation of words that end with the same consonants with words that are far-flung on different ends of the phonological spectrum makes for the rhythmical performativity that one would find being used by oral poets of Yoruboid languages like Igala.

The flaunting of her grounded feel for the oral skills of her ethnic heritage goes on with her enjambment of single words. She runs on these words which might make no sense in textual context but somehow possess extraordinary bravado when enjambed into a sentence: 'My mouth is a babel between/Subconscious/Tongue/ Teeth's/ And vocal chords' (@_havfy). In terms of syntactical arrangement, it is awkward to have subconscious-tongue-teeth's-vocal-chords in a single sentence, but the oral flair with which she reads it takes away from the awkwardness and clearly conveys the arduous process that a non-native speaker goes through to utter words that somehow catch between their minds and their mouths. By also enjambing incohesive words with oral braggadocio, Abdullahi is detailing a personal struggle with the English language; she is not communicating a struggle that she does not share. The struggle to reclaim her mother tongue is as real for her as it is for many other Nigerians.

It is quite telling that in the textual captions plastered onto the video, there are notable grammatical errors made, and despite the widespread popularity of the video, there has been no attempt to rectify it. This might be due to different reasons, but what is noteworthy is that the interplay between textuality and orality aided by the digital nature of the poem has yielded a new layer of significance to the poem. By having grammatical mistakes recorded textually, it is possible to infer that a thematic emphasis is being made in the process. For instance, consider this error: 'so escuse you, if my speach does not soothe you' [sic]. The presentation of 'escuse' instead of 'excuse' might be in line with the tendency of Nigerians to render x's as sibilants. And 'soothe' as presented here should have probably been 'suit'. Another instance is this: 'a clash of unyeilding cultures waring for dominance' [sic]. In purely written form, the mistaken use of 'unyeilding' instead of 'unyielding' and the spelling of 'warring' as 'waring' might have raised

Nigeria's Instapoetry 29

more than a few eyebrows. But presented in this digital format where the Yoruboidized-oral has more dominance than the Westernized-textual, it becomes logical to read it as a subtext, a semiotic signifier of the clash between two warring linguistic heritages.

In line with the use of ludo-semiotic sub-textuality in this Instapoem, Abdullahi code-switches fiercely between English and Igala, going from offering sophisticated English words to speaking in deeply indigenous Igala proverbs that the so-called girl in English class would not understand without translation. There is, therefore, a reclamation going on here; the apostrophic 'you', the 'Karens' have to subject themselves to the translatory practice that Nigerians often have to go through every time they move between spaces and crevices that privilege either or both English and their native languages: 'So cut me some clack/Agbiti megi neke logi ogi shin (Two elephants cannot pass a feeble bridge).../So to the girl in English class/Ewu shoduwe (What is your name?)/Its about time you learn my own language too [sic].'

Although part of the Yoruboid language system, the people of Igala form a distinct ethnic group in Nigeria, separate from the Yoruba ethnic group. Apart from the usual accentual difficulties experienced by Nigerians in general, minority groups or ethnic subgroups have specific challenges with enunciating certain words, and they are often jeered at for this. For instance, within the Yoruboid community, the Ikales of Okitipupa in Ondo state, the Eguns of Badagry in Lagos state, and the Igalas of Kogi state, where Abdullahi comes from, are usually mocked for their distinctive accents. Thus, Abdullahi's choice to code-switch in Igala shows that she is not just directing her criticism at an external body – at Western, imperial entities who peripherize our side of the world – her criticism is directed at her kinspeople who have internalized the assimilative policy of imperial forces and are mercilessly discriminating against their kinds.

Her literary activism is thus as inward as it is outward. Abdullahi drives home her inward activism through the production of, and participation in, skits where she combines powerful words, theatrical zest, ear-piqueing soundtracks, and collaborative presences to send forth messages of encouragement and rebuke to Nigerians. In one of the skits, titled 'Ode to the Nigerian Spirit', in which she alights from a Keke Napep and walks into a chaotic market street, Havfy commends the average Nigerian 'cycling the streets of palava dey catch cruise like we no send them because wahala has turned a popular joke that compels us to laughter'. In yet another skit, called 'This is not a Motivational Poem', in which she acts the role of a blindfolded, battered Lady Justitia chanting despite opposition from militating forces represented by coercive hands, she warns Nigerians whose 'tears are active participants in this play of prey, prey to [their] homes, prisoners of [their] own domes' to vote aright.

Abdullahi's inward form of activism is paradigmatic of how literary activism is practiced by contemporary Nigerian poets. This activism is geared towards ideological transformation. It is aimed at elevating self-worth and self-esteem as well as creating positive awareness of the unique streaks of black identity. Abdullahi is one of many Nigerian creatives whose form of activism takes this shape. Another prominent example of an Instapoet with this inclination for inward-looking activism is @waynesamuelle. Unlike @_havfy, @waynesamuelle is not exactly an internet viral sensation, but he has a considerable number of fans who follow his work of combining AI-generated visuals with emotive, emotionally charged, orally rendered poetic lines to create a surreal voice of advocacy.

Given that the images that accompany his oral lines are generated by artificial intelligence, they have an animated look to them – bright, beautiful colors, unrealistically human bodies, and perfectly crafted spaces that often depict Nigeria, his usual poetic setting, as a world of fantasy, a sci-fi utopia filled with people bearing ethereal appearances. His magical realistic depictions of Nigeria connote some kind of environmental activism and act as fodder for ecocritical analysis. As the images move and transition seamlessly in fricative, they tell a story and present a visual simulacrum that creates a collaborative interactivity between words, images, and sounds that could range from his voice to AI-enabled voices of others, like that one time he channeled David Attenborough's voice (narrator of the National Geographic documentary) to recite poetry about the 'mating signals' of the human female specimens (@waynesamuelle). The fact that a soundtrack is always added to the motion-picture-poem intensifies the immersive interplay between digitality and orality that his poems evoke.

Every other week, Wayne releases a new reel where he talks about the most mundane issues like Christmas chicken to more topical concerns like the corrupt, crumbling state of Nigeria. In one of his reels, titled 'ENDSARS REMEMBRANCE [sic]', posted on 20 October, 2023, he calls out to Nigerian youths to keep up the fighting spirit and not let down the banner of activism that started in October 2020. 'Wear your hijab', he says, 'Pack your dreadlocks/Slip on your Nike/ Wear palm or wear Crocs/Today, we step toward a future they have kept from us/Your "Male" will say it's dangerous/Your "Pale" will says it's a waste of time' (@waynesamuelle). As is noticeable, Wayne's choice of poetic words bears the same simplicity associated with Instapoetry, but even more, he uses culturally specific terms that signify that his audiences are Nigerians whom he intends to prod with the sharp stick of poetry.

To further register his interest in addressing the domestic polis as opposed to focusing on the generic, global internet population, Wayne also uses the apostrophic 'you' for individuals and personifies Nigeria and Africa with feminine pronouns, while always making sure to keep his lyricism spatially grounded. In a series of Instapoems titled 'If Nigeria was a Wedding', Wayne, in a deep, earthy voice, extols Lagos as the 'chief bridesmaid, the beautiful, quirky smart woman that everyone expected to marry first but somehow hasn't found her way to the altar. She belongs to everyone and no one. No culture, no creed, no religion has really been able to put a ring on it. She is an attractive free spirit, inviting many suitors from the far away hills of Kaduna and the red sands of Edo... She goes to church on Sundays, on Mondays, worships Sango, visits Fela's shrine on Fridays' (@waynesamuelle). Edo state, on the other end, is the 'spiri-koko aunty who brings her pastor to officiate the wedding' while boasting of a handsome, skinny-jeans loving son, Benin city, who is full of rizz and is as razz as they come (@waynesamuelle). He also uses the metaphor of a wedding to praise the 'picture perfect, sun-kissed' divas and patriotic intellectuals of the East (@waynesamuelle).

In lyrically metaphorizing the Northern woman, Wayne collaborates with another Instagram wordsmith @thelagostourist (Hamda Koya), who is from the North. Together, they depict Northern Nigeria as a woman who paints the lovely henna of the bride but is 'beautiful but misunderstood... a [woman] who's got modesty and beauty'. She would 'enter a wedding hall with head held high like the ancient Kano Walls, like Farin Wura Falls, her hijab falls...'. Wayne uses the wedding motif to also describe other African countries like Kenya, who he says is a 'lovely quiet girl [accompanied by] her more outgoing friend Nairobi... dressed in Kitenge with kinky hair alluring as a breath of fresh air'. No doubt, it is impossible to miss the ecocritical perspectives @waynesamuelle brings to his works by spatializing women and 'womanizing' citied spaces. Cajetan Iheka conceptualizes this creative spatial punning practiced by creatives like @waynesamuelle in his book *African Ecomedia*. He says, 'Ecomedia that focuses on urban space in Africa constitute the urban as a site of everyday precarity, a space for geopolitical-cum-ideological contestation that endangers the human

32 Oluwafumilayo Akinpelu

and nonhuman bio-sphere, and a space for articulating future possibilities' (187). The spatially conscious Instapoems of @waynesamuelle fit right into this description.

Furthermore, @waynesamuelle's personification of Nigerian regions and countries in Africa as fantastical, vivacious females full of unique personalities does more than just paint a picture of the multifaceted cultural delights of Nigeria, it also arouses pride and dignity in the country. Readers-listeners-viewers cannot help but feel a sense of gratification for being a Nigerian from any of these regions. Many Nigerians in the comment section express the warm feeling of belonging the poetry series gives them. @rabialiyuumar__ says, 'This is so beautiful I feel represented'. Another commenter remarks, 'As a Kenyan I miss home now 😢😢😢😢 thanks for the beautiful piece 💜 can't get over it 😍🥹 it's a masterpiece 🥲'. Even when commenters don't agree with the depiction of some states and regions, the conversations their antagonism generates are often enlightening. About the portrayal of Lagos as 'belonging to everyone and no one', @ujunwadiogo comments, 'Wait o!! Y'all need to stop this nonsense about Lagos belonging to no one. The traditional name of Lagos is Eko. It was the Portuguese that visited in the 1500s that called it Lagos. Before there was Nigeria, Eko was and it is. Eko has people and it has culture. Don't erase her history…' (@waynesamuelle). A lot more comment along this line was presented as well.

The genderized nature of Wayne's Instapoems touches on all of his themes. Often, he elevates the personality and outlook of the feminine self by personifying important phenomena as women. The woman is the iPhone, 'the pretty daughter of a visionary named Steve Jobs' (@waynesamuelle). The woman is 'Lady Justice' who meets Nigerian politicians 'at the corridors of power' (@waynesamuelle). The woman is a Barbie girl living in a dollhouse called Nigeria where they can't 'walk the streets like every night is girls' night' (@waynesamuelle). The woman is the human heart which keeps 'receiving shipments from Cupid's arrow' (@waynesamuelle). The woman is Twitter who makes 'bold statements [yet] does the devil's work [and becomes the instrument with which people] chas[e] clout like a storm chases wreck' (@waynesamuelle).

Positioning women at the centre of his poetic discourses not only projects his platform as a hub of feminist activism but it also allows for the kind of self-reflexivity that contemporary literary activism engages in. In one of the Insta poems titled 'Your Personal Mami Water', he attacks the common misperception that women are seductive succubi who cause the downfall of men. He spits out clearly, 'Our enemy is

Nigeria's Instapoetry 33

not without, she is within... All your village people are living rent-free inside your own head. Your Mami water is just a projection of your own self, the creature lurking deep inside the waters of your consciousness...' (@waynesamuelle). At the heart of this poem and many others created by Wayne is a call for ideological transformation, an advocacy for Africans to be proud of their heritage while also aiming for self-improvement by disavowing themselves of negative stereotypes and participating in the fierce struggle needed to ensure political emancipation.

Thus, as earlier stated of Abdullahi, through his Instapoetry, Wayne engages in inward-looking, ideological activism. One poem that best embodies the ethos of ideological activism in full force is 'If Nigeria Was Disneyland'. Here, Wayne appeals to Western pop culture and appropriates Walt Disney's Land of Magic to metaphorize the current socio-political climate of Nigeria. In its appropriated format, President Tinubu is the evil stepmother who looks at a magic mirror in Aso Rock and asks, 'Who is the Jagabanest of them all' (@waynesamuelle). Afrobeats would be 'Sleeping Beauty waiting for True Love's first kiss from Made Kuti as mainstream artists make it their duty not to stay woke and only convince the Humpty Dumpty masses to shake their booties' (@waynesamuelle). The japaists (those who emigrate from Nigeria) are Moanas ('Maanas') looking for greener pastures, the proliferating skit makers are Mickey Mouses, and Gen-Zs are represented by the activist Shrek who fights against the kingdom's status quo and the non-corrupt politician Simba who 'will one day be king' (@waynesamuelle).

Obviously, @waynesamuelle believes that the salvation of postcolonially decrepit nations like Nigeria lies in its Generation Z. In ideological, inward activism, the mandate is often ascribed to Gen-Zs who are open-minded and whose disillusionment with the old ways of perceiving and receiving the world has radicalized their attitude towards politics, religion, sociability, economy, and just about every way of life. This belief has held strong since the protest culture and hashtag activism that started with the #ENDSARS movement and continued vehemently with the Obidient movement. Generally, the practice of inward, ideological activism is also a by-product of the aesthetics of Gen-Z activism. Unlike millennials and baby boomers, whose focus was on revolutionizing political institutions from the top-down and defending the socio-political and cultural legitimacy of Nigeria to the outside world, Gen-Z activism centres on self-actualization, social and mental empowerment, and on enacting political changes through a re-orientation of the mind.

34 Oluwafumilayo Akinpelu

It is no wonder then that Piquet compares Instapoetry to self-help literature. Beyond Instapoetry, content creators like @layiwasabi, @taaooma, and @mrmacaroni1 are known for sarcastically personifying archetypal grassroots Nigerians whose unscrupulous ways contribute to the structural challenges faced by the country. Layi Wasabi, for instance, personifies the bribe-centric police officer, the hustling lawyer, and a network marketer who uses witty puns to entrap naïve customers in pyramid schemes. Beyond the entertainment value of their works, these new-age creatives recognize that to enact any kind of change, ideological transformation is first needed. What has enabled their ideological activism to thrive is the synergy between digitality and orality.

Even in more explicit forms of poetic activism that touch on exigent socio-political issues, orality is being augmented by digitality to achieve never-before-seen effects. For instance, during Nigeria's 2023 elections, well-acclaimed Nigerian poet Iquo Dianabasi Obot released an Instapoem on her page in which she recounted the horrors that had befallen Nigeria due to bad governance and called for Nigerians to rightfully exercise their voting rights (@dianaspeak). The poem's mix of oral vivacity and digital dynamism is an example of how even creatives with non-juvenile inclinations are tilting towards Instapoetry to extend the reach of their literary activism and appeal to the aesthetical shift of the current era.

It is worth emphasizing that the proliferation of Instapoetry in Nigerian literature and the tilt towards inward activism echo how people of colour around the world are using digital storytelling to tackle prejudices and injustices perpetrated against them. The convergence between the vibrant, protest art of the #ENDSARS movement and the #Blacklivesmatter movement in 2020 is an example (Nwakanma). This is not surprising considering that Black poetry, be it in Africa or the diaspora, is linked to poetry rendered by the griots of West Africa, for whom performance and orality were important (Niane). Conclusively, while many scholars have created concepts around new genres of poetry that have emerged from social media, there is yet to be a concrete establishment of how these new developments affect the very nature and definition of poetry. For one, contemporary poetic innovations call for a wholesome acceptance of multimodal convergences and the blurry interstices between literature and pop culture. Also, the fact that Instapoetry, as a prototype of inward literary activism, is at the nexus between Africa's oral poetic heritage and written poetry is worth canonizing in future conceptualizations of poetry. Masters is therefore right when he posits that the poetry of this epoch has less to do with textual constrictions and more to do with amplifying the vibrations of the soul (308). Instapoetry in all its different manifestations is a testament to this truth.

WORKS CITED

Akinpelu, Oluwafunmilayo. '21st-Century Digital Techno-Cultural Trends in Nigeria and the Pseudoism of Globalization in Africa.' *Espergesia*, vol. 8, no. 2, 2021, pp. 15–21.

Barnes, Cedric, and Tim Carmichael. 'Editorial Introduction Language, Power and Society: Orality and Literacy in the Horn of Africa.' *Journal of African Cultural Studies*, vol. 18, no. 1, 2006, pp. 1–8. JSTOR.

Belcher, Sara. 'Rupi Kaur's Plagiarism Controversy Has Resurfaced After New Viral Video.' *Distractify*, 31 Dec. 2019, https://www.distractify.com/p/rupi-kaur-plagiarism.

Berens, Kathi Inman. E-Literature's #1 Hit: Is Instagram Poetry E-Literature?

Feldner, Maximillian. Narrating the New African Diaspora : 21st Century Nigerian Literature in Context. Palgrave Macmillan, 2019.

Gunner, Liz. 'Africa and Orality.' The Cambridge History of African and Caribbean Literature, edited by F. Abiola Irele and Simon Gikandi, 1st ed., Cambridge University Press, 2000, pp. 1–18. DOI.org (Crossref), https://doi.org/10.1017/CHOL9780521832755.002.

Hafsat Abdullahi - LIPFEST22 Poetry Slam (First Round) || Orange Poetry. Directed by Orange Poetry, 2023. YouTube, https://www.youtube.com/watch?v=pqOF5tBRBnY.

Hafsat Abdullahi (@_havfy) Instagram Photos and Videos. 15 Mar. 2023, https://www.instagram.com/_havfy/.

"Hafsat Abdullahi, Nigeria - #YouthActOnEDU Spoken Word Winne." World Bank, https://www.worldbank.org/en/news/video/2022/09/06/hafsat-abdullahi-nigeria-youthactonedu-spoken-word-winne. Accessed 15 Dec. 2023.

Iheka, Cajetan. African Ecomedia: Network Forms, Planetary Politics. Duke University Press, 2021, https://doi.org/10.1215/9781478022046.

Iquo DianaAbasi (@dianaspeak) Instagram Photos and Videos. https://www.instagram.com/dianaspeak/. Accessed 16 Dec. 2023.

Knox, JuEunhae. 'United We 'Gram: Scrolling through the Assimilated Aesthetics of Instapoetry.' *Poetics Today*, vol. 43, no. 3, Sept. 2022, pp. 479–532. DOI.org (Crossref), https://doi.org/10.1215/03335372-9780403.

Kovalik, Kate, and Jen Scott Curwood. '#poetryisnotdead: Understanding Instagram Poetry within a Transliteracies Framework.' *Literacy*, vol. 53, no. 4, Nov. 2019, pp. 185–195.

36 *Oluwafumilayo Akinpelu*

Masters, Edgar Lee. 'What Is Poetry?' *Poetry*, vol. 6, no. 6, 1915, pp. 306–308. JSTOR.

Miller, Alyson. 'A Digital Revolution? Insiders, Outsiders, and the "Disruptive Potential" of Instapoetry.' *Arcadia*, vol. 56, no. 2, Nov. 2021, pp. 161–82. www.degruyter.com, https://doi.org/10.1515/arcadia-2021-9029.

Niane, Djibril Tamsir. Sundiata: An Epic of Old Mali. [London] : Longmans, [1965], 1965, https://search.library.wisc.edu/catalog/999469522402121.

Nnodim, Rita. 'Configuring Audiences in Yorùbá Novels, Print and Media Poetry.' *Research in African Literatures*, vol. 37, no. 3, 2006, pp. 154–75.

Nomu, Kéchi Nne. 'Who's Afraid of Nigerian Literature?' *The Republic*, 27 July 2023, https://republic.com.ng/june-july-2023/nigerian-literature/.

Nwagbara, Dr Uzoechi. 'Political Power and Intellectual Activism in Tanure Ojaide's The Activist.' *Nebula*, Jan. 2008.

Nwakanma, Adaugo Pamela. 'From Black Lives Matter to EndSARS: Women's Socio-Political Power and the Transnational Movement for Black Lives.' *Perspectives on Politics*, 2022/03/15 ed., vol. 20, no. 4, 2022, pp. 1246–59. Cambridge Core, Cambridge University Press, https://doi.org/10.1017/S1537592722000019.

Paquet, Lili. 'Selfie-Help: The Multimodal Appeal of Instagram Poetry.' *The Journal of Popular Culture*, vol. 52, Apr. 2019, pp. 296–314. ResearchGate, https://doi.org/10.1111/jpcu.12780.

'Tolu Akinyemi: Books, Biography, Latest Update.' Amazon.Co.Uk, https://www.amazon.co.uk/stores/Tolu%20Akinyemi/author/B00C4U61PW. Accessed 15 Dec. 2023.

Wayne Samuel (@waynesamuelle) Instagram Photos and Videos. https://www.instagram.com/waynesamuelle/. Accessed 15 Dec. 2023.

Williams, Adebayo. 'Literature in the Time of Tyranny: African Writers and the Crisis of Governance.' *Third World Quarterly*, vol. 17, no. 2, June 1996, pp. 349–66, https://doi.org/10.1080/01436599650035725.

A New Direction in Contemporary Nigerian Poetry

The Pandemic Poems of Tanure Ojaide and Kola Eke

OGAGA OKUYADE & EDAFE MUKORO

A new direction is emerging in contemporary Nigerian poetry. This is seen as poets from that geographical landscape of Africa capitalize on the realities of our present world, especially in light of the traumatic and brutal experiences that accompanied the coronavirus pandemic[1] and its associated panic, risks, global human fatalities, lockdowns and economic dysfunction. This poetic rethinking and musing on the pandemic has become the spark that is inspiring the growing trend of pandemic poetics currently re-energizing the creative landscape of contemporary Nigerian literature. Thus, this essay is approached from a national perspective within the African milieu. It adopts a blend of socio-scientific as well as literary commentary that is anchored in environmental materialism, or rather material ecocriticism, and begins with the premise answering: 'what is pandemic poetry?' – Pandemic poems are poetry (oral or written) that assert the musings of poets about a pandemic disease. They register the contemplations of poets about a contagious disease that spreads over a whole country or the whole world, as well as its accompanying devastations and wreckage of human psychology, cultural norms and socio-economic and political activities. Pandemic poems are products of pandemics that are either real or imagined. This is quite crucial because the business of poetry, as with literature in general, deals with both the real (factual) and the imagination. In that respect, we cannot ignore historical pandemics such as the Black Death (1331–1353), Spanish Flu (1918–1920), Asian Flu (1957–1958), and so on, and just recently the Coronavirus (COVID-19) pandemic, which is the core of the poets' pandemic ruminations in this chapter.

---

1 On 30 January 2020, the World Health Organization (WHO) through its Director-General Tedros Adhanom Ghebreyesus declared the global outbreak of COVID-19 as a global health emergency (Pandemic).

37

38 Ogaga Okuyade & Edafe Mukoro

The responses of African poets, with specific reference to contemporary Nigerian poets, to the coronavirus pandemic have been quite commendable. One is not unaware of the contribution of pandemic poems by some established Nigerian scholar-poets like Niyi Osundare, Tanure Ojaide, Abubakar Othman, as well as Ismail Bala with some fifty other poets (writing in English) and another sixteen poets (writing in the Hausa Language) in the bilingual pandemic poetry anthology entitled *Corona Blues: A Bilingual Anthology of Poetry on Corona Virus*. Still others, such as the renowned Nigerian female poet and one-time joint winner of the Nigeria Prize for Literature, Akachi Adimora-Ezeigbo, and newer poetic voices like Ikechukwu Emmanuel Asika, Iquo Diana Abasi (The spoken word poet), as well as the South African spoken word poet Mary Charmain Tshabalala contributed pandemic poems to yet another pioneering pandemic poetry anthology entitled *World on the Brinks: An Anthology of COVID-19 Pandemic*, which, to quote the words of the critic Isidore Diala, is 'one of the earliest poetry anthologies published on the subject of the COVID-19 pandemic, not only in Nigeria but in the globe' (World on the Brinks: 203). And in another essay, the critic appraises 'preliminary notes on topicality and recent pandemic poetry' (Preliminary notes: 210).

What is, however, evident is that the novelty of this genre of creativity in Nigerian literature, with its engaging demand on the cerebral sophistication of literary artists, has attracted a number of contemporary Nigerian poets' dedication to experiment and publish at least a corpus of pandemic poetry, that is, a book of poems, to reflect on the coronavirus pandemic. These poets along with the anthologized ones mentioned earlier are blazing the trail and charting the course of a new direction in contemporary Nigerian poetic discourse. In this respect, the books of poems entitled *Narrow Escapes: A Poetic Diary of the Coronavirus Pandemic* by Tanure Ojaide and *Covid-19 and Other Poems* by Kola Eke represent to a very large extent the new trend of pandemic poetry in the contemporary Nigerian poetic landscape. These texts are examined in this chapter demonstrate the private, public and universal concerns that pervade the vulnerabilities of a wider manifestation of our common humanity, using the Nigerian and by extension the African poetic milieu.

Reading the pandemic poems of Ojaide and Eke, one is reminded of the theory of trans-corporeality as postulated by Stacy Alaimo. The theory is actually a subset of environmental materialism, or rather, material ecocriticism. It emphasizes the 'interconnections of human corporeality with the more-than-human world [of]... material agency' (Alaimo, 2). The eco-critic asserts, thus:

Trans-corporeality reveals the interchanges and interconnections between bodily natures... [it] opens up a mobile space that acknowledges the often unpredictable and unwanted action of human bodies, nonhuman creatures, ecological systems, chemical agents and other actors (2).

The theory emphasizes 'the movement across bodies' because the word 'trans indicates movement' (2). At the same time the theory stimulates the scientific understanding behind zoonosis, which has to do with zoonotic pathogens jumping from nonhuman animals to humans, creating a biological disease within the host, known as zoonotic disease. It stretches our intuitions to grasp the reality that 'the human is always intermeshed with the more-than-human world [which further] underline the... human as ultimately inseparable from the environment' (2). To make this point clearer, the more-than-human world refers to material agents, invisible matter such as viruses, bacteria, chemical agents and other actors that interact with human bodies, wielding 'often unpredictable and unwanted action' that transform and distort bodily natures beyond its genetic self. The movement of the viral agent SARs-COV-2 virus (COVID-19) – a material entity and biological agent – into the human body sparks an 'unpredictable and unwanted' biological reaction that destroys the human immune system, activating severe and often fatal health complications such as fever, dry cough and fatigue and aggravating already existing medical challenges within the body systems. These complications arising from 'interacting biological forces' form the deadly global onslaught of the pandemic with 'almost 7 million deaths; causing severe economic upheaval, erasing trillions from GDP, disrupting travel and trade, shuttering businesses, and plunging millions into poverty' (Ghebreyesus), thus 'emphasizing the material interconnections of human corporeality with the more-than-human world', to quote the position of Alaimo for the last time (2).

From the above framework, this essay examines pandemic poetry as an emerging trend and direction in contemporary Nigerian poetry. It is observed that the genre is used to recapture in vivid imagery the pandemic-induced panic and risks, human fatalities and lockdowns that trail the virus outbreak. This is espoused through clever evocation of pictures of global anxiety laced with depression and isolation, debilitating risks that gnaw the hearts of millions in the face of a global outbreak of a public health emergency of international dimensions. Right from the preface of the book of poems entitled *Narrow Escapes: A Poetic Diary of Coronavirus Pandemic*, henceforth *Narrow Escapes*, Ojaide considers his responses to the pandemic as a 'spiritual journey

40 *Ogaga Okuyade & Edafe Mukoro*

to better understand the meaning of life' (xv). This thought aligns with his allegiance to his Urhobo culture and tradition, from where he draws his inspiration in the course of his writing the diary. He is emphatic here:

> Throughout the period [of the pandemic], I was inspired by my Muse, Aridon, the god of memory and poetic inspiration in my Urhobo culture. These poetic entries in the diary are gifts to me... I had to wake and write – often not sleeping well to take advantage of the inspirational spell. Aridon will not leave me alone and I have to obey the call (xvi).

These 'gifts' from 'Aridon' form the pandemic musings of Ojaide, and they reveal to a large extent the responses of a poet who is overwhelmingly burdened by the novel realities that confront humankind during the period. 'Aridon' seems motivated by the prevailing temperament of the moment to bombard his client's memory with poetic inspiration and thoughts of the pandemic. In the poem entitled 'The World Revolves Around a Virus', Ojaide paints a graphic picture of the overwhelming panic and risk the novel virus infuses in the hearts of people. The irony of the situation is captured through the gripping influence that a 'tiny' thing could have and demonstrate to the world:

> The world revolves around a novel virus.
> Time the minutest of things caught attention.
> Worse still, it hedges all into quarantine.
> This is terrible, tiny to invisibility
> yet poaching the known world into panic-
> stricken enclaves for self-preservation.
> For a change the smallest of things
> Unleashes a stampede. Terrible, really so!
> Fear tiny things and their mortal rage!
> (Narrow Escapes 1)

There is a reminder here that there is a connection between the world of humans and the beyond-humans. One could sense Ojaide's subtle brilliance in drawing humanity's attention to the potentials of material agents that hitherto were relegated to the background by the forces of anthropocentrism. The 'stampede' of the coronavirus serves as a rude awakening to the Anthropocene as it 'hedges all into quarantine'. One is reminded (at the time of the pandemic) of the safety measures put in place by governments, such as quarantine, physical distancing and lockdowns, to curb the spread of the virus.

A New Direction in Contemporary Nigerian Poetry   **41**

It is therefore important to stress that the viral image in the poem exposes the vulnerabilities of humanity in the face of the 'invisibility' as well as the invincibility (as at the present time) of 'the smallest of things' in the world. Instructively, the novel virus is cast in the image of a poacher in the poem's fifth line, as the world becomes a wild that is 'panic-stricken' because of the 'terrible' onslaught of the poacher. The speaker, therefore, informs us in the poem's last line about the level of suffocating apprehension that gripped the world about 'tiny things and their mortal rage'. The irony strikes at the very core of the dilemma of human existence in a world bedevilled by the turbulence of environmental ignorance.

The 'mortal rage' of the viral agent assumes another dimension in the poem entitled 'flood of fire' (3). Here Ojaide recollects with poetic ingenuity how we 'wake to grimmer news' daily to hear of the astronomical rise of human fatalities as the 'blaze' of Covid-19 virus 'spreads beyond the imagination' (3). In the poem, the suffocating and searing heat of the pandemic is seen extending its reach to every corner of the globe as there is 'nowhere to escape to/ that's not already drowned/ in the terrible flood of fire' (3). The whole poem is cast through a meticulous handling of thermal and aquatic imagery to evoke pictures of the devastating influence of the coronavirus and the associated human casualties that followed.

Ojaide further dwells on the idea of human fatalities in another poem entitled 'Novel Fatalities'. The entry in the poetic diary is dated 28 March 2020. It reads thus:

> The monthly figures of gun fatalities dropped steeply
> from the exponential increase of past bloodied decades,
> shooters have been paralyzed by the novel fear
> of an invisible enemy on the loose in the boroughs
> that cares not from what side of the city, west
> or south, you have elected to plant your habitation
> Gender neutral, it seeks anyone to devour. Hide!
> (Narrow Escapes 25)

It is important to note that, as of the time of writing his poetic diary, Ojaide was already in the United States. In fact, he tells us in the preface to the diary that he got back to Charlotte from Nigeria on 8 March 2020 and, by 10 March 2020, 'the American Government started to take things [the outbreak of Covid-19] seriously after a rather unserious attitude before then'. (Narrow Escape vi). The location of the poet gives us a background understanding of the quoted poem

42 *Ogaga Okuyade & Edafe Mukoro*

above. Srdjan Ilic asserts that in relation to gun-related fatalities, 'the United States known for being one of the most heavily armed countries globally... is ranked third in terms of the highest number of gun deaths. This amounts to a staggering 13,001 deaths caused by firearm each year...' (1). The implication of the first line in the poem draws attention to the 'novel fatalities' caused by the novel virus whose 'exponential increase' of human fatalities dwarfs that of the 'gun'. In the poem, it is noticed that the virus's presence instils fear of paralysis in 'shooters' whose boldness is disabled by 'an invisible enemy on the loose in the boroughs'. They have gone into hiding as the destructive viral agent 'cares not from what sides of the city, west/or south, you have elected to plant your habitation'. Moreover, the 'tiny' thing has no consideration for gender, as its neutrality makes it all the more unpredictable and destructive. In a way, the 'shooters' have chosen the option to 'hide' as the 'novel fatalities' from the 'invisible enemy' outdo their gun performance.

Ojaide shows us further in the poem how the 'novel fatalities' caused by the 'braver alien warrior' who has 'sworn to bruising or knocking dead all on the way' skyrocketed 'to nothing emergency wards ever saw'. From all indications, there is a strategic humility of gun owners 'in the land of the brave'. One could sense the paralysis of 'those who own dozens of rifles' as the 'Hunters [who] are themselves hunted... throw down gun[s] and run blindly for life' (25). The virus attack is non-discriminatory with 'radicals and conservatives, straight and crooked folks' not spared in the onslaught. It is interesting to note the amount of humor that is generated by the poet in his crafting of this diary entry, even in a period of sober reflection.

The introduction of lockdowns by different countries during the pandemic as a way to curb the spread of the Coronavirus disease also received the attention of Ojaide. The unprecedented measure is captured with feelings of déjà vu in a poem of the same title. Hear him:

> I have always walked through
> a ghost town; no human sound
> and even birds taking a nap
> this early that I am up and alone.
>
> And so its nothing new
> The quarantine of the already
> entombed; indoors a lifestyle
> now legitimized by necessity
> (Narrow Escapes 12)

A New Direction in Contemporary Nigerian Poetry   43

In this poem, Ojaide leads the readers by a stroke of his imagination into the streets to underscore vivid pictures of a world under lockdown in a pandemic. The streets are empty 'with no human sound/and even birds taking a nap.' It is virtually a world where nature seems suspended and the beauties that are common to the auditory senses become elusive. Besides, there is evidence in the poem that the visual senses of the speaker are witnessing an unprecedented event in human history. He is pictured 'this early… up and alone' walking through 'a ghost town' made possible by the controlling influence and power of a 'tiny' thing. The eyes are far from being satisfied as the hustle and bustle of humanity and other ecosystems are bereft of the breath of life.

The feeling of déjà vu continues in the succeeding stanza as the speaker ruminates on the 'quarantine' regulations 'of the already entombed'. Ojaide's use of the word 'entombed' in this instance is quite suggestive and shocking. It triggers the picture of a tomb in the mind's eye. By implication, the poet considers the lockdown measure during the pandemic as an institutionalized act of interment of humans in a tomb. The atmosphere of the poem is suffused with the sensation of death, while the analogy takes the mind to the 'lifestyle' of the 'entombed' whose circumstances are 'legitimized' by death. In the same manner, staying 'indoors' becomes 'a lifestyle now legitimized by necessity'. No wonder the poet further asserts in another place in the diary that 'those who seek individual privacy/now have got their sovereign spaces', by virtue of 'self-isolation' through the agency of coronavirus (6).

In another poem entitled 'what they said', Ojaide takes us to Africa – specifically Abuja, Nigeria – to visualize the lockdown that trailed the pandemic there:

> No power could keep the millennial congregation out, they said
> Today is Sunday and Dunamis Church is closed for worship
> Folks said the traditional market never closes or get postponed
> Agbarho's biweekly main market shutdown on this market day
> (Narrow Escapes 27).

The 'Dunamis Church' (The Glory Dome) situated at Airport Road, Abuja, Nigeria is reputed to be the largest church auditorium in Africa, with a 100,000 seating capacity. It is a mega church with a 'millennial congregation', and every Sunday of the week it is packed full with worshippers. But on this 'Sunday', the speaker appeals to our visual senses to see that The Glory Dome is 'closed for worship' due to the lockdown policy of the Nigerian government to curb the spread of

44 *Ogaga Okuyade & Edafe Mukoro*

Coronavirus. Airport Road has become a 'ghost town' as the 'Dunamis Church' is 'shutdown on this market day'. The might of a 'tiny' thing has overcome the 'power' that boldly proclaims that the 'millennial congregation' cannot be kept out from the mega church. This is quite interesting as it underpins the uncommon fear that pervades human responses during the pandemic.

Moreover, another interesting insight from the poem is the speaker's infusion of the market image from his indigenous Agbarho community of Urhobo kingdom. There is evidence here about the commercialization of the religious centre as 'the traditional market' that 'never closes or get postponed'. The critical reader could see that the 'traditional market' is deprived of its bragging rights and rendered comatose by the deadly viral agent. It is unimaginable to fathom the disruption of the system brought about by the influence of the virus. The 'unimagined catastrophe' has thus shifted our perceptions about traditional thinking patterns and lets us know that 'established order cannot always remain sacrosanct' (Narrow Escapes 27).

For Eke, poetry is more than a 'spiritual journey', for he is more 'interested in how his society functions and operates'. (7). Reading his book of poems on the pandemic, henceforth *Covid-19,* it is observed that his message is the same as Ojaide's – Pandemic-induced panic/ risk, human fatalities, lockdowns and so on – yet the poet's dexterous handling of imagery fascinates the imagination in a rather unique way. It grants us better understanding of the significance of material agents in a vastly interconnected world of diverse ecosystems. In the poem entitled 'fisherman', Eke uses imagery from the world of fishing to suggest his thoughts on the pandemic-induced panic/risk in the world. Here Covid-19 is captured as a 'fisherman' that

> Catches both rich and
> Poor oysters
> with his fish trap
>
> ...
> Casting his net into
> The sea of death
> Catches many crabs
> (Covid-19, 56)

The implication of the poem's introductory lines suggest that corona-virus is not subject to sentiments. Its ruthless aggression is palpable to all and sundry. There is a feeling of panic in the world of both the rich and the poor as the novel virus de-recognizes class stratification. The reader of this poem needs to move his/her imagination into the world of fishing to recognize the degree of panic that envelopes humanity during the pandemic. It has been discovered that the 'alarm pheromones' known as 'Oligosaccharides of Chondroitin-4-sulfate and Chondroitin-6-sulfate' is responsible for panic signals in some fish as they 'skitter, dart or dash, while others freeze or go into hiding, yet others rise to the surface, even jumping out of the water' (Stensmyr and Maderspacher 185–186). These behavioural patterns in the world of fish are critical to understanding humanity's responses during the threat of the pandemic. The poet further heightens the level of panic in the second stanza to the level of death through a deft use of metaphor laced with aquatic imagery. One could perceive that the whole arena is suffused in the deluge of 'death' and confusion, as the 'fish trap… catches many crabs'. Similarly, Eke shows us with graphic skill in another part of the poem how the 'fisherman conveys numerous lobsters/to isolation centers/with his trawler', as well as 'searches the/bottom of rivers/using his dragnet/infesting fishes with coronavirus' (56). This is a poetic recreation of the victimization of millions of people by the deadly virus. By all stretch of imagination, the novel virus exudes dominance and confidence as it spreads panic, fear and death across the world.

Another area that attracts attention in the reading of Eke's pandemic poems is the picture of human fatalities. The poem entitled 'No respecter of persons' conveys vivid images:

> Ambassador plenipotentiary of
>   Death
> strikes with the
> First born plague
> …
>
> Ambassador of pains
> And woes
> knitting the cardigan of
> Death and Destruction (Covid-19, 17).

The title of this poem registers the poet's sense of appreciation for biblical allusion. The expression is drawn from the book of Acts 10:34: '… then Peter opened his mouth, and said of a truth I perceive that God is no respecter of persons…' (King James Version). This reference gives vent to the indiscriminate onslaught of COVID-19 on humanity. Another interesting feature of the poem is the speaker's use of the ambassadorial image to espouse Coronavirus as a representative

46 *Ogaga Okuyade & Edafe Mukoro*

from the sovereign of death. In this instance, the emissary is conferred with 'plenipotentiary' powers to unleash the diplomatic weapon of 'death' on the citizens of the host country. In another meticulous use of language, Eke elucidates the idea of human fatalities during the pandemic with another shrewd use of biblical allusion. This time the reader's mind is taken to the ten plagues of Egypt in the Bible and most specifically the 'first born plague', which is the last plague to be unleashed against the Egyptians. The reference is drawn from Exodus 11:4-6. One must concede that the scourge and savagery of the death-laden virus is seen through the poet's recourse to biblical analogy.

It is an established fact that there was a 'great cry' across the world as the 'Ambassador plenipotentiary' wreaked havoc as human fatalities from the United States to India as well as from Brazil through Africa to China reached a devastating level. In the same way that there was wailing and gnashing of teeth in biblical Egypt, humanity across the world was dazed by the scale of death-laden attacks instituted by the emissary. The spread of death across the length and breadth of the world knows no bounds as it strikes with lightning speed that is beyond human comprehension. By extension, one could recognize the 'pains/and woes' in the hearts and souls of millions of people who are victims of the brutal envoy. In fact, it is noticed in the poem that the 'ambassador' is further pictured in a rather metaphorical manner as a knitter of the 'cardigan of death'. He is seen using his knitting tools such as knitting needles, stitch markers, stitch holders as well as scissors to interlace and intertwine yarn loops, creating stitches of patterns of 'death and destruction'. The visual appearance of the knitwear therefore becomes a cartographical display of 'death and destruction' on the world's map.

The introduction of lockdowns by different governments of the world likewise did not escape the poetic radar of Eke in his pandemic poems. The disruption of human activities by the policy is captured with striking images in the poem entitled 'Covid-19 II':

Covid-19
Like army worm
Has consumed the grain
Crops of academic activities

Covid-19
Like army worm
Has stolen the
Leaves and stem of Learning
(Covid-19, 14).

A New Direction in Contemporary Nigerian Poetry   47

This time, the poet moves the reader's imagination to the field of agriculture to underpin how the outbreak of the virus and the consequent introduction of lockdown to curb its spread disrupt 'academic activities'. The 'army worm' is a pest of the noctuidae family that destroys grain crops such as corn, rice, wheat and grasses. Its outbreak behaviour is similar to the invasion of an army, resulting in the destruction of crops within weeks. This image forms the dominant thought of the poet's espousal of COVID-19 lockdown here. In the poem, Eke shows us how the pandemic-inspired lockdown disrupts 'academic activities' in the same way that an 'army worm' destroys the entire crop in a grain farm. There is a total lockdown of the grain farm as the 'army worm' invades the territory with devastating speed. The worms leave a trail of destruction behind as they feed voraciously on the grain crops in the farm. The analogy is quite interesting as it grants the critical reader of the poem graphic pictures of the disruption of the academic calendar as well as other human activities during the pandemic. Moreover, the use of repetition in the poem is deliberate to emphasize the outbreak of the pandemic and the debilitating character of the virus. The dominance of the virus is further sustained in the poem both as an incapacitating consumer of human activities and as a plunderer of the 'stems of learning'.

Closely related to the above insight is the fact that the lockdown not only affected the 'plants of learning' and the 'premises of learning' but also rendered them 'stunted' as well as 'dearth of internodes' (14). The poet further extends the catastrophes of the lockdown into the world of business and commerce. In this case, businesses and corporate organizations are captured as grain crops facing damaging attacks from the outbreak of the virus. One could see through the mind's eye how these 'cobs of factories' are gnawed and masticated by the 'mandible and maxillae' of the lockdown (14). The image strikes at the heart of the death of commercial activities. From all indications, the lockdown is not only disruptive of commercial activities, but it functions as a structural and systemic element for economic downturn and dysfunction. It is said that 'the pandemic damaged more than a billion people's livelihoods in its wake' through job losses triggered by the lockdown while 'people in lower-income countries with large informal economies suffered in the largest scale' (Ray 1)

Drawing from the idea of economic dysfunction due to the lockdown, one could appreciate the poet's handling of imagery in another poem entitled 'Deforestation of workforce'. The poem emphasizes job losses during the COVID-19 lockdown in the most unique and profound manner:

Deforestation of workforce
cutting down the plants
on account of
Covid-19 lockdown

And the pandemic
Snowballs
Deforestation...
Defoliation of trees
(Covid-19, 27).

It strikes the imagination interestingly to recognise what Romanus Egudu refers to as the '*dislocation* of language' in the above quoted extract (7). In the poem, there is the exploratory use of words to align with the job losses during the lockdown. The word 'deforestation' is gifted with potentialities as its use triggers the imagination to grasp the layoffs that pervade the 'Covid-19 lockdown'. The picture becomes more vivid when one moves to an imaginary forest to witness the 'cutting down' of trees. The imaginative brilliance is further heightened as the 'cutting down of plants' becomes analogical for the job losses during the lockdown.

In the poem, the word 'deforestation' is repeated to stress the massive level of job layoffs, with livelihoods strangled of the basics and millions descend into the poverty bracket. The grove of commercial activities is depleted of its luxuriant 'trees', rendering a once forested arena almost empty of greens as 'deforestation' and 'defoliation of trees' take centre stage. As the lockdown persists from the first into the second and the third waves of the pandemic, many businesses and organisations 'fell down trees', while others 'deflower some plants' as they attempt to stay afloat. Without a doubt, the impact of the lockdown on millions and billions of people is quite catastrophic, and we must appreciate the sensitive manner in which the events are presented by the poets.

In conclusion, it has been the focus of this essay to establish that a new direction, known as pandemic poetics, is emerging in contemporary Nigerian poetry. The idea is drawn from the recent coronavirus pandemic and its associated devastation of human lives and cultural, socio-economic and political activities across the globe. The essay shows that Ojaide and Eke are leading the trend with their published books of poems on the pandemic and thus re-shaping the temperament of the contemporary Nigerian poetic landscape. Reading their pandemic poems, one notices that there is the injection of fresh poetic form (the diary genre) through the re-clothing of ideas and dexterous handling of language to capture the pandemic-induced panic, human fatalities as well as lockdowns. The poets' ruminations on the pandemic seem to have stretched their imaginations beyond familiar territories such as politics, social inequality, environmental pollution, feminism as well as bad leadership, which hitherto had dominated their poetic idiom. It is hoped that with the path cleared and the foundation laid, other poets on the national and continental levels of Africa will join the march of pandemic poetry, thereby expanding the corpus and frontiers of pandemic literature and writing in African literature today and in the future.

WORKS CITED

Alaimo Stacy. Bodily Natures: Science, Environment, and the Material Self. Bloomington Indiana UP, 2010.

Bala, Ismail and Khalid Imam, eds. Corona Blues: A Bilingual Anthology of Poetry and Coronavirus. Kano: Whetstone Publisher, 2020.

Diala, Isidore. 'A Review of Ikechukwu Otuu Egbuta and Nnenna Vivien Chukwu, eds. World on the Brinks: An Anthology of Covid-19 Pandemic'. In Africa Literature Today, 41 Africa Literature Come of Age, (2022): 198–203.

——— 'Preliminary Notes on Topicality and Recent Pandemic Poetry'. TYDSKRIF VIR LETTERKUNDE 59.3 (2022): 210–227.

Egbuta, Ikechukwu Otuu and Nnenna Vivien Chukwu, eds. World on the Brinks: An Anthology of Covid-19 Pandemic. Lagos: City Way Books, 2020.

Egudu, R.N. The Study of Poetry. Ibadan: UP, 2007.

Eke, Kola. Covid-19 and Other Poems. Ibadan: Kraft books, 2021.

Ghebreyesus, Tedros Adhanom. WHO Director-General Opening remarks at the Media Briefing. 5 May, 2023. Who.int.

Ojaide, Tanure. Narrow Escapes: A Poetic Diary of the Coronavirus Pandemic. Dever: Spears Books. 2021.

Ray, Julie. 'COVID-19 Put More Than I Billion Out of Work'. GALLUP. 3 May, 2021

Ilic, Srdjan. 'Gun Death by Country 2023: Behind the Numbers'. South West Journal. 4 August, 2023

Stensmyr, Marcus C., and Florian Maderspacher. 'Pheromone: Fish Fear Factor'. Current Biology 22.6 (2012): 183–186.

History and the Call of Water in
Romeo Oriogun's 'Nomad'

IQUO DIANAABASI

A migrant's voyage across borders can be triggered by a multitude of conditions, whether this be war, economic conditions, fear of persecution or human rights violations. This voyage undertaken with hope for a new (way of) life might be successful or otherwise, but it is always embodied in a complex trauma. Too often, the migrant is burdened with silence, the tongue knotted under the weight of history, blood and all that binds them to home. In *Nomad*, Romeo Oriogun unpacks this restlessness that represents the voyager's constant return to homeland, loss of roots, loss of language and the memory of those who never returned. In examining the tensions surrounding bodies and their back-packed heritage as they move across the world, Oriogun's *Nomad* becomes a sensitive cartography linking the relics of the transatlantic slave trade to the complicity of systems that force people to embrace uncertainty, loss, exploitation and the other migratory risks that are nonetheless more enticing than the familiar terror of home.

The International Organisation for Migration (IOM) defines migration as the movement of a person or a group of persons, either across an international border or within a state. It is a population movement, encompassing any kind of movement of people, whatever its length, composition and causes. This definition encompasses political refugees, displaced persons, economic migrants and people who move because of education or the wish to reunite with their families (IOM, 2011). The movement of people across international borders can be voluntary or involuntary; it can be legal or illegal; however, Oriogun is little concerned with these legalities, but more with the power imbalances that can motivate this movement and the effect of this movement on the migrant's physical, psychological and emotional wellbeing. He explores migration as an uncertain miracle of flight, a hunger wracking the migrant's body, across the waters of the Earth.

History and the Call of Water in Romeo Oriogun's 'Nomad' 51

Romeo Oriogun is a Nigerian poet who was awarded the 2017 Brunel International African Poetry Prize and has attained fellowships from institutions such as Harvard University, the IIE-Artist Protection Fund and the Oregon Institute for Creative Research. Before *Nomad*, he published the chapbooks *Burnt Men*, *The Origin of Butterflies* and *Museum of Silence*. He also published the poetry collection: *Sacrament of Bodies*. In this latter collection, water bears a strong motif of salvation and cleansing – this role of water is expanded in *Nomad*, where Oriogun interrogates migration and history and different cultural connotations of water. Poetry, with its distilled imaginary and sensitiveness, serves as the perfect vehicle for this engagement, and Oriogun does a great job of this through his tender attention to the migrant's internal struggles and his beautiful use of language.

In *Nomad*'s opening poem, 'The Beginning', we learn what the poet describes as the fear and the ritual of leaving, in the voice of one who was once tender, and loved their home city.

> The weight of a country will always be too heavy
> to leave in a strange park. There was music there:
> silent tears, travellers, the shifting of trauma
> through borders, the mingling of languages
> (Oriogun, 2021:1)

Leaving home is a burden and not always an easy one, and the poet paints it as a displacement from the familiar – 'The voice of exile is the murmur crossing rivers, and sea, crossing empty roads until it washes/over a man, a baptism of loss.' And in this condition of exile, the memory of lost ones – whether they be family lost on the journey or fleeing migrants drowned in the waves of the Mediterranean Sea – becomes something that pinches harder the farther one is from home. The traveller's reality is filled with the mystery of a sea swelling, pushing out every dead thing: migrants, fishermen, dead animals, women murdered and thrown off slave ships (Oriogun, 2021: 4). In wishing that humans could always take off like migratory birds when the seasons change the speaker tells of 'the river which is empty, yet mercy lives in its currents, as it moves towards other cities.../... I do not know how to choose/ myself, but the birds do. I would like to join them'. (Oriogun, 2021: 6).

The temporality of the poems in *Nomad* is nonlinear. In the words of John Drabinski, history and memory bear on this text in ways that sustain, enable and extend the meaning of its arguments and descriptions (Drabinski, 2019: viii). We engage with poems that gather

52 Iquo DianaAbasi

painful relics from the Transatlantic Slave trade: 'behind this market of oysters,/there was once a market for flesh,/in Ouidah, in rooms filled with Black flesh/in chains, branded like cattle, herded into pens...' (11). And then the poet strings these verses into a not-so-colourful bead, accessorized and completed by present day trafficking as sexual slavery: a smuggler whose work of terror suffers in the coldness of brothels across Bamako, Tripoli, Mauritania keeps a tight leash on his girls while they wait for their bus to get fixed, his eyes ruthless as he watches his flesh commodities (8). These poems are elegiacal, a tribute to those lost to slavery, alive now as it was hundreds of years ago. As Oriogun re-enacts the era of slave trade, so similar to the irregular migration of recent years, the poems seem to have been exhumed from a different era, complete with the markings, scars and colours of a past, which are almost indiscernible from the trappings of its present setting.

> ... Even in tears
> of origin. there is no atonement enough
> to restore a people lost to a ship's belly,
> no forgiveness, there is only the sting
> of cold air, the open Atlantic, only that.
> (2021:12)

It has been documented that almost 15 million slaves were transported from Africa to Europe and the Americas between the sixteenth and the nineteenth century (Castles et al. 2013). While thousands of deaths occurred in the Atlantic Ocean while the slave trade lasted, the Mediterranean Sea, being the world's deadliest migration route, has become the graveyard of many migrants who have unfortunately lost their lives while crossing its expansesing ordinary boats and dinghies (Ogu, 2017:56). The OIM estimates that about 22,400 migrants and asylum seekers have died since 2000 in their attempt to reach Europe (2018).

There are similarities between the backways syndrome – the contemporary seeking of passage between Africa and the developed West – and the Transatlantic slave trade, top of which is the age range of most of the migrants, most of who still have many productive work years ahead of them. There is also the likelihood that many migrants survive on menial jobs in foreign lands, and they face the risk of less access to rights than other people. These make the present irregular migration of Africans into Europe and North America into a second colonization, recalling the words of Vijay Prashad: immigration is always already about mobile capital and immobile race. Colonial rulers went where they willed, and they even moved people from one colony

History and the Call of Water in Romeo Oriogun's 'Nomad'   53

to another; but the colonized were not to be fully welcome in the heartlands of the empire, in Europe, in the United States. If they came, they were allowed in for their labor, not for their lives (2010: ii–iii).

In several of the poems, the poet sings of place like a bird examining the wonder of new lands, often through the eyes of his past, memory or with the longing to find a way back home. 'I have walked into where the mourning/of dolphins led to an eternal song under water/… I am always at the border of things,/always at the spot where what returns/is the emptiness of hope…' (2021: 70). The poet bemoans loss of language, loss of culture – 'when I said we love you, I knew I would speak these words/sitting before a fallen house, the baobabs too are going/extinct…' (2021: 81). This lament looks back at migration from rural communities to urban centres, in search of better livelihoods – a search which leaves villages in a peculiar state where houses are empty, existing as relics – 'Little pieces of remembrance on which their children once sat.' In this reflection we are reminded that a greater migration now plagues Africa, the kind of migration that leads to an emptying not just of the rural areas, but one which also clears the towns of young men and women. But the greatest loss is the death of language and culture. The custodians of these cultures do not live for eternity, the young and maturing ones flee the home of their birth, leaving little or no prospects for carrying the cultures forward. As the poet asks: 'We who have witnessed the death of language, what will become of us?' (2021: 81).

To be a nomad is to be a constant wayfarer, one with no fixed homestead for too definite a time. It is to be haunted with the knowledge that the home one carries within can never be wholly replicated on one's travels. It is also to be othered, a person on the periphery, different and seeking belonging in the new shores that one sojourns to. The migrant is often one who has no language for belonging, in a faraway land, walking through cities, soundless, like a bone thrown into a pit (p. 93). The sojourner is in perpetual bondage to memory, of home, of festivals and significant events triggered by specific symbols – pigeons at a park can become reminiscent of the pigeons set free as part of the Igue festival (107). Algae and earthworms become the echo of an immigrant's childhood (108). This longing is replicated across land and sea, from Cotonou to Ouidah to Togo, Chad, Bamako, Dakar, Libya, Lampedusa.

In appraising the burden of the migrant as a being tortoise-like, moving about with their house (history, memory, language, dreams, etc.) lifted onto their back, drifting from city to sea to desert to city, one cannot help gleaning glimpses of the complicity of the systems

54 *Iquo DianaAbasi*

that force people into voluntary exile. Systems that make it more appealing to risk exploitation, the dangers, the pain and the weight of movement and its accompanying uncertainty, than to stay in the familiar terrain that home is. 'Economic crisis, individual ambitions, political and armed violence rocking many parts of Africa have substantially forced and motivated inhabitants to move to different parts of the world' (Idemudia et al., 2020: 17). In 'Migrant by the Atlantic Sea', Oriogun posits that the hunger wracking a migrant's body is movement. To remain at home is to court the complexities that abound in the familiar, the systems that suck the air from many indigenes and force one to risk exploitation, loss and longing in exile. To stay is to risk a stunting, obscurity and hunger, while to live is to move, to traverse water, air and land in search of more fertile ground, greater opportunities to spread wings and glide aloft. Hunger pushes the migrant to search for comfort and adventure, yet they are wracked by a different kind of hunger for as long as they sojourn. The choice of migration is a risk greater than many comprehend, but as Oriogun says, 'The eagle knows the fish in water is the gateway out of hunger.'

In 'The Sea Dreams of Us' (2010: 95) we read:

for what burns the world quicker than desire?
there is no rest in exile, there is only the road echoing
in blood, the road echoing in water and we know it.

Water is channelled through every activity in this collection, through it we see that migration is a loss of peace that triggers memory – '… and if I drink a glass of rum/it becomes water from my ancestral lake…/there is no peace for those thrown out of a country.' (p. 18, An old song of despair). Further along in the collection, we read: 'There is thirst from exile,/rivers have become ice-skating rinks./… Desire sung into a void/ is still desire and I am left/ to witness the plunder of self.' (2021: 112). Also: 'Again, to decolonize water is to walk into the sacredness/of rituals, meeting my mother, the long line of women/in white, all chanting, water will always lead us home' (2021: 67).

In the eponymous poem, 'Nomad', Oriogun declares:

…Every river is a journey
and I went along, a pebble skipping
through water. Where I sink will be home,
alive in the language of exiled cartographers,
in maps seeking the way of water,
alive in a mother still waiting for a son
at the crossroads of life

History and the Call of Water in Romeo Oriogun's 'Nomad' 55

It is pertinent to note that Oriogun's use of water is mythological. It does not stop at signalling the element, water is in different places a metaphor for nature and the capacity of water bodies to provide movement for the migrant. But greater than all this, the poet uses water as a tribute to the deity Olokun. Okun means ocean, and Olokun (Owner of the Ocean) is regarded as god of oceans and fertility in the Yoruba, Edo and Urhobo ethno-linguistic groups. It is found not on the surface of the water, but within its depths. 'Olokun is the divinity who grants children to women. In Bini cosmology the land of the living is surrounded by water into which all great rivers flow. It is through these waters – the realm of Olokun – that human souls must pass either to be born or on their way to the spirit world' (Nevadomsky and Norma, 1988: 187). Therefore, when the poet says above: 'in maps seeking the way of water,/alive in a mother still waiting for a son/at the crossroads of life', the influence of his grounding in Edo cosmology looms large, and I read the lines as suggesting that his late mother awaits him in the river of life (Okun), which is a crossroads that they will yet meet again at, when he leaves the flesh.

The connection of water with origin is also apparent in the following verse from the poem 'The Sea Dreams of Us':

Before the sea became my journey, it was love,
folktales, it was our origin staring at us,
it was our shadows, then the ships of migration
came, reminding us that, years back, people left
in canoes loaded with hope, spices, seafarers
(2010: 95)

Before Oriogun, other poets have invoked water or her deities; Christopher Okigbo in *Heavensgate* sends an invocation to Idoto, the village river from which he drank in Nigeria's South-East: 'Before you mother Idoto/naked I stand/ Before your watery presence/a prodigal/ leaning on an oilbean/lost in your legend'. This sequence of verses is the beginning of a cleansing, the entry into the long ritual that Okigbo's whole collection is. And before Okigbo, there was Gabriel Okara in *Call of the River Nun* (1952), in which the poet, using vocabulary that is heavy with environmental and religious/spiritual significance, bears witness to the call from the river of his childhood in Nigeria's South-South. The river Nun is the beloved water body the call of which reaches the poet persona from far away, he being a sojourner, having left the land of his birth to earn an education and a living. Still, it is the river's call which he hears '…coming through; invoking the ghost of a child listening, where river birds hail your/ silver-surfaced flow'.

56 *Iquo DianaAbasi*

The call of water echoes and re-echoes throughout *Nomad*, as conveyor, as a stranger that knows the traveller's strength and desires, as a force that holds their thirst (82). The sea takes the fisherman away and returns him to shore with the day's bounty or regrets, in a boat anchored with the fisherman's longing for sand and home. However, the migrant's return is not so easily negotiated. Oriogun molds water into different shapes and attributes, and in the end, we see water not just as a cool refreshing liquid, not as the cleanser that it can be, 'There is history/in the clash of waves and in water/we are reminded, every name we know/is written in a language across the ocean' (2021: 16). We begin to believe that water is a repository of the violence of history and the unfortunate present. It was a tool of oppression as much as it is a symbol of freedom, it rises and falls, a devourer of many parts, aiding slave trade in centuries past as much as it contains the many shipwrecks and migrant ghosts lost on their way to Europe via the Mediterranean Sea on the coast of North Africa. One wonders along with the author: What mercy lives in water? What is devoured in darkness?

In Nomad, Oriogun chooses to write about history and his migrant experiences with a decidedly Africa-centric outlook. Wherever the migrant turns, water, land and air surrounds them in perpetuity, one unending whole, interdependent, each element different yet the same wherever the body encounters it. Wherever one sets foot, the land remains a source of fertility, of balance, deity and provenance, just as water remains unchanging, be it free flowing or bound within land, be it river or sea, lake or ocean. Oriogun attests to the consistent nature of water in more places, 'Here, in the midst of women dancing/ on the riverbank, I didn't discover the path/home, I only saw a goddess, the endlessness of water' (86). The poem 'It Begins with Love', opens with a fisherman's whispered prayers against the ill omen of happening upon a drowned and bloated body – in which case water would be cause of, and the conveyor in, death. The poem then talks about how love is interwoven into most facets of life and ends with a plea: 'Omi, spare us in death, spare us in life.' (113). Omi here means water, a direct reference to Olokun.

'Bini appreciation of the pragmatic qualities of the ocean provides a backdrop for a host of images, symbols, and semantic clusters concerned with wealth, fertility, joy, purity, and death' (Nevadomsky, 1988). Another Oriogun poem where the water deity towers is 'Lamentation':

Because my legs have travelled
to far places, I must sing

History and the Call of Water in Romeo Oriogun's 'Nomad' 57

with the iron bell, your praises
the mist of the morning. The river
full of mirrors is not enough
to show your beauty.

This poet persona, having travelled to far places, still attempts to sing the praises of Olokun. Key points to note here are the fact that bells are used to invoke the deity, and mirrors symbolise the purity of Olokun. The speaker continues by asking:

Will the ocean recognise me?
My song bows, who will raise it
Who will sing when the flash
of your skirt lifts the fishes?
Every deity becomes small
in translation…

In this piece, the speaker is a migrant son contemplating the inefficacy of rituals done by one who is adrift and unable to pay proper homage to Olokun. Water here is a lost deity, while the poet persona here is adrift in another man's land where 'the Priestess's feet are lost to wind, foamy waves are without cowries'. Olokun is symbolic in Oriogun's poems, and he is both deity lost and reclaimed, held aloft, revered in memory and verse.

In *Nomad*, Romeo Oriogun interrogates the past and present and shows a deep awareness and commitment to the politics of migration. Employing the poems in the book for a polemic conversation with postcolonial structures in present day Africa, Oriogun points out through impassioned verses the sad reality of the apparent unending cycle of migration, movements which are not always successful. Beyond the OIM discourse of migration – its numbers, inherent dangers and risks – Oriogun's *Nomad* gives us a historic, tender and personalized look at the continuous crossings from Africa to other parts of the world. The people-drain on the continent is reminiscent of the 400-year long slave trade, but where the transatlantic slave trade was forced and violent, the neo-colonial migration of people in twenty-first-century Africa is often voluntary, and sometimes violent. The poems in this book point to the complicity of governance structures in the continent. In this we see the indictment of ancestors who sold off their people into the slave trade rolling into the indictment of present leaders. Oriogun wraps up this tale of exile within the shroud of Bini mythology, using the ocean as deity, as origin and safety, as conveyor, as gravesite and repository of history. The waters in and around Africa

58 *Iquo DianaAbasi*

ebb and flow, and the citizens ebb with it, they dive into water knowing communion with the dead awaits them (2021: 105). The people are nagged by the burden of memory and loss, as the land itself droops under the weight of the drain of her skilled children. The sojourners rarely return, though, and if they can start new lives in the West, they remain there, hoping, waiting for a ray of light in the homeland. In the end, one cannot but agree with Oriogun, 'in exile there is no revenge against home,/there is nothing, only the waiting, the slow dawn of light' (2021: 85).

WORKS CITED

Drabinski, John E., et al. Postcolonial Bergson. Fordham University Press, 2019. Project MUSE muse.jhu.edu/book/67907.

Gbogi, Tosin. Against 'Afropolitanism: Race and the Black migrant body in contemporary African poetry'. *The Journal of Commonwealth Literature*, 2022, DOI: 10.1177/00219894221113767

Idemudia, Erhabor, et al. 'Patterns and current trends in African migration to Europe'. Psychosocial Experiences of African Migrants in Six European Countries: A Mixed Method Study (2020): 15-31.

IOM; 2011. Available at http://www.iom.int/V3S12_CM.pdf(SE)

McMahon Simon and Sigona Nando. 'Navigating the Central Mediterranean in a Time of "Crisis": Disentangling Migration Governance and Migrant Journeys'. *Sociology* 2018, Vol. 52(3) 97–514.

Nevadomsky J. and Norma R. The Initiation of a Priestess Performance and Imagery in Olokun Ritual.

Ogu, Patricia Ihuoma. 'Africa's irregular migration to Europe: a reenactment of the transatlantic slave trade'. *Journal of Global Research in Education and Social Science* 10.2 (2017): 49–69.

Okigbo, Christopher. Labyrinths with Path of Thunder. 1972

Oriogun, Romeo. Nomad. Griots Lounge, 2020.

Voice, Identity, Tradition in Postcolonial Modernism
T. S. Eliot and Kofi Anyidoho from the Perspectives of Posthumanism and Post-Deconstruction

MILENA VLADIĆ JOVANOV

Using comparative analysis to explore the intricate relationship between modernism and postcolonialism, this paper elucidates the philosophical underpinnings and interpretations of the poems by T. S. Eliot and Kofi Anyidoho. Through the concepts of voice, self-awareness, tradition, and identity, the notion of postcolonial modernism is delineated. In T. S. Eliot's poetry, the voice does not serve as the core of self-awareness and identity; rather, identity is constructed upon non-identity and *différance*. Fundamentals and origins are displaced, giving rise to a system that is not merely a dynamic poetic system but is also transposed. In Anyidoho's poetry, voices are manifold, akin to Eliot's, and can be both narrative and lyrical. They blend in a structural-semantic interweaving to construct clusters of themes that foster self-realization regarding the role of African culture in the development of the nation, as depicted in customs and contemporary socio-political situations.

The tripartite relationship of Anyidoho with fellow poets Edward Kamau Brathwaite and Derek Walcott, who employed modernist elements and techniques, emphasized precisely what Eliot desired for Western culture: a transformation and a living tradition that communicates with the past not as a lifeless monument but as a living, experiential entity, forming diverse Deleuzian plateaus [1] – see Gilles Deleuze and Félix Guattari, A Thousand Plateaus, Capitalism and Schizophrenia. (Minneapolis: University of Minnesota Press, 2005) – branching out in different dimensions. The domain of modernism expands through artistic methods and an understanding of the language and culture of postcolonial poetry. The question of exile is linked to the adoption and imposition of cultural patterns, but it is no longer solely about physical space. Postcolonial poets have shown that exile is not just a physical location but a state of consciousness of an individual who, without a group or foundation, becomes one among

60   *Milena Vladić Jovanov*

many, locked in their own world despite being surrounded by people in metropolises. Therefore, in the study of structures and fundamental philosophical assumptions, post-deconstruction and post-humanistic elements and values are introduced into modernist poetry in contrast to humanistic values in postcolonialism.

In this paper, a theoretical framework of deconstruction, which manifests as an interpretative approach in the analysis of the poetry of Anyidoho and Eliot, has been articulated. Subsequently, the paper will elucidate the deconstructive voids discovered in meaningful wholes that are contextualized by the introduction of new lines of inquiry into previously analyzed existing poems. Anyidoho advances beyond the modernist Eliot in his treatment of voids that acquire and construct meaning through their spatiality. In the poem 'Memory and Vision *for Children of Musu*', the following lines are encountered: 'A people once enslaved, they say/are too often too willing/to be a *People Self-enslaved*'[1] (Anyidoho 26), which not only materialize voids but also embody a distinctively deconstructive approach, suggesting that a nation has 'voluntarily' become an enslaved nation. Such deconstructive writing implies that this nation has been shaped under the influence of slavery. The graphic deconstructive expression indicates that it was subjected to enslavement but never acquiesced to it. The intricate metatextual quality implies that the poet is cognizant of the dual nature of slavery and articulates it in a deconstructive fashion. That both Eliot and Anyidoho connect tradition with voice is confirmed by the lines of the Ghanaian poet: '*And those who took away our Voice/They are now surprised/They couldn't take away our Song*'[2] (Anyidoho 31).

The initial segment of this paper is dedicated to exploring the similarities and differences in the ways Eliot and Anyidoho interpret the connection between tradition and voice. In Eliot's case, a substantial portion is devoted to examining the status of the poetic subject Tiresias, who, despite being capable of using the first-person pronoun *I*, cannot guarantee the firm sense that Poirier describes, but is, as the author suggests, in pursuit of meaning. Similar to Eliot, Anyidoho employs the relationship between voice and tradition, wherein his poetic subjects, whether in dramatic dialogues, *halo* poetry, or introspection about space and the narrativization of space-time as per Homi Bhabha, consistently maintain a stable voice.

---

1   Highlighted in italic by Milena Vladić Jovanov.
2   *Ibid.*

Eliot did not traverse the center of contemporary culture like Anyidoho but sought the center in cultural models deconstructively. Although Eliot and Anyidoho share similarities in linking voice with tradition, they do exhibit differences. Consequently, a section has been devoted to the analysis of the poetic subject Tiresias in Eliot's work, to demonstrate that even the sole subject in Eliot's poetry capable of declaring *I* is semantically distinct from the certainty and uniqueness of *I*. Anyidoho, on the other hand, even in the complex meta-qualities where he distinguishes between the twins of Europe and Africa, ensures that each possesses its own *I*, thereby establishing its own perspective.

In T. S. Eliot's 'The Waste Land', scholars such as Harriet Davidson, Charles Altieri, Helen Vendler,[3] and many others interpret the concept of voice as a means to achieve unity on a structural level. This entails finding a structural center that can govern the disjunctive and fragmented nature of the poem, ultimately uncovering a shared meaning. For the structural center,, they often select verses that are graphically marked and belong to Prufrock's 'Pervigilium', specifically lines 70 to 74, which do not belong to the published version of 'The Love Song of J. Alfred Prufrock'.

As Paul de Man suggests,[4] interpretation is simultaneously blindness and insight. In other words, as Derrida notes, the center of the structure is both within and outside it. 'The center is not center. The concept of centered structure – although it represents coherence itself, the condition of the *epistēmē* as philosophy or science – is contradictorily coherent. And as always, coherence in contradiction expresses the force of a desire.' (Derrida 1978) Derrida's notion of centred structures, where the center is both within and outside the structure, corresponds to Paul de Man's idea of interpretation as being twofold – it is both insight and blindness. Just as interpreters seek the center of the structure, hoping it will provide them with meaning, they

---

3   See Harriet Davidson. *T. S. Eliot and Heremeneutics. Absence and Interpretation in The Waste Land.* (Baton Rouge and London: Louisiana State University Press, 1985). Also see Helen Vendler. *Coming of Age as a Poet.* (Cambridge, Massachusetts: Harvard University Press, 2003) Also see Charles Altieri. *The Particulars of Rapture. An Aesthetics of the Affects.* (Ithaca. London: Cornell University Press, 2003). Also see his Lectures at Berkeley edited online.

4   See Paul de Man. *Blindness and Insight – Essays in the Rhetoric of Contemporary Criticism.* (New York: Oxford University Press, 1971).

62 *Milena Vladić Jovanov*

also search for a singular voice through which the poetic subject can address itself with the first-person pronoun *I*.

Peter Hühn emphasizes that the poem 'Portrait of a Lady' has a narrative character. There are narratives of the lady and the gentleman, which overlap and conflict. There is also a superior voice that shapes the self-awareness of the poetic subject, as the author highlights. I would like to add that there is also a reader's narrative, as it is the reader who reveals the connections between the lines of allusions in Shakespeare's 'Twelfth Night' and 'Portrait of a Lady', as well as 'Portrait of a Lady' and 'The Love Song of J. Alfred Prufrock.' If one takes a closer look, the poem has a dual structure without any leading voice. One is oriented towards the reality of the poetic subjects, describing the salon, an evening in the park, a concert, senseless conversations, polished manners, and so on, while the other is oriented towards culture and literature, with the latter lacking a single center or a single voice. No voice could be attributed to or be recognized in the lines that Peter Hühn calls the textual mark of the gentleman's self-awareness, alluding to Shakespeare's 'Twelfth Night': 'If music be the food of love, play on:/Give me excess of it, that surfeiting,/The appetite may sicken and so die./That strain again, it had a dying fall […]' (Shakespeare 93). In 'Portrait of a Lady,' one encounters the line, 'This music is successful with a "dying fall."' (Eliot 11) Unless the assumption is made that the poetic subject is metatextually given and reflects the poet himself, which is not the case here because the character of the gentleman could not have 'known' about the hidden allusion to Shakespeare, Eliot's poetic system provides interpretations with multiple conclusions. One of them is the depiction of reality through human characteristics: as people are, so is reality. Prufrock speaks of everything except love, which is indicated by the intertextual reference in the title of the poem. The gentleman doesn't hear the lady, and there is a complete absence of communication in the poem. Eliot employs a cultural model, relying on Shakespeare and his own internal poetic model, linking 'Portrait of a Lady' with 'The Love Song of J. Alfred Prufrock', as evidenced by the lines within quotation marks in the former, suggesting that Eliot is now quoting himself, without relying on Shakespeare as a foundation. Eliot equally values both voice and tradition, while critically questioning traditional values as well as contemporary ones, as he has not bestowed upon them a stable voice.

In Eliot's system, everything is displaced, and there is no foundation anywhere. In the poetry of Kofi Anyidoho, one finds a more humanistic world, full of voices of sorrow, joy, debate, but voices that are more

Voice, Identity, Tradition in Postcolonial Modernism 63

human. The poetic foundation is much clearer and is not, even when exposed to meta-qualities, separated and fragment. The disunity and fragmentation in Eliot differ from the divisions in Anyidoho. Turning to the 'compound ghost' from T. S. Eliot's 'Four Quartets', the division, which represents *différance* in creating identity in relation to non-identity – i.e. the external and the other in relation to the inner *self*, which, as J. Lacan would put it, is not singular from the beginning because it represents a Gestalt in motion – in a comparative analysis with meta-qualities and division found in Anyidoho, presents a different cultural model. The entire scene in 'Four Quartets' is permeated with elements of uncertainty and double meanings that lead from the linguistic level, where expressions such as 'metal leaves' (Eliot 140) create an atmosphere of uncertainty and ghostliness at the thematic level. The time of the encounter is unknown because the encounter is 'in the uncertain hour before the morning' (Eliot 140), nor is the place of the meeting known since 'of meeting nowhere, no before, no after' (Eliot 140). Not even the appearance of the dead teacher the poetic speaker encounters, the 'compound ghost', is known. This scene, no matter how much it contains the negation of the conscious by what constitutes it, shifting its basis away from the center, thus leaving it in an aphoristic passage where questions are posed and answers are given but never final, has one of the hallmarks of modernism that Eliot brilliantly used: the division of the self which reflects the divisions and differences in culture, gaps that are irreconcilable.

At the same time, this semantic level reflects and intertwines with the structural one, opening a new poetic theme: a dialogue with oneself. Not just any dialogue but a time-bound dialogue in which one self speaks to its other self from another time, connecting the selves of different times into a new self. Such a transformation is vividly portrayed but is surrounded by an eerie atmosphere that suggests that the encounter of such selves within one person can take place on the level of self-encountering imaginary spectral beings. All of this makes the world Eliot describes deeply post-humanistic, unreal, just as the cities and characters he describes are both unreal and real, with London, topographically described, being realistic, while the faces are overlapping instead of being singular, which he states through the character of Tiresias in the footnotes of 'The Waste Land'. The cultural example he chose has already undergone a transformation in the sense that it was once within the body of both a woman and a man. When the poetic speaker in 'Four Quartets' hears himself in this scene, he hears the other's shout. The relationship between the two is strongly emphasized.

64 *Milena Vladić Jovanov*

Such a relationship will also follow in Anyidoho's poetry, with the difference that, in his poetry, especially in the poem 'The Song of a Twin Brother', the voice will be clear, as well as the messages it conveys. The foundations won't bury each other, and the culture he describes is the culture of individual life and the life of the African community within. Their intertwining builds the idea of the identity of exile in a foreign space that becomes imbued with culture, no matter how much the given space changes. Since Eliot's voice and the role of the poetic speaker are duplicated, yet the foundations of that voice unclear, the difference in verses allows for more clarity to ensue.

Anyidoho writes about two twin brothers. The fact that they are twins suggests that they are the same but also different. Similar to Eliot's poetic speaker, who takes on a double role, being the same but still different, and who hears his own voice as if it's someone else's, Anyidoho portrays an imagined dialogue between twin brothers who are similar but different because they have chosen different worlds: one African, the other Western. In this dialogue, akin to the critical stances and dialogues of W. B. Yeats and Ezra Pound and the play of personae, Anyidoho conveys the role of an individual in African society and what it means to be in one's own country yet in exile. The same but different, the twins are like the face of the god Janus, representing the Western and African worlds. The twin who stayed in Africa tells his brother that, without roots, there is no future. Furthermore, concepts such as name, voice, word, and song have a special meaning in Anyidoho's poetry. The twin brother gives his name to the winds: 'I give your name to the winds./They will roam the world and find your ears' (Anyidoho 55). Voice and song have not only a metatextual form but also deep political nuances. In the poem 'Lolita Jones', 'and so they says my name is Lolita Jones?/But that ain't my real name/I never has known ma name our Name./[…] Ma Name cud`a been Sculptured/ Into Colors of the Rainbow/Across the bosom of our Earth' (Anyidoho 29), he goes on to carve out the political and cultural nuance: 'But you see: Long ago your People sold ma People./Ma People sold to Atlantic's Storms./The Storms first it took away our name/And it tried to strip us of our Soul.' (Anyidoho 29) A poem is not just an artistic piece; it is a communal song of an African nation – the song of the people.

The notion of tradition can be similarly applied to poets like Kofi Anyidoho, a Ghanaian poet, and two Caribbean poets, Derek Walcott and Kamau Brathwaite, who are part of African culture. Postcolonial poets have constructed their own traditions; they haven't merely inherited and adapted them. In their works, more clearly can one of

Voice, Identity, Tradition in Postcolonial Modernism   65

the most important aspects of Eliot's understanding of tradition from his famous essay 'Tradition and the Individual Talent' be observed, and that is the quality of metamorphosis. 'This historical sense, which is a sense of the timeless as well as the temporal and of the timeless and of the temporal together, is what makes a writer traditional.' (Eliot 5) Such a poet is Kofi Anyidoho. Tradition in his poetry merges the contemporary spirit, as required by individual talent, and portrays the socio-political reality. At the linguistic level, the poet playfully engages with modernist elements in a postcolonial context. Anyidoho simultaneously weaves three levels: the linguistic, the socio-political-thematic, and the cultural-African. Linguistically, two lines are to be followed: the historical-etymological, as in the name of the African state Zimbabwe and the river Zambezi that flows through Zimbabwe and Zambia. Anyidoho playfully introduces graphical elements in a modernist fashion, separating the initial three letters 'Zam and Zim' from 'Bia-Bezi-Babwe-Zambia', creating a wordplay and a connection between the great Zambezi River, the state of Zimbabwe, and Zambia. The linguistic level is also political because it introduces the historical context of colonial dominance and Western culture over Zimbabwe, as well as later uprisings and Zimbabwe's liberation. The intertwining of linguistic and historical-colonial experiences suggests that none of the three levels is independent.

In other words, each exists within the other but does not undermine the other. The critical aspect, which also exists on the linguistic level, is reflected in the historical-contemporary perspective: those who ruled, like Queen Victoria, and those who colonized are now facing the changing nature of water. The concept of water and the metaphor of water are ancient symbols of transformation, power, and the dual nature of creation and destruction. From a poetic and philosophical standpoint, the question arises: which of the two aspects predominates – creation, the birth of nature through water, or destruction, the downfall of civilizations through floods? Eliot employs the metaphor of water in 'Four Quartets', particularly in 'The Dry Salvages', within lines 'I do not know much about gods; but I think that the river/Is a strong brown god – sullen, untamed and intractable,/Patient to some degree. [...] Then only a problem confronting the builders of bridges./The problem once solved, the brown god is almost forgotten/By the dwellers in cities – ever, however, implacable,/Keeping his seasons and rages, destroyer, reminder/Of what men choose to forget' (Eliot 130). The river is a destroyer deity, yet 'His rhythm was present in the nursery bedroom'.

66   *Milena Vladić Jovanov*

In contrast to Eliot, who emphasizes both the constructive and destructive powers of the river, Anyidoho emphasizes the river's constancy, contrasting it with the images of societal constructive and destructive forces. The constancy of the river, which is African and persists regardless of changes in power, whether colonial, corrupt, or liberating, is highlighted. The river is a blessing for all, for humans, animals, and nature as a whole. Eliot is tied to an urban landscape, featuring images of the river's presence in a child's room and garden. In contrast, Anyidoho is connected to images of the sky, the earth, and the entirety of nature. Zambezi is not just a river passing through Zambia and Zimbabwe, just as the Danube is not just German, Austrian, Serbian, or Romanian. Zambezi is an African river, just as the Danube is a European river. Therefore, the poetic subject in Anyidoho's work conveys, 'History is but the Future/We should have known in the Past' (Anyidoho 48).

Reality is also presented from a political perspective. Anyidoho plays with the names Victoria Falls and the reign of Queen Victoria. These names also allude to both water and the reign of the English monarchy. It's important to note that Anyidoho's verses also hint at the kingdom that existed in Zimbabwe: 'The mysteries of these lands/ Are deeper, loftier than/The Empire Builder's dreams' (Anyidoho 48). Kofi Anyidoho also engages with personal pronouns. Initially, he plays with the pronoun in the third person singular, which relates to Queen Victoria, and subsequently, he employs the pronoun in the third person plural, which pertains to the knowledge of governance and various rulers of Zimbabwe, cities, as well as the African people who should be familiar with their history. By saying that, 'one of these days/ Old Victoria shall have/to Gather her Wayward Children Home/If only she knew' (Anyidoho 48), the transition from the personal pronoun in the third person singular to the third person plural is accompanied by historical and political elements and is reflected in the linguistic choice. 'Mutare Rusape Harare/Chirendzi Chipinge Chirundu/Chimanimani Bulawayo Mbaalabala/The Souls of these Names/Are older than the Time/We count across our Mind's spaces. [...] If only they knew. If only' (Anyidoho 49-50) further demonstrates his play with personal pronouns, where he reverts to the third person singular, focusing on Victoria, who symbolizes the decline of her rule, signifying the fall of colonial governance. This transformation is also evident graphically in the language: 'So one of these days/Poor Victoria shall have/To trek her dreams across her own safari of pain/Poor Victoria shall have/To go back home to her QueenDom Gone. [...] Victoria FALLS ....!'

Voice, Identity, Tradition in Postcolonial Modernism   67

(Anyidoho 50). Linguistically, Anyidoho exemplifies the essence of Eliot's concept of tradition using a practical illustration. It is not merely about the past merging into the present and vice versa, but rather a Heideggerian[5] sequence of presents. In this understanding, tradition, as a concept, exists contemporaneously with the future. The present provides a sequence of pasts and insights into the future, emphasizing a constant modification of the past into the future.

Heidegger also emphasizes that being, as an individual, is grounded and phenomenologically appropriated by an event. Moreover, Being, as essence, as Logos, is also appropriated by an event, while simultaneously bestowing the event upon a multitude of beings. *Sein* is a part of *Da Sein*, and vice versa. In other words, there is no pause in Aristotle's conception of time as movement, where the present, identified with the presence of Logos, would be a singular point, nor does it align with Hegel's interpretation, where the present equates to *Jetzt*. Heidegger[6] considered this view of time vulgar, as it fails to recognize that movement exists even within the point itself, which serves as the center, with one half encompassing the past and the other, the future. Thus, the present is inherently fluid and constantly erased. What does this essentially mean for the poetry of postcolonial poets?

Kofi Anyidoho espouses poetic convictions aligned with Heidegger's discourse on a modified present, as exemplified in the verses from 'Memory and Vision': 'Time before Memory./Memory beyond Time' (Anyidoho 22). The expression 'Memory beyond time' can be intertextually connected to the phrase 'The endless saga of AncestralTime' (Anyidoho 22), while 'Time before Memory' articulates a reimagined reality and temporal experience, inviting the poet's compatriots on a journey: 'We all must make into our Past/in order to come to terms with our Future' (Anyidoho 23). The poet reconfigures the past and present into an altered present since 'For Five Hundred Years and more we have/journeyed into various spaces of the Earth./ And everywhere we go we must confront/dimensions of ourselves we did not know were there' (Anyidoho 23).

Structurally, these lines not only resonate with Heidegger's reflections on time but also with Anyidoho's previously discussed

---

5   Martin Heidegger: *Beiträge zur Philosophie (Vom Ereignis), Gesamtausgabe*, band 65, Herausgegeben von Friedrich-Wilchelm von Herrmann (Frankfurt am Main, Satz und Druck: Poeschel & Schulz – Schomburgk, 1989), 27.
6   See M. Heidegger. *Being and Time* (New York: Harper and Row, 1962).

68 *Milena Vladić Jovanov*

engagement with deconstruction theory. The contextualization is inherent within the text itself. Thus, the lines can be interconnected both internally, through textual mechanisms, and externally, through contextual means, resulting in thematic enrichment. The theme of political and geopolitical emancipation from Western influence on the African continent is introduced, as evidenced in the lines: 'It cannot must not be/that the rest of the world came upon us/picked us up/ used us to clean their mess/dropped us off into trash' (Anyidoho 24).

Simultaneously, Heidegger's conceptualization of time can be linked with Anyidoho's poetry and the perspectives of Homi Bhabha, who is significantly influenced by deconstruction. In the essay 'DissemiNation: time, narrative, and the margins of the modern nation', the title itself embodies the impact of deconstruction, signifying the dual meanings of the concepts of dissemination and nation. These concepts can be considered both separately and in conjunction. Initially, the term pertains to the concept of dissemination, followed by the dissemination of a specific concept, namely, the nation. The nation, akin to the philosophical notion of dissemination, is precisely realized through altered, modified concepts of time, which entail a modification of space, or the present, which, through its temporal pattern, transforms space and endows the nation inhabiting that space with the attributes of nationality and the ownership of identity, ranging from individual identity to the tradition of identity.

As Bhabha highlights in his essay, citing European poets, particularly Goethe, the focus is on distinct nations and spaces. Nevertheless, he also asserts that modernism is problematic precisely due to spatial boundaries, as they are reinvigorated in 'ambivalent temporalities of the nation/space' (Bhabha 294). Bhabha engages with phrases that are positioned deconstructively, not in terms of either/or but rather both/ and. The nation is part of space and vice versa, yet it is essential to temporalize different spaces, achievable only through narrativization, that is, through song and narrative, recounting the history of the nation and its future prospects through the modification of the present, which encapsulates the lived experience of the nation. Thus, Bhabha playfully engages with the concepts *Out of many, one* and *The many is one* in a deconstructive manner. This leads to Anyidoho's understanding of identity.

During a conversation with him upon his receipt of a lifetime achievement award in Serbia,[7] he articulated his view on the identity

---

7   Kofi Anyidoho received the lifetime achievement award 'Golden Key of

of his nation and his literary expression of it, stating that identity is rooted in heritage. I then referenced Edward Kamau Brathwaite, who also endeavored to reconnect with African traditions, particularly through the deity Ogun, to establish a new tradition shaped by the presence of colonialists and conquerors. Notably, Brathwaite incorporated modernist poetic conventions in his work, which extend beyond a mere graphical or visual style, akin to that of Paul Claudel, to a complexity and maturity comparable to the expressions of both Eliot and Anyidoho. In a certain regard, Anyidoho has transcended Eliot in the graphical articulation of meaning, a feat Poirier deems challenging within modernism. The spatial voids in Anyidoho's poetry exhibit a more pronounced impact than the fragments in Eliot's work. These voids, along with the influence of modernism on African poets and the reciprocal impact of postcolonial poets on modernism, evoke the concept of exile, previously discussed in this paper. Eliot, Anyidoho, Brathwaite, and Walcott share the experience of exile, unified by their use of the English language. According to Bhabha, this implies the adoption of the terms of the occupying nation. Hence, their exile can be perceived as twofold: they exist in exile but also transcend it by locating their roots and exerting their influence within the linguistic and cultural sphere of the English language and its associated nation.

Eliot's reader assumes a more elevated role than that of a semantic reader, involving the development of various semiotic reader roles, whereas Anyidoho addresses readers from African culture, and surprisingly, although they are all different, they are comprehensible to readers in various spaces and times. The political role is not solely about the preservation of African art but also its new development. The fragmentation and disintegration of colonial culture after the Great War influenced a multitude of artists. For Wallace Stevens, Pound, and Eliot, culture becomes a project to rescue art. From an artistic perspective, the poetic texts of these poets reflect not only a dual relationship with culture, in terms of the search for a foundation that will negate modernity due to the lack of communication, empathy, and humanity in contemporary interpersonal relationships, but also the impossibility of actualizing the cultural manners of the previous

---

Smederevo' in the Republic of Serbia at the international poetry festival 'Smederevo Poets Autumn' in 2022. The award committee consisted of Prof. Dr. Milena Vladić Jovanov, president, and committee members Prof. Dr. Boško Suvajdić and M. A. Tatjana Lazarević Milošević. Predrag Pešić and Milena Vladić Jovanov translated selected poems into Serbian.

70 *Milena Vladić Jovanov*

era because civilization has surpassed them. Richard Poirier, in *Poetry and Pragmatism*, therefore, states that modern art is actually not a search for meaning but a search for hints of meaning. Poirier mentions in the context of Robert Frost's poem 'For Once, Then, Something' that the very title of the poem 'indicates a willingness to celebrate not a gift of meaning but only an inconclusive promise of it' (Poirier 145). Is the meaning clear, or is it only a hint, or does it already exist in Kofi Anyidoho's position?

The political moment is also a play on words between the name 'Victoria Falls' and the fall of Queen Victoria. In African culture, as well as in a Western context, it is quite clear what this means. But what transpires here is a conversation about the impossibility of finding a center, a voice that would be common to the entire West, and such a voice did not exist in the twentieth century. Such a voice has emerged in the twenty-first century within the media narrative, but it shares its fictional nature and thereby becomes exactly what it is not: a departure from the idea of any truth, acquiring manipulative characteristics. If it is homogenized, the question arises as to what makes African culture unique. Brathwaite is from the Caribbean islands, Walcott as well, and Nancy Morejón is from Cuba. However, in all these poets, including Kofi Anyidoho, a poetic image appears that is clear to all readers. One of them is the singing of songs, the creation of poetry, which, in Kofi's case, is associated with the history of ancestors, music, and the art of eloquence that can compete with any Western tradition. In Brathwaite's case, it's the graphic form of poems that he shares with Kofi Anyidoho, which somewhat resembles the musical scales of live song performance that Western poetry cannot afford because it lacks the musicality and the relationship of the poet as a bard to his own poetry. In the case of Walcott, there is a critical moment of Western culture as he speaks of modern African cannibals who will eat the body of Christ, reminiscent of biblical symbols that refer to the most potent prayer, 'Our Father, give us our daily bread.' It also alludes to the symbolic communion in which Christ's body becomes bread, and His blood becomes wine. Nancy Morejón talks about the body of a black girl that occupies the space of her movements but spreads like an image of African culture over Cuban culture.

Readers of Anyidoho's poetry would all understand it, just as they would understand Morejón's poetry. They are all interconnected intertextually with their unique inner echoes. However, Anyidoho also addresses contemporary themes of exile, movement, and migration, both departure and arrival. He emphasizes his origins similarly to

Voice, Identity, Tradition in Postcolonial Modernism **71**

Kamau Brathwaite when he sings of Ogun. However, he also has a metatextual and critical moment shared with Walcott when Walcott writes about Crusoe's journal, reviving in the reader's consciousness the first outcast, Crusoe, who imposed his culture and the trials he went through, realization for greater clarity of what his culture is in comparison to all the 'good Fridays', as Walcott states in his poem. Crusoe is alone in 'Crusoe's Journal', and he imposes rules that are not in harmony with the nature he finds himself in. By imposing the rules of 'white culture', Crusoe goes into self-exile. Defoe's first modernist novel showed that at its core, Crusoe is alone.

Neither Eliot nor Pound, when he claims that a poet is one who has ambitions to change the world, and thus the culture, and that poets – contrary to Shelley's statement – are the true legislator of the world, managed to create a community that would respect or at least apply these laws. Although he refers to his origins – the troubadour poets – in 'Piere Vidal Old', Pound didn't succeed in forming a community. In the poem about the contemporary poet 'Hugh Selwyn Mauberley', even though he complains about the conditions and themes that modern poets describe, he fails to invoke a cultural community in the consciousness of the contemporary reader. Eliot, on the other hand, won't be understood by any community that follows the culture he invokes until they feel what that culture has felt. At the same time, both poets are solitary, and both poets refer to a culture that needs to be known but whose time has passed. Although they refer to an educated reader, whom they create through the act of reading their poems, leading to new insights into what that culture was and what was lost within it, both poets, despite the collaborations they had, remain solitary. For example, they might not have had a twin brother, someone who is different but whom culture and community call to return. I think they didn't have one when I compare the role of the poet and the poetic work as well as its echo with Anyidoho's 'The Song of a Twin Brother'. Unlike Eliot and Pound, where an individual voice turns to culture, Anyidoho's poetry turns to African culture, which stands like a Janus-faced sculpture, turned towards itself and the whole world.

In 'The Song of a Twin Brother,' Anyidoho illustrates exile in a markedly different manner. Exile isn't merely a physical place; it's a psychological space, a state of consciousness: it's being estranged from one's own culture. These two brothers differ in that one embraces Western customs while the other calls him to return to Africa. One has departed while the other remains. However, in that act of remaining,

72 Milena Vladić Jovanov

poetic destiny conveys to us what has occurred in the absence of his twin brother, embodied in his other *self*. Anyidoho navigates through the realm of the English language, as it's his secondary language alongside his mother tongue. With this secondary language, he has also adopted another culture. Have we adopted African culture? Do we comprehend his poems, which have been embraced by the younger generation, with contemporary music often using his verses? This prompts the question of what the twin brother symbolizes within the framework of English language and culture.

For instance, Eliot sensed this when he expressed in a letter to his friend Mary Hutchinson[8] that he was a 'metic'. As a member of that culture by language, Eliot doesn't feel entirely at ease. The reason for this discomfort lies in the subtleties to which he doesn't feel connected in the culture he writes about. The space he belongs to is not the space that Anyidoho or Morejón have. It's not the black female body or the twins who speak in the same voice about departure and remaining in the same culture. It's Eliot's voice, an American in the English tradition. This is also demonstrated in the lines in Eliot's 'Four Quartets' in the form of 'compound ghosts'. Eliot's poetic persona converses with himself, with an instructor, who is himself – sometimes familiar and known, sometimes entirely unknown. He is one and many from the culture to which Eliot's poetic persona beckons. However, the two don't recognize each other, and if they do, they do so in a post-human world where the leaves on the asphalt are metallic.

Anyidoho's twin, although possessing metatextual qualities and metaphorically invoking himself as a twin, does not contain post-humanist elements. On the contrary, it is presented in the form of a lament that is not condemnatory. The dialogue unfolds as both turn to African culture, one who has departed and the other who has remained. In the space of their dialogue, a political thought emerges as to why one left and the other stayed.

Far from believing that Western culture's adherents wouldn't understand, they are separated only by wars. It's difficult for someone of Austrian origin to understand that Italians took away South Tyrol, where Austrians still reside. I believe that everyone is in exile from their own cultures, the boundaries of which have been transcended by postcolonial culture, becoming something one must not only consider part of modernism and contemporary times but something one wants to embrace.

---

8   See T. S. Eliot. 'To Mary Hutchinson', *The Letters of T. S. Eliot*. Volume I. 1898–1922. (New York: Harcourt Brace Jovanovich, 1988).

Anyidoho has developed a different role for the poet, in which he represents the heir to his ancestors and continues the poetic lineage of his own people, where poetry has been sung and written. The poet is a word gatherer, sharing them like a tree, reminiscent of Kamau Brathwaite's poem 'Ogun'. They create objects for a new civilization and words for a new culture. In light of the theoretical insights presented, it is feasible to contemplate the notion of postcolonial modernism or modernist postcolonialism, considering the significant contribution of postcolonialism to the modernist poetic tradition as delineated from the aforementioned world.

WORKS CITED

Anyidoho, Kofi. Ancestrallogic & Caribbeanblues. Trenton, New Jersey: Africa World Press, Inc.

———— Earthchild with Brain Surgery. Accra: Woeli Publishing Services, 1985.

———— Seed Time: Selected Poems I. Accra: DAkpabli & Associates, 2022.

———— PraiseSong for TheLand: Poems of Hope & Love & Care. Accra: Sub-Saharan Publishers, 2002.

———— Elegy for the Revolution. New York: The Greenfield Review Press, 1978.

Ahluwalia, P. Politics and Post-colonial Theory. New York: Verso, 1999.

Bhabha, Homi K. 'DissemiNation: time, narrative, and the margins of the modern nation' in Nation and Narration. London and New York: Routledge, 1990.

Boscagli, Maurizia. Eye on the Flesh: Fashions of Masculinity in the Early Twentieth Century. Boulder, CO: Westview Press, 1996.

Davidson, Harriet. T. S. Eliot and Hermeneutics. Absence and Interpretation in the Waste Land. Baton Rouge and London: Louisiana State University Press, 1985.

Deleuze, Gilles. Guattari, Félix. A Thousand Plateaus. Capitalism and Schizophrenia. Minneapolis. London: University of Minnesota Press, 1987.

Derrida, Jacques. Writing and Difference. Chicago: The University of Chicago Press, 1978.

———— Aporias. California: Stanford University Press, 1993.

———— Dissemination. Chicago: The University of Chicago Press, 1981.

Eliot, T. S. The Complete Poems and Plays 1909–1950. New York: Harcourt Brace & Company, 1952.

———— Inventions of the March Hare. Poems 1909–1917. Ed. by Christopher Ricks. New York: A Harvest Book. Harcourt Brace and Company, 1996.

———— Selected Essays 1917–1932. New York: Harcourt, Brace and Company, 1932.

———— The Letters of T. S. Eliot. New York: Harcourt Brace Jovanovich, 1988.

74 *Milena Vladić Jovanov*

Egudu, R. Modern African Poetry and the African Predicament. London: Macmillan, 1978.

Griffiths, Gareth. African Literatures in English. East and West. London and New York: Routledge, 2014.

Heidegger, Martin. (1989) Beiträge zur Philosophie (Vom Ereignis), Gesamtausgabe, band 65, Herausgegeben von Friedrich-Wilchelm von Herrmann, Frankfurt am Main, Satz und Druck: Poeschel & Schulz – Schomburgk.

Kenner, Hugh. 'The Urban Apocalypse' in Eliot in His Time. Editor A. Walton Litz. Princeton, New Jersey: Princeton University Press, 1973.

Madden, Ed. Tiresian Poetics. Modernism, Sexuality, Voice, 1888–2001. Madison, Teaneck: Fairleigh Dickinson University Press, 2008.

Mayer, John T. T. S. Eliot's Silent Voices. New York. Oxford: Oxford University Press, 1989.

Ngugi, W. T. Moving the Centre: The Struggle for Cultural Freedom. London: James Carrey, 1993.

Okon, F. Politics and the Development of Modern African Poetry. English Language and Literature Studies, 2013.

Pound, Ezra. Poems and Translations. New York: The Library of America, 2003.

Richard Poirier. Poetry and Pragmatism. Cambridge, MA: Harvard University Press, 1992.

Shakespeare, William. The Complete Works. General editors Stanley and Gary Taylor. Oxford: Clarendon Press, 1998.

Vladić Jovanov, Milena. Dinamični poetski sistem T. S. Eliota. Beograd: Službeni glasnik, 2014.

Walcott, Derek. Collected Poems 1948–1984. New York: Farrar, Straus and Giroux, 1986.

Xiros Cooper, John. T. S. Eliot and the Politics of Voice: 'The Argument of the Waste Land'. Ann Arbor, MI: UMI Research Press, 1987.

Xiros Cooper, John (Ed). T. S. Eliot's Orchestra. New York and London: Garland Publishing, Inc. 2000.

Yeats, W. B. The Collected Poems. New York: Scribner Paperback Poetry, 1989.

Personal Reflections on Niyi Osundare, Oríkì Praise Tradition, and the Journey Motif in If Only the Road Could Talk

ADETAYO ALABI

This essay focuses on Niyi Osundare's engagement with the Yoruba oríkì praise tradition in relation to cities in *If Only the Road Could Talk*. The essay discusses Osundare's representation of the various cities he visits in Africa, the Pacific, Asia, and Europe in relation to their epithets, achievements, and challenges. The paper also examines how Osundare weaves his own stories into those of the cities he writes about.

I devoted part of *Oral Forms of Nigerian Autobiography and Life Stories* to a discussion of the Yoruba oríkì panegyric tradition and the works of Niyi Osundare. In the book, I analysed how Osundare uses the oríkì genre autobiographically to represent himself, his family, his friends, community, and nation. In this paper, I explore Osundare's auto/ biographical engagement with the Yoruba oríkì panegyric tradition in relation to travel and the various cities he visits and writes about in *If Only the Road Could Talk*. Osundare succeeds in the poems in representing the different cities he encounters, including Lagos, Accra, Johannesburg, Cairo, Alexandria, Taipei, Kuala Lumpur, Berlin, and London, in terms of their panegyrics and critique like the traditional oríkì poet does. Osundare ultimately transports the oríkì tradition from its Yoruba origin to an international trope to unite various cities in the world and to put them in a comparative relationship. I also explore the interactions between the biographical representation of the cities and Osundare's own autobiographical stories within the stories of the cities he writes about.

A discussion of Osundare's *If Only the Road Could Talk* can be contextualized within the Yoruba panegyric tradition, to which I devoted three chapters in *Oral Forms of Nigerian Autobiography and Life Stories*. In the book, I wrote a chapter on the place of orí or head as ordinary and metaphorical head in relation to the praise tradition as well as on four foundational texts on the oríkì tradition, namely,

76 *Adetayo Alabi*

Olatunde Olatunji's *Features of Yoruba Oral Poetry*, Adeboye Babalola's *The Content and Form of Yoruba Ijala*, Karin Barber's *I Could Speak Until Tomorrow: Oríkì, Women, and the Past*, and Toyin Falola's *In Praise of Greatness: The Poetics of African Adulation*. In a second chapter, I discussed the overwhelming use of the oríkì tradition in Nigerian music. The third chapter on the praise tradition was on how Niyi Osundare has used the praise tradition for auto/biographical purposes in his writings over the years. This paper continues my work on the praise tradition in relation to Osundare's poems, and I will concentrate on his book *If Only the Road Could Talk*.

A popular definition of the Yoruba oríkì is provided by Karin Barber in *I Could Speak Until Tomorrow*. Barber defines oríkì as:

> a genre of Yoruba oral poetry that could be described as attributions or appellations: collection of epithets, pithy or elaborated, which are addressed to a subject... They are composed for innumerable subjects of all types, human, animal and spiritual; and they are performed in numerous modes or genres. They are compact and evocative, enigmatic and arresting formulations, utterances which are believed to capture the essential qualities of their subjects, and by being uttered, to evoke them. They establish unique identities and at the same time make relationships between beings (1).

As I noted in *Telling Our Stories: Continuities and Divergences in Black Autobiographies*, 'Oríkì are not always praise poems in the sense of lauding their subjects. They are often very critical of their subjects. Also, the history of various Yoruba communities is taught through the oríkì of the town or those of its most prominent citizens' (10).

One very significant attribute of the oríkì genre that is germane to my current discussion of Osundare's work is that it could be composed for inanimate subjects. As I mentioned in *Oral Forms of Nigerian Autobiographies and Life Stories*, Adeboye Babalola 'gives considerable attention in *The Content and Form of Yoruba Ijala* to the oríkì of animals and inanimate objects like trees and crops in the environment. Babalola's examples of oríkì to animals and plants include praise poems in honour of the duiker, the elephant, the bush fowl, the domestic fowl, the iroko tree, cassava plant, etc. (19–22, 87–116). The oríkì for plants, animals, and the environment are particularly important because many people and communities take personal and lineage oríkì praises from animals and communal natural endowments like rocks and rivers in their communities' (36).

Personal Reflections on Niyi Osundare 77

What Osundare does in *If Only the Road Could Talk* is similar to Adeboye Babalola's representation of the oríkì of nonhuman subjects in *The Content and Form of Yoruba Ijala*. Osundare in *If Only the Road Could Talk* assembles the oríkì, epithets, and the panegyrics of the various cities he visits like the traditional oríkì poet. The poems in the collection are, therefore, largely biographical about the cities, landscapes, and seascapes Osundare writes about. An interesting twist to Osundare's biographical representation of the cities, landscapes, and seascapes is that he weaves himself into the poems such that many of them are both autobiographical and biographical. Osundare, in line with the oríkì tradition, also offers some subtle criticism of some of the cities he adulates. Osundare structures his representation of the cities he visits around the journey motif, as shown in his subtitle for the book: 'Poetic Peregrinations in Africa, Asia, and Europe'. The poems in the collection are about cities in Africa like Lagos, Accra, Johannesburg, Cairo, Alexandria, Buea, Assilah, and Volubilis; Pacific cities and countries like Taipei, Malaysia, and South Korea; and European cities like Berlin, Amsterdam, Prague, Paris, Toulouse, Ljubljana, Stockholm, and London.

Naming is a very central issue in oríkì studies. On almost all occasions, whoever or whatever is being praised is eulogized through naming, which is a typically meaningful and illuminating process among the Yorubas. Several attributes of the praised are identifiable in the different names used in the panegyric process. This importance of naming for eulogizing subjects is responsible for the name adopted by Osundare in celebrating his encounters with Lagos, the former Nigerian capital city, the wealthiest and the most densely populated and cosmopolitan city in Nigeria, and the headquarters of Lagos State. Osundare foregrounds Eko and Lagos, the two names of the city in the poem titled 'Eko' (9-13):

Two names the City has, two souls:
one native and inexpressibly deep,
the other a rapid baptism from a foreign altar;
the two sometimes kiss, and sometimes quarrel (10)

Eko, the name adopted by Osundare for Lagos in the poem, is the traditional precolonial name of Lagos. The name comes with a string of praises that are clearly manifested in musical compositions for Eko over the years. Some of the lines showing this string of praises associated with Eko are:

78   *Adetayo Alabi*

Eko Akete, ile ogbon	Eko, city of wisdom
Arodede maa ja o	The one that hovers precariously
	without dropping
Aromisa leegbeleegbe	Billowing eternity of water (9)

Eko is described as the city of wisdom because of the belief that, if someone is not street-smart in Lagos because of the complexities of urban living, the person can't literally be wise anywhere else. This section about Eko's wisdom suggests that the knowledge any inhabitant of Lagos gains from the city will be paramount in the individual's interactions with other people and cities around the world like those that Osundare visits and writes about in the book. Eko is the one that hovers precariously without dropping because it has always been the centre of Nigeria's modern economy, and it has been affected by major events in Nigerian and African history like slavery, colonialism, independence struggles, and the creation of a modern city and a modern economy. Eko is the billowing eternity of water because it is surrounded by the Atlantic Ocean and the lagoon.

In presenting his encounters with Eko/Lagos, Osundare uses repetition, which has always been a major tool in the hands of the oríkì poet. The lines that are repeated throughout the poem and serve as a refrain are Arodede maa ja o/Aromisa leegbeleegbe (The one that hovers precariously without dropping/Billowing eternity of water). This repetition throughout the poem establishes the image of Lagos and creates its looming magnificence throughout the poem. The lines in Yoruba also make the poem musical, and of course musicians have always used the oríkì genre to praise their subjects, as I discussed in Chapter 3 of *Oral Forms of Nigerian Autobiography and Life Stories* (41–56). The fact that the song/refrain is in Yoruba is also important. It indicates clearly that the Lagos speech community is not monolingual. It is multilingual and foregrounds the importance of and consistent use of Yoruba language in the community even in the postcolonial era. The repeated refrain also shows the call and response musical pattern of the poem. This is a format that is often employed by the traditional artist to include audience participation in performances. The use of Eko – which is a name from the Yoruba language of the indigenous people of Lagos – in the poem also functions as part of Osundare's effort to thematize precolonial history and write back to the colonial naming of Lagos and the colonization of the region by the British.

Osundare also presents the culture and additional epithets of Lagos in the poem through the Eyo festival that is recreated in the

Personal Reflections on Niyi Osundare   79

text. This is reminiscent of Osundare's representation of other festivals like Olosunta and Ogunoye festivals in his previous works. Osundare brings out some of the praises for the Eyo masquerade, which is associated with Lagos. Some of the repeated lines/refrain in Yoruba with Osundare's English translation are given below:

Eyoo o, Eyoo o	Eyoo o, Eyoo o
Eyo baba ta wa to nfi goolu sere	Eyo of our ancestors for
	whom gold was plaything
Awa o le sanwo onibode, o	No border tributes; home
dileeee	straight we go

The song praises Lagos's resilience and wealth by describing Eko as the place where the ancestors had so much gold that they used it playfully. This recalls the image of Mansa Musa of the Mali Empire, close to Lagos, who had so much gold that it caused a slump in the world gold market in the medieval period by his excessive use of gold on a pilgrimage to Mecca. The poem further celebrates Lagos's resistance streak by asserting that it will not pay border tributes. This is probably a recollection of Lagos's resistance to British colonization and taxation.

Another set of epithets celebrating Lagos through the Eyo festival are as follows:

Mo fun ruuruu ke ruuruu	I am clad in flaming white
Ki 'ku ri mi saaa	Let death see me and run

The lines' reference to flaming white recalls the immaculate white garment of the Eyo masquerade. This is associated with purity and uprightness. The line is followed by a prayer for longevity.

Osundare also uses the autobiographical I in the poem to give further agency to the Eyo masquerade by bringing out his voice. What is equally significant here is Osundare's clever conflation of the I to include himself and the whole community in the Eyo celebration of Lagos and its culture. The staff that the Eyo masquerade carries attracts attention by Osundare as the Eyo claims that the staff is not owed to any forest. It is primordial, and it is the staff that the Eyo uses to part the waves of the billowing ocean in Lagos and to create a space for itself in the community of cities as follows:

I owe the egret more than the harmattan can pay...
I owe my staff to no forest...
With it I part the way, part the waves...
I can dance from now till the coming season (11–12)

80   Adetayo Alabi

There are some other notable lines that serve as praise and epithets for Lagos in its duality in the poem. Lagos is the 'Cause and the curse.' It is 'saint and sinner.' (10) It is where 'Lust ripens into love' (10) with 'night angels, (11), 'politicians winged fables' (11), and 'magic and maggot' (11). Lagos is the centre for different religions – 'the venal Hallelujah of Pentecostal noises/the soporific Allahu Akbar of sword-wielding Saracens;/God, the Blackman's Nemesis, his drug, his dragon,/watched countless prayers crushed by pagan waves' (11). Lagos is about prosperity with the contradictions in 'a god called Money:/its crown is gold, its sword reckless like a drunken pirate's' (11). It is the home of 'Masks and magic' (11). It has 'Room for all comers/promiscuous like a marketplace' (13). It is 'heavenly hell with choir of slipping angels... face too wide for a partial mask' (13). The poem concludes by celebrating the sea in Lagos in the repeated line that conflates the two: 'The Sea is Lagos; Lagos is the Sea' (12 and 13). Osundare's representation of Lagos in its duality either in its names or its inhabitants, history, and activities, recalls the use of duality for representation by Derek Walcott in his poems, particularly *Ruins of a Great House* and *Another Life*.

Osundare has two poems on Egypt, titled 'Cairo' and 'Alexandria', in *If Only theRoad Could Talk* to commemorate his visit to the country in 2003, at the beginning of the second America/Iraq war, for the African Literature Association conference. These two poems are particularly significant to me because I was with Professor Osundare on that trip, and I saw much of what he saw in Cairo and Alexandria. While in Cairo, we visited the national museum of Egypt, where we saw some excavated royal corpses and the Sphinx. We also went into the pyramids at Giza. In Alexandria, we visited the library of Alexandria. These visits were part of what inform the panegyrics of the two cities in the poems. Osundare represents Cairo as the city that swirls. It is where '[t]he stars are singing,' where '[t]he moon's fingers rap the tambourine/to a talkative delight' (17). It is where the lotus 'bats its eye/On the ledge of/A sprawling swamp' (17). It is the city where '[h]ouses swarm/like seeds/in a fertile pod' (17). It is the city with 'Pharaoh's golden swagger' reminiscent of the achievements of Egyptian Pharaohs, many of whom were buried with gold. It is the city where the past joins the present apparently in reference to the past glory of Egypt, including the monumental pyramids that we visited when on that trip to Cairo and the famous ancient library in Alexandria.

Osundare's 'Alexandria' celebrates the location as the city of both medieval and contemporary knowledge. It starts by describing the city

Personal Reflections on Niyi Osundare 81

as one that rose 'from the ashes of burnt letters' and as 'a United-Nations of books' (18) where 'papyrus held History/Between its veins' (18). Unlike the ashes of the past, 'The ruins have risen again/On another page of the sky' (18). He also refers to the emperors who once ruled the region as 'fame-famished' people who '[l]eft iron footprints in these sands' (18). The ashes of the city tell 'the tale of incendiary despot/Who darkened the ancient world/With the spectacle of burning books' (18). These descriptions recall how the Alexandria city library was burnt twice, once by Roman Emperor Julius Caesar and the second time by Roman Emperor Theodosius in 391 CE. The library was rebuilt by the United Nations in 2002. Osundare also recalls in the poem some significant historical events in Alexandra like the Pharaohs who 'foraged free', the pyramids that 'assayed consent', and the Sphinx that 'witnessed it all in stony silence' (18).

Legendary Cleopatra, who was born in Alexandria in early 69 BC or late 70 BC, and her famous picture with a cobra, also get some attention in 'Alexandria'. Osundare describes Cleopatra as 'cobra coiffured' (18) to commemorate her headdress picture with a cobra. According to Osundare's lines, Cleopatra 'held a powerful empire between her legs/Stunning the world with the goddessly/Grace of a fated beauty' (18). This is an apparent reference to Cleopatra's relationship with Roman Emperor Julius Caesar. She was supposed to have stayed at Caesar's villa when in Rome on some occasions. The affair was said to have resulted in the birth of Caesarion, who later became her Egyptian co-ruler as Ptolemy XV. Cleopatra also had another celebrity affair with Mark Anthony after Caesar's assassination.

The autobiographical poems 'Touchdown Taipei' and 'Malaysian Moments' are in the Pacific section of Osundare's peregrinations. 'Touchdown Taipei' is about Osundare's sixteen-hour flight to Taipei. The poet informs his readers of his love for language and how he learnt some words in Chinese from a fellow flyer to thank the air hostess. He also informs the reader that he travelled several time zones on his way to Taipei:

> Grey morning
> Crisp like the tangy touch
> Of a long-expected dawn
> My jet-weary feet
> Commune with the Eastern earth.
>
> I thank the air hostess
> In a Chinese learned
> From a fellow flyer...

82 *Adetayo Alabi*

Sixteen long hours
In the belly of a flying whale
I have crossed several time zones
Pursuing a tender sun
to its Eastern roost (50)

Osundare's 'Malaysian Moments' is elaborate and in thirteen movements. Osundare describes Malaysia as a 'forest of rains' with 'silk and laundered cotton' and the *tunku* cap of 'velvet crown' (53) in the poem. He foregrounds the Malaysian yellow juicy mango that he compares to 'a sunrise sky' and 'magic in the mouth' (51) and Malaysian coconut of the 'rarest juice' for his evening rice (56). He mentions the friendliness of Kuala Lumpur, the country's capital city, which he describes as the city with 'the golden mud' and the 'muddy memory' (52). Next, he focuses on the multilinguistic nature of Malaysia by associating three of the major languages of the country with the three meals of the day:

I breakfasted
    In Malay
Lunched
    in Chinese
Supered
    in Tamil

Osundare also comments on the Kelantan (a state in Malaysia) kite 'gliding gracefully/surging with the wind/close to the moon/closer to the sun' (56). The kite is a symbol for Malaysia's economic growth; hence it has to avoid 'the hawk of the sun', 'tree branches', and 'the roofs' (57).

Osundare's lines on Malaysian oil palm are particularly relevant to and critical of the post-independence mismanagement of the Nigerian government. The 'oil palms flourish/in tidy rows/wide-girthed/heavy-fruited/luxuriant leaves/glistening in the sun' (58). Osundare now rhetorically asks in obvious reference to Nigeria where Malaysia was reputed to have obtained the oil palms that it went to grow in Malaysia:

Is it really true
That the seed of this bounty
Came from a country
Which, once a supplier,
Is now supplicant
On wobbly knees? (59)

Personal Reflections on Niyi Osundare **83**

This section on oil palm is particularly relevant to the 'Eko' poem, discussed earlier, because good leadership would have harnessed the oil palm wealth of Nigeria, and this could have been one of the achievements to celebrate in relation to Eko.

Osundare dedicates the last movement of 'Malaysian Moments' (xiii) to Mohammed Salleh, a prominent Malaysian poet. He endows the poet with several epithets to show his significance and major contributions to Malaysian culture and the arts. Osundare describes Salleh as 'Poet, priest, patriot/swift-footed traveler/whose heels are wet/with many waters/poeticizing in Penang/singing in Singapore/... crowing like an/ample-combed cock/in Kajang' (59).

'At Bertolt Brecht's House, East Berlin' is, in a way, a biography of both Brecht and East Berlin. Here, the human represented by Brecht is interwoven with the city of East Berlin. The poem is oríkì praise for both Brecht and the city of East Berlin. The poem is also autobiographical because of how Osundare's own story is woven into it. It is an account of his visit to Brecht's house and his city. The opening lines of the poem describe Brecht's house as the setting for the poem: 'He wrote those plays here/His cigar between his lips/His pen the sixth finger/ of a restless hand...' (83). The poem also describes the features of the house, including its furniture, whose 'wood still raw/From the wound of the saw' (83). The poem also pays attention to Brecht's bedroom and the kitchen. Finally, the poem focuses on Brecht's death and grave which Osundare describes as the 'Last act' in apparent allusion to the conclusion of a play. Of course, Brecht was a famous playwright, and in this case his death is the last act for him by God, the ultimate playwright. Osundare also foregrounds the landscape of East Berlin in the concluding stanza of the poem. The grave is in the 'bowered backyard/In the midst of pundits and philosophers;/Flowers grow tall above your sleep/Petals bloom into smiles so reminiscent/Of your parting lips;/Here you rest/Now that all the world is your stage' (85).

Berlin features in both 'Checkpoint Charlie' (90) and 'Berlin 1884/5' (91). Apart from a biographical representation of the Berlin Wall in both poems, they are both autobiographical because they recall Osundare's visit to Berlin and his representation of the fall of the Berlin Wall. Osundare recalls the irony of the fall of the Berlin Wall and how some businesspeople profited from the historicity of the fallen wall in 'Checkpoint Charlie:'

Our guide told the story from his own side
as I took another look at the boy

84 *Adetayo Alabi*

who sold "The Wall" for tourist dollars
'Come buy History, come buy History!', he screamed again, his voice
vanishing into the late morning traffic.

The infamous scramble for and the partition of Africa in 1884/1885
features prominently in 'Berlin 1884/5'. The catchy epigraph to the
poem is 'Come buy History! Come buy History!' from the wall seller
in the poem 'Checkpoint Charlie.' 'Berlin 1884/5' is a critique of the
European division of various African kingdoms and ethnicities among
themselves. Osundare describes this greed for faraway lands as the
'cruel arrogance of empire,/Of kings/queens who laid claim to rivers,
to mountains,/To other peoples and other gods and their histories' (91).

Osundare sets the tone for 'Amsterdam' by first identifying two of
the most famous Dutch painters and showering them with memorable
oríkì praises. The city 'Goes to bed/Wrapped in Rembrandt's canvas'
[and] 'Floats her dreams in the watercolour/Of Van Gogh's telluric
imagination; The Ocean laughs' (92). From the renowned painters,
the poem focuses on the city itself and its planning. Osundare refers
to the city's canals as 'fluent chapters/Of tales told by singing tunnels'
(92). He also writes that the windmills of the city 'swirl to the sway/
Of the wind, flail their arms/To the whirring tonality of its drum' (92).
Osundare concludes the poem by drawing attention to the city's flyer
and shopping bag inscription of See, Buy, and Fly by reminding the
reader that many cannot participate in the advertised rendezvous of
buying, selling, and flying because of different reasons ranging from
immigration policies, racialization, sexism, and classism. Osundare
notes that 'There is a liberal lilt/To the laughter in the streets/Many are
those who SEE, BUY but cannot FLY' (92).

Osundare's 'London' was inspired by his several visits to the city
and the Summer Olympics of 2012 that it hosted. Osundare celebrates
London as a city whose laughter 'Is sometimes louder than its voice'
(106) because of the different languages used in the multiethnic city
and its heightened commercial activities. He describes the city as
'Old, never aged'. The history of London and empire building come
to the fore as Osundare describes the city as 'Once golden apple of
an Empire's eye' (106). Osundare details some of London's landmarks
and monuments like the River Thames, Big Ben, Brixton, Westminster,
Buckingham, Trafalgar, Hyde Park, the Union Jack, and the Anglican
denomination of Christianity, and he gives them epithets that create a
city that has affected the destiny of several other cities and civilizations
through empire building and colonialism. For examples, Osundare
describes the Thames as 'Giant artery' in London's 'crowded heart'

Personal Reflections on Niyi Osundare **85**

(105), Trafalgar as 'fair and square' (106), and Hyde Park as 'Where Freedom fumes and frets in a corner/Ringed by the charmed circles of a complex speechocracy' (106).

Osundare also brings various British achievers, writers, and inventors like Blake, Wordsworth, Shakespeare, Newton, and Adam Smith to foreground the several contributions of this city to human civilization. He refers to William Blake's famous poem titled 'London' by inferring that the London he describes is different from Blake's with the line 'Not exactly Blake's chartered streets' (106). He also refers to William Wordsworth's 'Romantic imagination' (106), Isaac Newton's 'meticulous mathematicization' (106), Adam Smith's 'immortal credo', and to William Shakespeare as '(good Ol' Willy)/Still ambles along the Strand, his gait primed/To the iambic tonality of a rap-enamored era' (106). I found Osundare's allusions to various British achievers instructive because part of the praise for their city of London and country belongs to them. In praising the city, Osundare praises the achievers and vice versa. How Osundare brings the British achievers to the poem is like how Derek Walcott brings several writers to comment on the evil of colonization of the world in his 'Ruins of a Great House.' Osundare also refers to London as the city that never sleeps but sometimes snores (106). This is reminiscent of an Ekiti oríkì about Umọlẹ̀ kọmàrì sùn í hùn, meaning the masquerade who doesn't sleep but snores. Osundare concludes the poem autobiographically by referencing the Shakespearean quotation from Davy in *Henry IV*, Part 2, Act V, Scene 3 that 'I hope to see London once ere I die.' Osundare's representation of that famous quote is: 'I saw London, indeed/And guess what?/I never died!' (107). The saying about seeing London and not dying is, according to Osundare's note in the poem, 'A quip on "See London and Die", a common jocular saying in Nigeria in those days' (107). This declaration of seeing London and not dying recalls Coyote's famous statement in Canadian Thomas King's poem 'Coyote Goes to Toronto'. After she is racialized in the city, Coyote says in the poem that she has been to Toronto, and people from the rez sarcastically say they see it:

I been to Toronto Coyote tells
    the people.
Yes, everybody says,
We can SEE that.

In conclusion, Osundare graphically represents his travels in Africa, Asia, and Europe in *If Only the Road Could Talk* with road symbolism throughout the collection. As Osundare mentions in his preface to the book, 'the road never forgets' (xiii). Like the road that never forgets, Osundare remembers and recalls his encounters with different locations on his trips. The issues of memory and remembrance that Osundare emphasizes early in the book thematize the autobiographical content of the text. This is in relation to how Osundare weaves himself and his stories into the poems in honour of the different cities and endowments in the text, including a beautiful recollection of his mother's prayer that the road that will take him to different places will always bring him back (xiv). So, like the different locations he encounters, Osundare becomes an autobiographical subject in the collection as he travels from place to place.

Like the traditional Yoruba oríkì panegyric poet, Osundare foregrounds different epithets and personalities associated with the different cities, landscapes, and seascapes he encounters to present their major attributes and contributions to civilization to the reader. He, therefore, represents the Yoruba oríkì as a common denominator to different world metropolitan centres. Some of the poems in this collection share some intertextual similarities with some of Osundare's previously published poetry. An example is the acknowledgement and praises for landscapes and seascapes in the newer book just like in the older ones. It is in Osundare's *The Eye of the Earth* and *Midlife* that he personifies himself and claims his descendance from Olosunta Rock in Ikere. It is in *Moonsongs* that Osundare identifies the differences between the moon in a wealthy location and in an impoverished setting. In the new book, the praises for the landscapes and seascapes are woven into the praises for the cities and individually as natural phenomenon like the sun, the sea, rivers, forests, and the sky are featured repeatedly in the poems. In this acknowledgment of landscapes and seascapes, Osundare dedicates a whole poem to the Pacific including its ocean (49), another to a stone orchard (101), another to the Irish Sea (108–109), and another to a mountain (121).

There is another level of intertextuality going on in *If Only the Road Could Talk* which is in relation to performers and writers. Osundare directly alludes to various important performers and writers and their works to show connections between them and their various locations. Prominent in this regard are references implying the art of the traditional Yoruba oríkì poet and performer in 'Eko,' to Ghanian Highlife Music and to the West African talking drum (9 and 14), to Misse Ngoh's music in Cameroon and to Bate Besong's plays and poems from Cameroon (23), to Tchicaya U Tamsi's Congolese poems

Personal Reflections on Niyi Osundare **87**

(30 and 31), to Kenyan publisher Henry Chakava (37), to Bertolt Brecht's home in East Berlin, to British William Blake's poem 'London', to William Shakespeare's *Henry IV* and his other plays, and to William Wordsworth's romantic poems (106).

A final example of intertextuality in relation to *If Only the Road Could Talk* is the connection between Osundare and Derek Walcott and Thomas King. The connection with Walcott here lies in Osundare's representation of duality in 'Eko' and allusions to various writers in 'London' to Walcott's method of providing the same contrasting representation and allusions in his autobiographical poetry in *Another Life* and the focus on empire and plantocracy in 'Ruins of a Great House.' The Thomas King connection is in relation to Osundare's 'London' and King's 'Coyote Goes to Toronto'.

WORKS CITED

Alabi, Adetayo. *Oral Forms of Nigerian Autobiography and Life Stories*. London and New York: Routledge, 2022.

———— 'Orality as Counter-Narrative in Niyi Osundare's *Midlife*', presented at the Association of Canadian College and University Teachers of English Conference, Halifax, Nova Scotia, 28–31 May 2003.

———— Telling Our Stories: Continuities and Divergences in Black Autobiographies. New York: Palgrave Macmillan, 2005.

Babalola, Adeboye. *Awon Oriki Orile Metadinlogbon*. Ikeja: Longman, 2001.

———— *The Content and Form of Ijala*. Oxford: Clarendon Press, 1966.

Babalola, Adeboye and Alaba, Olugboyega. *A Dictionary of Yoruba Personal Names*. Lagos: West Africa Book Publishers Limited, 2003.

Babalola, Adeboye (Ed). *Awon Oriki Borokini*. London: Hodder and Stoughton Educational, 1975. Ibadan, Nigeria: Nigeria Publishers Services Ltd., 1981.

Barber, Karin. *I Could Speak Until Tomorrow: Oriki, Women, and the Past in a Yoruba Town*. Washington DC: Smithsonian Institution Press, 1991.

Falola, Toyin. *In Praise of Greatness: The Poetics of African Adulation*. Durham, North Carolina: Carolina Academic Press, 2019.

King, Thomas. 'Coyote Goes to Toronto'. Ramraj, Victor J (Ed). *Concert of Voices: An Anthology of World Writing in English*. Peterborough, On, Canada: Broadview Press, 1995, 214–215.

Olatunji, Olatunde O. *Features of Yoruba Oral Poetry*. Ibadan: University Press Limited, 1984.

Osundare, Niyi. *If Only the Road Could Talk*. Trenton, New Jersey: Africa World Press, 2017.

———— *Midlife*. Ibadan: Heinemann, 1993.

———— *Moonsongs*. Ibadan: Spectrum Books, 1988.

88 *Adetayo Alabi*

———— 'Mountain in Image and Word in English-Speaking World: The Landscape Figured and Disfigured', delivered at Universite de Toulouse-Le Mirail, on 4–7 October 2007.

———— *Pages from the Book of the Sun: New and Selected Poems*. Trenton: Africa World Press, 2002.

———— The Eye of the Earth. Ibadan: Heinemann Educational Books Nigeria Limited, 1986.

———— 'The Mother Who Was Also My Muse (A grateful son remembers…)'. *Sahara Reporters*, 17 January, 2016.

Walcott, Derek. Another Life. New York: Farrar, Straus and Giroux, 1973.

———— 'Ruins of a Great House'. Ramraj, Victor J (Ed). *Concert of Voices: An Anthology of World Writing in English*. Peterborough, On, Canada: Broadview Press, 1995.

Lost and Gained in Translation

Navigating the Contours of Kofi Anyidoho's Bilingual Poetry

MAWULI ADJEI

Kofi Anyidoho's poetry, spanning half a century, covers a large body of works in Ewe and English. The poet has performed his Ewe and English poems extensively on various platforms and commemorative occasions and also on radio, television and audio recordings. As the appreciation and appetite for Anyidoho's poetry grows, so is there a growing need to make his Ewe poems accessible to a wider audience outside the Ewe linguistic circle – in English and other languages. As someone currently engaged in co-translating selections of Anyidoho's Ewe poems from *Ghananya* into English (with Professor Patron Henekou of University of Lome, Togo), in this paper, I explore, from theoretical and practical perspectives, the burden of translating poetry across linguistic zones, with particular reference to Anyidoho's Ewe poems. I will critically discuss my engagements with the selected Ewe poems, drawing attention to Ewe as a tonal language steeped in deep-layered idiomatic texture; how poetic diction and imagery adapted from Ewe folklore, mythology and philosophy are captured in Anyidoho's Ewe poems with a touch of artistic complexity and aesthetic sublimity, and the intricate balancing act of conveying the nuances of such poetic language into English – employing various translation techniques, including semantic equivalence/reformulation, modulation, approximation, etc., without much injury to the original texts.

There are several translation theories, methodologies and techniques, as well as a groundswell of studies that explore and discuss the subject from varying angles (Newmark, 1988, 1989, 1991), Fawcett (1997), Munday (2001), Palupi (2002), Glynn (2021), Inggs & Wehrmeyer (2021), among others. According to Newmark, 'translation is rendering the meaning of a text into another language' (1988, p.5). However, translating from one culture to another needs

90 *Mawuli Adjei*

the experience in one's language, in determining its uniqueness from among other languages and skills in multicultural mediation. Therefore, translation or any form of transference cross-linguistically is more than simply translating the words, it is also translating the concepts; concepts belonging to a specific civilization, concepts that belong to a people with their own way of thinking, with equal focus on the source text as a work of literature.

THE TRANSLATOR, RESOURCES AND METHODOLOGY

With regard to translating Ewe poems into English, Nayo's translation of celebrated Anlo-Ewe poet-cantor Henoga Akpalu Vinoko's dirges into English (1964), Kofi Awoonor's translation of selected poems of some of the greatest Anlo-Ewe poets/singers in *Guardians of the Sacred Word* (1974), as well as Anyidoho's own attempts at translating some of his original Ewe poems into English, and the other way round, constitute a working template, to some extent, which can be adapted to the present project.

Translating Kofi Anyidoho's Ewe poems into English presents a daunting set of challenges due to the Ewe language's rich literary and cultural heritage. Without overstating it, Anyidoho's works are deeply rooted in Ewe oral poetry, folklore, history and worldview. Therefore, translating his poems requires not only linguistic skills but also a deep understanding of Ewe culture and literature. The translator of Anyidoho's poems must, therefore, take on board a good knowledge and understanding of Ewe culture, which, like any other culture, has its unique symbols, values and norms that influence its literature. The translator should be able to critically navigate the cultural significance and intricacies of the sociolinguistic implications of metaphors and convey them effectively in English. The translator must also bear in mind that Ewe and English are two different languages with their unique idiomatic expressions, colloquialisms, collocations, semiotics and cultural references. There is also the poet's use of innovative style and use of the Ewe language, including coinage of new words and expressions. The overall objective, therefore, is to establish a level of sensitivity to the poems' metaphors, rhythm, music and cultural context in order to produce a high-quality translation that captures the beauty and meaning of the original poems.

LOST AND GAINED IN TRANSLATION: KOFI ANYIDOHO'S POEMS IN TRANSLATION

In the following paragraphs, I shall discuss some samples of my translations of Anyidoho's poems from Ewe into English, based on the preliminary propositions above.

To begin with, a major issue to contend with has to do with Ewe titles, names, phrases, terms, maxims, metaphors, etc. that are used in Anyidoho's poems. Ewe names, in particular, have meaning and context, and most derive from Ewe philosophy, worldview, history, social organization and spirituality (Gbolonyo, 2009; Aziaku, 2016). They, therefore, carry a huge baggage of cultural implications that are virtually lost in translation if one loosely adopts word-for-word, semantic equivalence or any kind of substitution in translation. The names must, therefore, be subsumed in the general fabric of layers of meaning and aesthetic appeal of the poems.

Each poem in the collection has a Ewe title, including *Ghananya* itself, the collection from which the selections for translation were drawn. The immediate dilemma for the translator is: whether to retain the Ewe titles, or to render them in translation for the benefit of the English reader. Take 'Ghananya', for instance: Translating it as 'Ghana Palaver', 'Ghana Affair' or 'Ghana Matter' would convey the intended meaning due to the implied sense of unpredictability, confusion or danger that characterizes Ghana's socio-political discourse, if one does not tread cautiously. 'Palaver', in my view as translator, just about captures the connotations of the word in Ghanaian usage across linguistic hierarchies – from educated Ghanaian English to pidgin. However, in a literary sense, 'Ghanaya', which is repeated ten (10) times in the poem, each time with incremental allusive and sarcastic tenor, transcends the limited import of 'palaver' or 'affair' or 'matter'. What this implies is that the reader comes to terms with the original Ewe titles and names and makes meaning of them in the context of the entire poem.

Let us take, for instance, an excerpt from the poem 'Agbesinyale', which opens as follows:

There go **Agbesinyale and Agbelengɔ**
Waving flaming torches rehearsing war games
Threatening hellfire spewing venom
Towards **Zadokelikɔfe**

92 Mawuli Adjei

> They say all the affairs of the world have become Thunder-god's
> sacred axe
> Stuck between the teeth of the Deity

The two names 'Agbesinyale' (the title) and 'Agbelengɔ' present no contextual problem for Ewe readers who know and understand the loaded meanings of those two names and can easily relate them to the ravages of life which the names, derived from Ewe worldview and spirituality, convey, and which pervade the entire poem. 'Agbesinyale', or, literally, 'It is in the hands of life that matters are', idiomatically translates as, 'If one lives long, he'll succeed in life'. 'Agbelengɔ', on the other hand, translates literally as, 'There's life ahead'. The thrust of the message in the poem is thus borne by these two names, and which become clearer by the end of the poem. 'Zadokelikɔfe' makes very little sense if translated as 'Eclipse of the Sun Village' (quite a mouthful for the name of a village) in the metaphoric sense in which it is used in the poem. Similarly, in 'They say all the affairs of the world have become Thunder-god's sacred axe/Stuck between the teeth of the Deity', the Ewe idiom 'Sofia', which has been rendered literally as 'Thunder god's sacred axe' (from 'So' – 'Thunder-god' – and 'fia' – 'axe'), with its qualification as 'sacred' by the translator (which is not in the original text), does great disservice to the poem in terms of the religio-spiritual sense in which 'Sofia' is used, with reference to the Ewe Thunder-god and the myths, rituals and folk knowledge associated with it.

'Agbosege' in 'Agbe Ƒe Avi' (literally 'Life's Cry'), translated as 'Life's Lamentations', a recurrent mention in the above poem (and a couple of others), is much more than 'sea turtle' in both connotation and denotation. There is a sense in which the name is meant to carry what it represents in terms of size and weight, captured forcefully in its trisyllabic composition: 'Agbo/Se/Ge'. 'Agbo' stands for 'ram', but it also denotes 'big size' (same in the Ga language); 'Se/ge' (tonally with a grave accent on both syllables and where tone is a unit of semantics), on the other hand, has to do with heavy weight, particularly weight that hangs heavily and ominously in the air and which, when borne on the head by someone, is impossible to carry. And this is exactly what the poet-personal laments in the entire poem. See excerpt below:

> All my life's story has become okro soup unable to stand firm in the
> ladle's hold
> The travails of the world have become the Agbosege
> I carry on my bare head

Navigating the Contours of Kofi Anyidoho's Bilingual Poetry **93**

In terms of poetic diction, therefore, 'sea turtle' does not carry any such semantic import, hence Anyidoho's persistent use of 'Agbosege', with all its implications in the contexts in which it is used – as an enormous existential burden. The poem also features a number of other interesting constructions which, for constraint of space, are not captured in this discussion. However, what is not lost, in totality, is the resonance of orality, rooted in the speaking voice of the persona in his engagement with the audience.

A poem like 'Eʋe ho aʋa' (by far the longest poem in the selection), which takes a panoramic sweep of the entire Ewe landscape, from community to community, and their geographical, historical and cultural traits, presents its own problems of translation in respect of the names of towns and their traditional appellations, which are better left untouched. The closest one comes to translating 'Eʋe ho aʋa' into English is: 'Eʋe on the warpath'. It is the note on which the poem opens, in a two-line incremental repetition. In my estimation, 'ho aʋa' conveys a much more dramatic scenario of activities than merely being 'on the warpath'. The two words taken together evoke a sense of tumultuous eruption captured especially in the word 'ho', which literally means 'uproot', with implications of a forceful mass action of movement of people. Compounded with 'aʋa' ('war'), the martial picture is more engaging than what the simplicity of 'on the warpath' captures in English. However, as an example of semantic equivalence, it comes in handy, as in other cases of similar renditions in English. In terms of generic form, like Wole Soyinka's 'Idanre' (which uses Yoruba myths and symbols to construct a Yoruba creation myth), the entire poem comes across as an Ewe creation myth, and a fast-paced free verse narrative that graphically mimics people on the warpath. Take note of the opening lines of the poem:

Ewe on the warpath
The Ewe have waged a war
Ewe enclaves are embedded in gunpowder
All the way from Betsi to Bedo
Ferocious beasts and wild animals
Are engaged in a scuffle on the forehead of the Adaklu Mountain

The main focus in this discussion is on the title poem 'Ghananya', which will be analysed in detail; a redacted presentation of the *Halo* poem 'Awoyo', as well as 'Agbe Ɉe Avi' (in full).

GHANANYA

Hmmm Ghananya!
Ghananya is a marshland
Also clayey morass
It's as slippery as okro soup poured on mirror
Ghananya is so slippery   5
Deer, reindeer, antelopes, leopards
And other four-footed animals
Survey the sky with keen eyes scan the ground
Probe deeper still into the crust of earth
Before they leap onto Ghananya   10

Ghananya is so slippery
Even mudfish have to tug at each other's tails to move ahead
I say Ghananya is a marshland
So slippery the tongue that speaks it
A creative tongue it must be   15

Therefore any child that for want of care
Pokes his **long pointed mouth**
Into Ghananya **with reckless glee**
If all his affairs do not turn into **drib-drab mish-mash slime**
Some surely would   20

Ghananya is just like wetland
Baptized by dawn, noon and sundown drizzle
**Mesmerizing swathes of lush glistening gleaming dreamy
greenery**

But woe betide the infant who knows not the mysteries of the
    hunters' world
Who **tiptoes gingerly gingerly gingerly**   25
Chest held high, balancing on one leg
Then plunges with a **thunderous splash** in Ghananya
He would tumble roll somersault till he lands in Underworld

I say, it was Crab that said
He's endowed with eight feet   30
And two mighty claws for good measure
But when he encounters Ghananya

Roller-coasting like a boulder downhill
**The distant untrodden footpaths…the lonely orphaned
trails
The coastline margins…the far-flung fringes** 35
Would he tread cautiously warily guardedly
Ei! GHANANYA.

'Ghananya' opens with a muted invocation: 'Hmmm Ghananya!' This invocation is at the centre of the entire narrative. As with other poems in the collection, it is contemplative, reflective/reflexive, and conversational: 'I say Ghananya is a marshland'; 'I say, it was the Crab that said/He's endowed with eight feet/And two mighty claws for good measure…' It features a plethora of descriptive Ewe words and phrases are almost impossible to render in English translation. The translator can only scramble approximations in English. For instance, how exactly does one translate Ewe figures of speech and imagery that invoke the five (or even sixth or seventh) human senses: the visual, auditory, tactile, gustatory and olfactory? Often, in Anyidoho's poetry, one encounters sophisticated imagery that seem to defy easy translation, particularly polysyllabic words, structures of compounding and reduplication as well as neologisms (the poet's own coinages), because there are hardly cross-linguistic forms of mediation between Ewe and English in that regard. 'Ghananya' features a number of expressions such as '**drigbadrigba**'/'**drigbedrigbe**' (diminutive form of the former), '**mlɔmlɔmlɔ**', **minyaminyaminya**', '**goŋu goŋu goŋu goŋu**', '**fuuu**', '**gboyaa**', ' **tsyɔʃui**', etc. These expressions have their renditions in English, arrived at in translation by adopting a dynamic semantic approach without recourse to the words in the original Ewe text. Ideally, they are better assessed when the source text (ST) and target text (TT) are placed side by side in full. However, below are how the expressions in reference have been translated into English:

- **minyaminyaminya** (visual/auditory imagery)

This polysyllabic expression is self-revelatory of an action undertaken stealthily, warily, quietly, gingerly. In translation, I opted for a single word 'gingerly', which, in my view, can replicate the action repetitively:

> But woe betide the infant who knows not the mysteries of the hunters'
> world
> Who tiptoes **gingerly gingerly gingerly** (lines 24–25)

- **fuuu** (auditory/onomatopoeic imagery)

96 *Mawuli Adjei*

The expression is used to describe the sound made when an object is immersed in water. The lines have been translated as:

> Therefore any child that for want of care
> Pokes his long pointed mouth
> Into Ghananya **with reckless glee** (lines 16–18)

The emphasis here has shifted from the auditory/onomatopoeic to something to do with recklessness, an unguarded moment when a careless person, literally, plunges into something, especially a matter he/she better steer of. The sound, which cannot be adequately captured in English translation, is here implied.

- **gboyaa** (auditory/onomatopoeic imagery)

As in 'fuuu' above, and in the same context, the expression is reduced to a dynamic equivalence in the English translation where 'gboyaa' becomes 'a thunderous splash' – in which case the onomatopoeic resonance is lost – as seen below:

> But woe betide the infant who knows not the mysteries of the hunters' world
> Who tiptoes gingerly gingerly gingerly
> Chest held high, balancing on one leg
> Then plunges with a **thunderous splash** in Ghananya (lines 24–27)

- **drigbadrigba/drigbedrigbe** (auditory/visual/tactile imagery)

Quite a sophisticated description of a slippery state of being in the Ewe language, to limit its equivalence in English to 'slippery' would lose the poetic intricacy of 'drigbadrigba'/ 'drigbedrigbe' as well as the phonemic/phonological and reduplicative verbal composition of the expression – especially the poet's play on tonal contrast where the first word is repeated but with a different tone. It is translated as follows, with emphasis on getting as close to articulating the phonic word-play as possible:

> If all his affairs do not turn into **drib-drab mish-mash slime**
> Some surely would (lines 19–20)

The word 'drib-drab' (my own coinage) is a crude attempt at replicating 'drigbadrigba'/'drigbedrigbe' while mish-mash together with 'slime' compensates for the state of being slippery.

- **mlɔmlɔmlɔ** (visual imagery)

Navigating the Contours of Kofi Anyidoho's Bilingual Poetry　97

Although just a reduplication of the root 'mlɔ', the visual image it conveys, which is, a wide swathe of luxurious/verdant vegetation that is alluring and thus appeals to one's sense of visual impression as far as the eye can see, requires such emphasis and word jugglery as would depict its proper context of usage. Note how it is descriptively translated below, employing a succession of cognate adjectives:

> Ghananya is just like wetland
> Baptized by dawn, noon and sundown drizzle
> **Mesmerizing swathes of lush glistening gleaming dreamy greenery (20–23)**

- **tsyɔʃui** (visual imagery)

The word 'tsyɔʃui' translates loosely as long and pointed. In its description of a mouth, it has been translated simply as:

> Therefore any child that for want of care
> Pokes his **long pointed mouth**
> Into Ghananya with reckless glee (lines 16–18)

However, as in our earlier discussions, something is lost in translation, contextually and linguistically; in terms of insult, for instance, 'long pointed mouth' does not compare in depth of impact with 'nu tsyɔʃui' in Ewe. Note that, as a spoken word poet, Anyidoho crafts his poems for performance. Thus, in a performance situation with regard to this poem, the facial muscles, in concert with labio-palato-dental features that are harnessed in articulating the word, particularly the way the performer would depict such a mouth pictorially, are lost in the English translation 'pointed mouth'.

- **goŋu goŋu goŋu goŋu** (visual/auditory imagery)

The expression 'goŋu goŋu goŋu goŋu' is no simple mimicry of an ideophonic depiction of the crab's slow and methodical gait, but embedded in that rhythmic construction is a whole philosophical statement bordering on loneliness, ennui and extreme caution, disposition and virtues/values, which, in totality, drives the crab to walk on the margins and fringes rather than the communal thoroughfares with the dangers such a choice would entail. In the context of the poem 'Ghananya', that constitutes the final thrust of the poet-persona's exhortation to the audience. Again, the option here for the translator is two-fold: a choice between maintaining what pertains

98 *Mawuli Adjei*

in the source text ('goŋu goŋu goŋu goŋu'), with footnotes, or other forms of explanatory glosses, and an attempt at semantic or dynamic equivalence translation. I opted for both: it does not quite capture, practically, the musicality and other poetic cadences of 'goŋu goŋu', but then what is lost in translation in that wise is perhaps gained in the extended metaphorical sense through semantic translation in English for the benefit of non-Ewe speakers. The translation of 'goŋu goŋu goŋu goŋu' is captured in the final segment of the poem below (lines 34–36):

> I say, it was Crab that said
> He's endowed with eight feet 30
> And two mighty claws for good measure
> But when he encounters Ghananya
> Roller-coasting like a boulder downhill
> **The distant untrodden footpaths…the lonely orphaned trails**
> **The coastline margins…the far-flung fringes 35**
> **Would he tread cautiously warily guardedly**
> Ei! GHANANYA.

It must be emphasized that the reader/audience would be captivated solely by the repetitive rhythmic thump-thumping and sing-song modulation of 'goŋu goŋu' and not its philosophical or socio-cultural import. This, again, raises a number of technical issues: how can the gulf between a poem composed basically for performance in Ewe be mediated in translation on the printed page; in effect, from the stage to the page; how can voice modulation, tone, pitch and the entire baggage of pyrotechnics involved in the performative delivery before an audience (particularly an active one) be transferred to the page in translation? The reader/audience can only bridge that gap based on their reception and appreciation of the poem in translation, not necessarily its fidelity to the source text.

The Anlo-Ewe poetry of abuse/insult known as 'Halo' (see Anyidoho, 1982; Avorgbedor, 1983, 1994; Campbell, 2002), which has fascinated both Awoonor and Anyidoho as Ewe poets who draw extensively on the Anlo-Ewe oral tradition, does not lend itself easily to translation into English. Halo texts are extremely descriptive, allusive and highly metaphoric, employing language of abuse at a level only accomplished poets in the tradition can deliver. Awoonor describes it as 'verbal overkill' on account of its exquisite and aggressive use of poetic diction and language. To achieve the maximum effect by way of inflicting verbal violence – insult that really hurts the referent to the marrow, breaking

Navigating the Contours of Kofi Anyidoho's Bilingual Poetry **99**

all the rules of decency in public discourse – and to induce humour at the same time, halo poets often overreach themselves in terms of their mastery of the Ewe language and technicalities of oral poetry. Both Awoonor and Anyidoho have experimented with this traditional poetic form, Awoonor mainly in English, Anyidoho in Ewe and English. This can pose great difficulty for the translator. Anyidoho's poem 'Awoyo' is one example. In translating 'Awoyo', which is a fairly long poem (because halo poems often dwell on padding, association, allusion, storytelling, address, etc.), I have had to settle for equivalences of descriptive transferences that do not capture the full weight of the source language. On the whole, the narrative segments of the poem (to do with morality, family history, mother's public image, etc.) are better captured in translation than the purely descriptive sections that dwell on the person of Awoyo (physique, personal hygiene, gait, etc.) Below is a redacted version of my (full) translation of 'Awoyo':

AWOYO
Awoyo Sagada Koklovie
Plodded her way clumsily and crossed my path
Spat straight into my face
Like a duck delivering its smelly shit.
I didn't as much as stir.   5
She again hobbled and landed those spindly legs
In a brush of cactus.
She turned back nonchalantly
Bathed my face with early morning hot spittle.
I didn't even move an inch   10
Much less fart in her direction.
She dawdled, gathered herself
Convinced in her mind that she was laughing
Unbeknownst to her it was an ugly cry
Evil cry she was laughing   15
I have sworn to myself to uphold my composure
In my corner somewhere
Juggling thoughts in my head hoping
Perchance she'd dare provoke me again
Then I'd use my sickle-sharp knife   20
To carve a Hausa tribal mark on her face
Slash her knotted cheek
Administer pepper in the fresh wound
Daughter of a witch

Her hollowed-out face like the Owl's   25

Awoyo come back for your rant
Do come back here
Do you recall that day?
You breached the dawn, night sleep's rheum still in your
    eyes
Seeking audience with stick   30
Seeking audience with rope
Pleading that they stand and hear your loaded tales.
You invoked all the earthly deities
And invoked the celestial ones ensemble
You said you saw Agbenɔxevi   35
On top of me
Doing what exactly behind your stinking mother's broken
    fence?
Daughter of a witch, perpetual night stalker
If you slept at night
Then we might say you dreamt a bad dream   40
Awoyo come back
Do come back again
So I unleash your baggage of shame in your ears
Come let me jolt your mind back to a very serious matter
The unspeakable matter Agbenɔxevi told you in public   45
Agbenɔxevi said
Even if they multiply you Awoyo
By Awoyo ten times, multiplied by ten
He would not accept you
Not even as a dash   50
Agbenɔxevi further said
When at Christmas time
Your mother holds you down
Bathes you in a whole barrel of lavender
And pampers your body with exotic spices   55
With gold, diamond, emerald and lazuli chains
Around your emaciated neck
And you glitter
You glitter
Like a comet   60
And a mother turkey with eggs
In addition to your person dumped on him

Navigating the Contours of Kofi Anyidoho's Bilingual Poetry **101**

He said he Agbenɔxevi
Would with the swiftest dispatch
Return you to Amedzɔfe 65
Back to Dada Bomenɔ

....

Awoyo, come...come with cocked ears
Let me explain a few matters to you 90
I am not the daughter of a mother-harlot
Like you Awoyo
Come and let me tell you a few things from yesteryear
Come and let me remind you of some old secrets
That mother of yours with the battered underside 95
Your notoriously gossipy mother,
Your mother, promiscuous slut, queen-mother whore
One with the withered underside.
She would offer herself to any object,
To stick, to rope 100
Dangle her lean backside in the air
Haul it down to the ground
People say she's a mother-hen
She said pleasure is not confined to one location
So she became communal wife 105
Gifted that thing of pleasure to children.
First of all,
Did she have the presence of mind
To whisper some guarded secret in your ear?
Whether you belong to Atsu! 110
Whether you belong to Etse!
Or are you Edo's child?
Would you remember that
They said the day your mother died
All the Elders heaved a heavy sigh of relief 115
Poured libation on her grave
With incantations and
Rebuke of her soul warning that
If she ever dreamt of coming back to life
She should endeavour to mend her conduct a little 120
Awoyo, child of a witch
Hollow face

102 *Mawuli Adjei*

Like an Owl's
I dare you to ever cross my path again
I will spread your shame on the ground 125
For you to roll on in public
As a form of entertainment for all the children
To see.

Anyidoho's closeness to the 'halo' genre of poetry comes into play in 'Awoyo'. As a literary piece, it adheres to the main technicalities required of a halo poem, most notably the typical opening of the halo poem where the poet-persona lays down the gauntlet for combat, as an artist provoked and, therefore, with a license to insult. In 'Awoyo', this is captured in lines 1–11 (highlighted in bold). The poet-persona then proceeds to roll out a litany of insults, laced with vulgarities and invectives. As indicated earlier, most of these insults have lost their finer details and artistic sophistry in translation.

Moving on to other poems, we concede that there are also poems where the density of Anyidoho's craft yields to pure lyricism bordering on romanticism. Such poems lend themselves to a much easier translation once the translator can match the English translation with the poetic diction and language of the source text without diminishing the poet's emotive cadences, or attachment to the poem and its subject matter. An example of one such poem is 'Agbe Ƒe Avi'. Below is the full translation of the poem:

AGBE ƑE AVI

Life's lamentations
If only I could glean some meager respite
From life's infirmities
If only I could unshackle myself from these fixations of
 morbid fear
I'd walk the gallant walk of warriors 5
Through the wilderness of life
Yeah, I'd travel with night
Knock on Dada Segbo's door
I'd plead with her for a little tete-a-tete
All my life's story has become okro soup unable to stand
 firm in the ladle's hold
The travails of the world have become the Agbosege
I carry on my bare head

Navigating the Contours of Kofi Anyidoho's Bilingual Poetry **103**

So long have I bottled grudges in my stomach
Farted b-o-o-m in public
Now I shriek and ululate to the high heavens   15
For all my life's story has become okro soup defiant of the
    ladle's scoop
And the travails of the world have become the Agbosege
I carry on my bare head
There are people chuckling and sucking their teeth in
    contempt
There are others hissing-hissing whining-whining   20
Persistently asking –
I an infant born only yesterday dawn
What have I been ear-witness to?
What exactly have I heard with my eyes?
Such that I mount the rooftops trumpeting my self-adulation   25
Desecrating the minds of great thinkers
Those with sparkling teeth
Those with coolness of chest
You around whose necks the fortunes of the world have
    wrapped their arms
Strut your majestic gait along the streets of life   30
Laugh. Drink. Feast.
But do not foul-mouth my person with idle prattle and
    jabber
Because the forces that pushed Swallow by the occiput
To Underworld with a big bang
The forces that killed Dumega Dumenyo's heart in his   35
    stomach
Dragged him roughshod all the way to Great Beyond
If we dispatched Kɔsivi Afi
To probe the mystic vaults of the greatest Afa diviners
They would search and search for him to no avail
Therefore, do permit me the luxury to hum a little song   40
For the troubles of life
Have become the Agbosege I carry on my bare head
I grumbled ceaselessly in my innards
Bombed a fart in public
My life story has become okro soup dribbling in the ladle's
    groove.

Translating 'avi' ('cry') as 'lamentations' alludes to Anyidoho's
grounding in the Anlo-Ewe dirge tradition. The poem bears many

104 *Mawuli Adjei*

features of the Anlo-Ewe dirge in terms of the poet-persona's laments about how unfairly life has treated him which is captured in the varying renditions of the refrains: 'All my life's story has become okro soup unable to stand firm in the ladle's hold' and '...all my life's story has become the Agbosege/I carry on my head.'

As work in progress, a lot of tweaking and fine-tuning is on-going. The final product, in collaboration with my co-translator and the poet himself, will reflect the convergence of ideas and harmonization of approaches for a credible translation of Anyidoho's Ewe poems into English for the benefit of a wider audience. As translators, our approach is framed by a multiplicity of renditions that are filtered through a maze of cross-cultural, cross-linguistic and translation methodologies, including turning parts of the source text into 'new originals' within acceptable limits. As we indicate in the Translators' Note:

> (T)here is something enthralling in Ghananya whose power dwells in qualities such as the poet's mastery of Ewe... the modulated paces that come with varied feelings, the crispy mystery of its emotional cadences, among others. To capture these features in their natural Ewe habitat, and transfer them into English, was for us more a question of creation than a matter of translation.

WORKS CITED

Anyidoho, Kofi.2022. *Ghanaya*. Accra: Bureau of Ghana Languages.

———— 'Kofi Awoonor and the Ewe Tradition of Songs of Abuse (Halo)'. *Towards Defining the African Aesthetic*, ed. Lemuel Johnson et al., Washington DC: Three Continents Press, 1982.

———— 2022. *SeedTime*. Accra: DAkpabli and Associates.

Avorgbedor, Daniel. 'Freedom to Sing: License to Insult: The Influence of Halo Performance on Social Violence Among the Anlo Ewe'. *Oral Tradition* 9/1 (1994), pp.83–112.

———— 'It's a Great Song!: Halo Performance as Literary Production'. *Research in African Literatures*, Vol.32, No.2, pp. 17–43.

Awoonor, Kofi. 1974. *Guardians of the Sacred Word: Ewe Poetry*. NOK Publishers.

Aziaku, Vincent. 2016. *A Linguistic Analysis of Ewe Animal Names among the Ewe of Ghana*. Koln: Rudiger Koppe Verlag.

Campbell, Corrina. 'A War of Words: Halo Songs of Abuse of the Anlo Ewe'. SIT, Legon, 2002 & *African Diaspora*, ISPs 44, 2008.

Fawcett, P. 1997. *Translation and Language*. Manchester: Jerome Publishing.

Gbolonyo, Stephen. 'Indigenous Knowledge and Cultural Values in Ewe Musical Practice: Their Traditional Roles and Place in Modern Society'. University of Pittsburg, 2009.

Glynn, Dominic. 'Qualitative Research Methods in Translation Theory'. *Sage Journals*, 18 August, 2021.

Munday, J. 2001. *Introducing Translation Studies*. London: Routledge.

Nayo, Y. Z. 'Akpalu and His Songs'. Institute of African Studies, University of Ghana, Legon, 1964.

Palupi, Muji Endah. 'The Techniques of Translation and Methods Using the V Diagram Methods'. *Journal of English Language and Literature*, Vol.6, Issue 1, March 2021.

Poetry and Performance
The Spoken Word Poetry as a Reincarnation of African Oral Literary Tradition

PARAMITA ROUTH ROY

Oral literature has a central position in African literature and culture. While it took years for the West to appreciate and theorize performance, Africa had done it way before with their dynamic poetic tradition, which merges performance with literature. The Eurocentric understanding of episteme has always prioritized writing over oral literary tradition or the text over performance, and thus 'the suppression of the oral in favour of the printed text is a feature of literary studies worldwide' (Brown 1). But that limited understanding of literature has blinded them to the rich history of African literature and prompted them to claim superiority over the African nations and their literature.

The Apollonian approach to poetry, where there is a specific structure, rhyme, and tradition of writing poetry, has limited the scope of Western poetry and has restricted readers from experiencing dynamism in poetic tradition, which is essential in the African poetic tradition. There is a notion of the carnivalesque in African poetic tradition where, through the performance of oral literature, the literary piece takes a new shape and evolves out of an Apollonian approach. This Dionysian element in African poetry provides a poststructuralist approach, where each time an oral poem is performed, the content gets revised through the evolving performance of the piece. According to the Western standard, the oral poetic traditions 'do not fit neatly into the familiar categories of literate cultures', and that might be the reason behind African literature not receiving its due importance and respect (Finnegan 3). It is interesting to note that, while European literary culture celebrates the Dionysian aspect of its dramatic tradition, it turns a blind eye towards the rich old roots of African poetic tradition, which is centred in orality rather than written literary practices. Because 'the oral tradition has largely been "written out" of literary history', African poetry has never found its canonical positioning in the

106

Poetry and Performance **107**

world forum (Brown 5). Between the binary understanding of written and oral literature, where the first term enjoys hierarchy, the second term is always perceived in relation and negation to the first term. While discussing African poetry or poetry from the different nations of Africa, one cannot miss the historical oral tradition of African poetry only to emphasize the written ones, which were produced as a result of the colonial interventions.

While it is highly improper to perceive written poetic tradition as not essential to African literature, still, a discussion about African poetry almost always privileges a thorough understanding of the oral roots of this literature. Owing to the dearth of proper and unbiased research on African poetry, it would be unjustified to claim that the written tradition is not essential to the literatures from Africa. It is true that colonial exposure popularized written literary culture or might have catalysed such a literary practice among African poets, but one needs to do credible research on the topic to find out if there was any form of written literary tradition in any parts of Africa before the colonial advent. Eurocentric criticism of African oral or performative poetry viewed African oral poetry as 'crude and artistically undeveloped formulations' because they 'are harder to record and present, and, for a superficial observer at least, they are easier to overlook than the corresponding written material' (Finnegan 3). But with the advent of the modern genre of spoken word poetry, this kind of criticism will not stand strong. It has been a decade since spoken word poetry gained popularity on the world forum. The way Western culture has adopted and popularized the format, it seems ironic that this same culture once nullified the credibility of the African poetic tradition based on the ground that more than performance it is the written text that demands and deserves validity. This paper will discuss some of the most popular African performers of spoken word poetry and their works, which have been gaining importance amidst the white-washed aspects of the spoken word poetry tradition. Some of the artists of spoken word poetry, such as Hafsat Abdullahi, Nomfundo Khambule, Onome Enakerakpor, Bothale Boikanyo and Xabiso Vili, will be the focus of this research. Through a qualitative analysis of their poetic performances, it will be shown how traditional African oral poetry has evolved into a form where the oldest roots of this literary culture have been revived by modern age poets.

The ramifications of colonialism were instrumental in suppressing the traditional poetic practices of the different African nations and introducing the written form as the only valid form of composing

108 *Paramita Routh Roy*

poetry. The Western poetic 'model leads us to think of the written element as the primary and thus somehow the most fundamental material in every kind of literature – a concentration on the words to the exclusion of the vital and essential aspect of performance' (Finnegan 6). In the Eurocentric format, it is work of the poet that is considered to be the active piece while the poet remains in the background as the passive creator. It is only in relation to the poet's biographical references that at times the meaning of the poem is decoded. So, the poet in the Western poetic tradition does not have a very active role in delivering the meaning of the poem, rather he or she maintains distance from their work. On the contrary, in the African oral poetic tradition, the poet has an active role in hinting at the meaning of the text through his or her performance of the piece. African poetry does not happen in isolation from the poet or the creator, rather it takes place with and because of the poet who performs the creative piece in front of the audience. 'Oral literature is by definition dependent on a performer who formulates it in words on a specific occasion', and that is something that makes it unique and poststructuralist in essence (Finnegan, 4).

As the African nations came in contact with the colonizers, they adopted their cultures and traditions along with their specific literary practices. But that does not make modern African poetry something which is not essential to its culture. Rather it shows the dynamism of a culture that can easily adapt to new styles of writing and develop its own essence in doing so. One cannot deny the fact that the 'significance of performance in oral literature goes beyond a mere matter of definition: for the nature of the performance itself can make an important contribution to the impact of the particular literary form being exhibited' (Finnegan 5). Due to the lack of recorded archives of traditional oral poetry and insufficient research on them, it is impossible to comment on that content, but a modern manifestation of that oral poetic culture can be found in the spoken word poetry from Africa that is making rounds on the internet. It can be said that 'the effort in contemporary African poetry is geared toward recovering that traditional image of the poet' who used to perform the piece and pass it on to the next generation as a part of oral tradition (Okpewho 13). Just like every performance is unique in its own right, so is the case with the oral poetry of Africa, which always takes a new shape once the same piece is performed by different people and on different occasions. This modern trend of spoken word poetry has 'driven the literate poets to reidentify themselves with the oral traditional roots of their craft' (Okpewho 23).

Poetry and Performance **109**

A close analysis of recent works of African spoken word poetry will show how they draw upon the traditional poetic practice where the poet was at the centre of the poem just by virtue of being the performer who generated the intended meaning of the literary piece. Just because something has no written record, one cannot discount the credibility of a literary tradition of a specific culture which has a long history. The modern age African poets thus stand as symbols of revolt, who are trying to revive their traditional poetic practices on the world forum to hint at the long history of the African literary tradition that has been marginalized by Western critics. The Nigerian poet Hafsat Abdullahi's poem 'Mother Tongue' is a brilliant example of that endeavour where the traditional role of the African poet as the dynamic performer can be noticed. Through her work and her performance, she tries to communicate the discrimination and pain that every African culture has suffered in the face of the exclusionary trends of Western culture. Her poem speaks of her rage towards those who try to humiliate her for her indigenous English accent. The way she performs her poem, with the use of specific pace, tone and gestures, underscores clearly how bothered she is about the trends of those cultures which try to marginalize the diverse accents of the English language by standardizing one single accent as the yardstick of perfection. When she says that 'this accent is a story of my survival, tells how my mother tongue endures till this day, See my mouth is a battlefield, a clash of unyielding cultures waring for dominance, see my tongue is a traumatized survivor', her anger is clearly communicated through all the kinesics she uses (Abdullahi 2022).

It is important to note that, in relation to traditional oral poetic practices, 'tone is sometimes used as a structural element in literary expression and can be exploited by the oral artist in ways somewhat analogous to the use of rhyme or rhythm in written European poetry' (Finnegan 6). Hafsat's use of a specific tone, her swift delivery and her rap-like pace of performance adds a dimension to her poetry that would not have been possible if it was only a textual presentation and not a verbal one. The way she uses her hand gestures to emphasize her points, the way she uses facial expressions to express deep feelings or the way her dress acts as an add-on to her performance allow her to enhance the dynamism of the work. Traditionally speaking, poets in African oral performances always paid considerable attention to the way they presented themselves, and thus one can easily notice resemblances of such traditional elements in the performance of spoken word poetry by poets like Abdullahi. In reference to the work of poets like Abdullahi, it is natural that 'we cannot hope fully to

110 *Paramita Routh Roy*

understand their impact or subtlety if we consider only the bare words on a printed page' (Finnegan 7).

Researchers who work on the traditional oral poetry of Africa have noticed how 'an appropriate pace and level of excitement for the words which are chanted at considerable speed' bear much significance (Okpewho 11). If it were not for the pace and the tone of Abdullahi, the message she wants to communicate would not reach her audience. As mentioned earlier, the Dionysian element in the African oral poetic tradition sets it apart from a structured notion of written poetry. Unlike the Apollonian essence of following a restrictive prosodic pattern with emphasis on a regular pattern of sound and rhythm, Hafsat's poem breaks free from any such restrictions, and, with irregular pace and rhythm, her performance gives way to an open interpretive structure. To cite an example, when Hafsat utters the last line of her poem that 'It's about time when you learn my own language too', she makes a particular gesture with her hands which symbolizes power and confidence, almost a gesture of challenging those who try to bring down people like her (Abdullahi 2022). This line can be performed in many ways to suggest different kinds of emotions. While Hafsat makes a gesture of challenging and defiance, one might simply utter this line with a neutral pace and pitch and without such a gesture to communicate a toned-down message. This is where one can notice the poststructuralist essence in the spoken word poetry or for that matter the oral poetry.

The sense of carnivalesque is also at play here because the genre of spoken word poetry becomes a platform where the hierarchical order seems to become upside-down, which allows African poets like Hafsat to communicate their messages through performative poetry and re-establishing the significant position of oral poetic tradition in Africa. Rather than being a passive creator, poets like Hafsat actively perform their poetry to deliver the message they want to circulate. Just like a traditional African poetic performance, Hafsat performs her poem by using kinesics to a greater extent. Unlike the traditional African poetic performances, which were accompanied by some musical instruments, Hafsat alters that element with the effect of an echo in the audio. The way her voice reverberates seems to symbolize how the years of effort to silence the African poetic voice is being challenged with the echo of a revolting poetic voice that attempts to destroy that silence. As an evolved form of the African oral poetic tradition, Hafsat seems to incorporate all the traditional elements but in a fresh way to make her poetry more relevant to the present-day audience.

South African poet Nomfundo Khambule's poem 'Walk with me' is yet another example of spoken word poetry that shows how these new-age African poets are bringing back elements of the traditional African oral literature and catalysing the evolution of the form with their technological innovations. The use of background music in the poem shows how 'much of what is normally classed as poetry in African oral literature is designed to be performed in a musical setting, and the musical and verbal elements are thus interdependent' (Finnegan 6-7). The emotional tone of this poetry is expressed using the specific colour scheme of the visuals, the walking gestures of the poet, her expressions, her attire and the slow-paced melancholic background score. In case of a poetic performance 'a verbal evocation of mood' happens 'also by the dress, accoutrements, or observed bearing of the performer' (Finnegan 7). Reflecting upon the poetry of Nomfundo, it becomes clear how the adaptation of the traditional style has allowed the poet to reinvent the oral poetic tradition of Africa. Her work emphasizes her experience of overcoming various barriers to make her voice heard. With the recorded version of the poems, poets like Nomfundo have been able to overcome the Eurocentric criticism that denied African oral poetry its credibility because oral poetry did not have any valid record. With the advancement of technology, this barrier has been destroyed, and that has allowed spoken word poets like Nomfundo to reclaim the credibility of the African poetic tradition. When in her poem 'Walk with me' she says that 'I no longer fight using my wrists but now it is with my voice, my key weapon', the rage and melancholy become even more highlighted (Khambule, 2020).

One can call this new-age spoken word poetry an extension of the African oral poetic tradition only because this recent poetic trend mirrors the evolved version of that tradition. The active movements, the vitality, the celebratory tradition of African oral poetry can be found in the recent spoken word poetry of those African poets who incorporate all the traditional elements in a way that represents their poetic heritage but with an evolved outlook.

On the other hand, Onome Enakerakpor's work entitled 'A poem about the African' speaks about the pride of being a Black person, or more precisely, the pride of being an African. The poet speaks about the significance of the African identity and how that identity speaks about the history of the continent. It seems to be a reaction against the colonial understanding of Africa, which was almost always fettered with bias. Through the mode of oral poetry, or to be more appropriate the mode of spoken word poetry, the poet tries to appeal to the

112 *Paramita Routh Roy*

audience by making them feel deeply about their identities as Africans. To understand how this poem breaks away from the Eurocentric model of poetry, we need to focus on the fact that the essence of the poetry rests in the performance more than the written words on paper. The fact that Africans had always been concerned with the impact of their literary creations made them concentrate on the performative aspect of the creative piece rather than the passive reading value. There is no specific prosodic structure, and the varied use of pace, tone and pronunciations make the performances even more appealing to the audience. For instance, when he says 'I am made of black' and he pauses for a few seconds before moving on to the next line, it is the subtle and intricate pause that communicates to the audience the message of pride and confidence of reclaiming Blackness as a powerful part of identity (Enakerakpor, 2018). The background, the dress code, the body language and the voice modulations of the performance seem to resonate the traditional trends of oral poetry in Africa.

A very careful analysis of these performances also reveals that African poets always have a tendency to make exaggerated gestures and voice modulations in their poetry performances in comparison to any Western performer. On this note, it can be said that the spoken word poets from African nations also have been able to keep that essence to project the rage that is mostly the subject matter of their creations. It is with the exaggerated voice modulations and body language that they show their disgust towards the Western world that had always been disdainful to people of African descent.

The South African poet Xabiso Vili's rendition of 'Forget how to die' also echoes a similar message, where the constant struggle to fight back against the history of racism seems to be hinted by the poet through his performance. As he utters the lines 'I am tired sighs the breath of my breath, from here I will pull all the strength I have left', the pain of the experience is communicated by his fluctuating tone and violent hand gestures (Vili 2022). In this regard 'an oral poetry performance may be usefully compared to a dramatic monologue in which the performer supports his verbalization with a due amount of "semantic component," in the form of gestures, grimes, etc.' (Okpewho 8). So, there is no doubt about the fact that the modern genre of spoken word poetry can be read as a reincarnation of the older oral poetic tradition. A close look at this performance shows how the weight and pain of the written words have been delivered with perfect emotions by the performer to ensure that the audience can relate with the pain that has been bothering a whole community for so long. The line where Vili

Poetry and Performance **113**

says: 'My kind have nooses for blood, and bullets for eyes, knives in their throats that shows when we smile', the cry within reverberates through his voice (Vili 2022).

In most of the popular spoken word poetry by African poets, it is noticeable how they voice their migrant experiences, which have been troubling the Black community for eons. Keeping in tune with the carnivalesque essence of traditional African oral poetry, the spoken word poets from Africa make the social media platform a medium to celebrate the power of different voices, opinions, experiences and perspectives. It seems to be a celebration where the hierarchy is altered, and every voice is given equal space to develop and rebel.

The question of double consciousness has time and again surfaced in the matter of spoken word poetry. These poets are seen speaking about how colonial exposure has forced them to live two lives, where their ethnic identity tries to come out of suppression and express itself. This makes the new age poets of the spoken word poetry genre closer to the image of the 'griot' who was 'the traditional oral artist' (Jones et al. 1). For in the written poetic tradition, one gets no scope to revise the piece based on the reaction of the audience, but in case of a performer of oral poetry, the individual can sense the audience reaction and thus mould the speech accordingly. In the African oral poetic tradition, most of the time, the performers also make dance movements to enhance their performance, and that element can be seen in Bothale Boikanyo's poem 'It is our light, not darkness', where she makes slow dance movements to accompany her poetic verse and the background score. What is it if not a carnival dance? These modern spoken word poets have been able to incorporate old elements in a new way through their interpretive poetic performances. It is the performance that enhances the dynamism of the poems and that indeed points towards the superiority of this genre for going beyond the codified norms.

Spoken word poetry has become a way through which the suppressed voices and histories of the African oral poetic tradition are trying to find a voice. Their 'use, for instance, of vivid ideophones or of dramatized dialogue, or manipulation of the audience's sense of humour or susceptibility (when played on by a skilled performer) to be amazed, or shocked, or moved, or enthralled at appropriate moments' is central to these poetry performances (Finnegan 7). Just like the traditional African poet, who considered his surrounding, his audience and the mood of the event for enhancing his performance, so it is the case with the modern poets from the African nations, who

114 *Paramita Routh Roy*

have taken to the platform of social media to rediscover the oral poetic tradition that has been an important part of African literary history.

The dynamism of oral poetry rests in the fact that an 'essential factor is the audience, which, as is not the case with written forms, is often directly involved in the actualization and creation of a piece of oral literature' (Finnegan 12). This interaction between the poet and the audience makes the performance even more dynamic in nature as 'a performance takes place as action, interaction, and relation' (Schechner 30). For example, we can notice in the video of the poem by Onome Enakerakpor and Xabiso Vili how these poets are looking at the audience and framing their gestures and voice modulations to ensure that they are successfully able to communicate feelings through their performance. The way Xabiso Vili makes rapid movements of his head while performing the lines of poetry reflects the sense of discontent that he tries to communicate with the audience. These intricate details in the performance allows the genre of spoken word poetry to break free from the Eurocentric overindulgence with Apollonian aspects of poetry and celebrate the traditional aspects of African oral poetry, which embodies the essence of openness. It is this poststructuralist approach to poetry that directs one to understand the genre of spoken word poetry as an extension of traditional African oral poetry that has always been looked down on owing to the overwhelming privileging of written literary forms over oral literatures.

While the theorists from the West took until the 1960s to begin a discussion on performance, African literature has been doing it for centuries through their traditional poetry by merging performance with poetic composition. But, owing to the one-dimensional understanding of the West about poetry as a written form, the unwritten oral forms have never been considered by the Western canon as valid literature. It can be mentioned in this regard that 'oral literature (often in this context called "folklore") was relatively undeveloped and primitive; and this derogatory interpretation was applied to oral literature both in completely non-literate societies and when it coexisted with written literary forms in "civilized' cultures"' (Finnegan 17). These 'unlettered performers' did not seem important until the advent of the internet and the celebration of this tradition in the name of spoken word poetry (Okpewho 4). In that connection the modern age poets from Africa who have taken on the onus of representing the authentic African culture of oral poetry have blended that tradition with their modern consciousness to reach a larger audience.

Poetry and Performance **115**

It must be noted that 'performances mark identities, bend time, reshape and adorn the body, and tell stories' and these new-age poets are here to tell those stories about Africa and their experiences as we can notice in the performances of Hafsat Abdullahi, Nomfundo Khambule, Onome Enakerakpor, Bothale Boikanyo and Xabiso Vili (Schechner 28). Even though it was believed that with 'the spread of writing, however, the traditional poet may be becoming more of a performer, treasured but no longer central to communal life as he once was', still, due to the modern transformation of the form, both the content and the performance have equal priority (Jones et al. 1). Spoken word poetry is more open than the written form of poetry because it allows diversity. As the performer performs a piece of his or her poetry, they try to communicate the meaning of their works even more clearly so as to avoid the ambiguity that surrounds the written form. While in a written form the creator has no control over the production of the meaning of his or her text, in the oral poetic tradition or spoken word poetry, the poet has scope to easily communicate the message directly to the audience. In spoken word poetry, every aspect of the performance bears meaning, either in a symbolic form or directly, which contributes to enhancing the meaning of the work. It is high time that we 'have to liberate our understanding of the term poetry from the constraint of words or the specific order in which they are arranged so that we can catch something of the more dynamic process of poesis' (Okpewho 8).

WORKS CITED

Abdullahi, Hafsat. 'Mother Tongue-Spoken Word'. Unzipped Stories Africa, 10 Nov 2022. https://www.youtube.com/watch?v=qIrN4I1qX20.

Boikanyo, Bothale. 'It is our light, not darkness'.Got Talent South Africa, 30 Nov, 2017. https://www.youtube.com/watch?v=vpJfMYgzrNU.

Brown, Duncan. *Voicing the Text: South African Oral Poetry and Performance.* Oxford University Press. 1998.

Butler, Judith. 'Performative Acts and Gender Constitution: An Essay in Phenomenology and Feminist Theory'. *Theatre Journal*, vol. 40, no. 4, 1988, pp. 519–31. JSTOR, https://doi.org/10.2307/3207893. Accessed 26 Nov. 2023.

Enakerakpor, Onome. 'A poem about the African'. TEDx Talks, 22 Feb, 2018. https://www.youtube.com/watch?v=Mm2BC4603H4&t=37s.

Finnegan, Ruth. *Oral Literature in Africa.* 1st ed., vol. 1, Open Book Publishers, 2012. JSTOR, http://www.jstor.org/stable/j.ctt5vjsmr. Accessed 3 Dec. 2023.

116 *Paramita Routh Roy*

Jones, Eldred Durosimi, et al. editors. *Oral and Written Poetry in African Literature Today 16.* James Currey,1989.

Okpewho, Isidore. 'African Poetry: The Modern writer and the Oral Tradition'. In *Oral and Written Poetry in African Literature,* Jones et al (ed).1st ed. Woodbridge, Suffolk: James Currey, 4–23.

Schechner, Richard. *Performance Studies: An Introduction.*Routledge.2013.

Vili, Xabiso. 'World Poetry Slam Champion 2022, Brussles'. World Poetry Slam Organization, 8 Oct, 2022. https://www.youtube.com/watch?v=vF0k2IYYycI&t=111s

Interviews

ALT Interview with Professor Kofi Anyidoho – Scholar, Critic, and Award-Winning Poet

Venue: ALA Conference, Knoxville, Tennessee, Friday, 26 May 2023

INTERVIEW TEAM: ERNEST EMENYONU, CHIJI AKOMA, AKACHI EZEIGBO, OBI NWAKANMA, ROSE SACKEYFIO, CHINYERE EZEKWESILI, AND IQUO DIANA ABASI

ALT: A few days ago, you won, deservedly, African Literature Association's highest award – 'The Fonlon Nichols Award' for outstanding creativity, and defence of Human Rights. Congratulations! So, let us begin by asking you to tell our readers a little bit about yourself – Kofi Anyidoho, the man, the poet, and his beginnings.

Kofi Anyidoho: If I were to identify myself, I often say, I am a teacher by profession and a poet by preoccupation. Due to family circumstances, I did not have the initial advantage of going to secondary school, but at that time, Teacher Training was available and free. So, that was the option I took, and I believe honestly, that God had His own plans for me. It has turned out that the teacher training option was the hand of destiny, for which I am most grateful today. The very first classroom I went into was a Primary One classroom. There was a little girl in that class who made it very clear to me that she was more intelligent than I was. She was quick; she was sharp and she was very careful not to offend me. I learnt from that point that, as a teacher, I could encounter students who were better endowed naturally than me. The advantage I have would be age and experience. I was a teacher at one level, but I was also learning from my students all the time; so having had the chance to teach at the elementary, secondary, Teacher Training, and university level, in that order, has defined me in many ways. However, the point of our gathering here in Knoxville is related to my work as a creative artist. I started through a creative writing program, which was in place in Ghana at the time. Initially, it was for students in Teacher Training Colleges and Secondary Schools with Sixth Forms. It was some kind of apprenticeship. You form a creative writing club in your school under the guardianship of one of the English teachers.

118

ALT Interview with Professor Kofi Anyidoho   **119**

Students wrote and their work was corrected by the English teachers. Later, the programme was officially adopted and accepted by the Ministry of Education, with people like Efua Sutherland and, Dr E. O. Apronti and later, Dr K. E. Agovi, as patrons. They would go through the most promising pieces submitted from all the schools and follow it up with a workshop. The workshops were held during Christmas and Easter holidays, and a bigger one at the national level, during the long vacation. Eventually, they selected what they considered the best pieces, to be published under the title *Talent for Tomorrow* officially by the Ministry of Education in large quantities and distributed free to students in the schools. Therefore, you can imagine me as far back as then, seeing my writing among those published at the national level!

ALT: When was this?

KA: This was in the early to mid-sixties and went on into the mid-seventies. I consider this important because one of my writings in Ewe was selected for publication. I was excited. Then somewhere along the line, the school discouraged me from writing in what they referred to as vernacular. I was told to write in English if I wanted to be a serious creative writer, so I abandoned what I already had and started writing in English. Then, I started receiving invitations for poetry festivals. On one occasion, when I went home my elder sister Aku Kpodo complained about how everybody else benefitted from what I did as a creative writer except my own family. I was reminded of the fact that I got my gift from the family and they expected some kind of giveback.

ALT: So, to contextualize what you have just said, how important is the history of creative performance in the family to your own production as a poet? As you just narrated, your grandfather Abotsi Korbli Aanyidoho and mother Abla Adidi Anyidoho were great poet-cantors in the oral tradition. How did that influence your production in English?

KA: Well, that is the beauty of the impact of tradition. That it works best if you acquire it, if it grows in its own soil before you try to export it later. As an academic, I developed a theory of what I call 'The Fertilizer Theory of Knowledge Production'. We are led to believe that fertilizer is very beneficial but the truth is nobody sows a seed in a pile of fertilizers. The seed must first take root in its own soil.

ALT: What is the main thrust of your writing? What thematic preoccupations do you focus on in your poetry?

KA: In general, what one writes about is defined by significant moments in one's life. The early part of my career coincided with difficult moments in the history of our country as African people, the

120 *Emenyonu, Akoma, Ezeigbo, Nwakanma, Sackeyfio, Ezekwesili, & Abasi*

political and economic challenges that we had, the interventions of the military, etc., so I had to respond to these. Throughout my period at the university when I began to take my creative writing seriously, every school year was interrupted by student protests. The general population had been silenced, the journalists were afraid to write the truth. It was the young people, especially the university people, who took up the challenge. I was part of that generation. You find some of my poems dedicated to colleagues who were shot dead during the protests. The military pretended they were working in the interest of the people while their selfish interest was their top priority. These were the preoccupations of some of my poems. At the same time, because my grandfather and my mother specialized in the composition and the performances of funeral dirges, reflections on death and life also dominated part of my poetry and has continued to do so. Now that I am getting closer and closer to my time, I see very dear colleagues, mentors being called away and in my most recent collection 'See What They've Done to Our Sun Rise' (yet to be published), there is a whole section on poetic tributes to departed colleagues, some of whom I had very personal relationships with, some not so well-known but made very prominent contributions at the national and international level. So, I will say my focus is not limited to any particular theme. Whatever happens around me, that's what drives my work as a poet.

ALT: Thank you for this wonderful insight into your life and your artistry. Earlier you talked about the teacher's need for humility since there are possibilities of his learning from his students as well. Chinua Achebe's essay, 'The Novelist as a Teacher' also comes to mind here. Could you speak more about your experiences as a teacher and how it has impacted the way you engage with your creative work.

KA: Well, it so happens, maybe because of my closeness to the poetic tradition of my people at a personal level, that it became the focus of my research project as a scholar. In fact, as an undergraduate the long essay that I wrote was on the life and work of a traditional composer of funeral songs, Kodzo Ahiago Domegbe, who when he became too ill to continue passed on the leadership of the group to my mother. That focus on traditional forms of creativity, as a long-term research project, has worked very efficiently in complementing what I have been learning about in the classroom from Shakespeare and all the other people whose footsteps we are following. I have been a life-long beneficiary of what I call the elders. Our generation benefited from the path that was cleared for us by the Achebes the Okigbos, the Efua Sutherlands, the Soyinkas, the Kofi Awoonors, the Okot p'Biiteks, the Ama Ata Aidoos, the Mazisi Kunenes, the Dennis Brutuss, the Kamau

ALT *Interview with Professor Kofi Anyidoho* **121**

Brathwaires, etc. My work fortunately was to bring me into personal acquaintance with some of these people. So, yes, some of my works have a stamp of tradition but that tradition did not come only from my mother and grandfather. It came from that whole generation of creators who gave a particular shaping and impetus to our search for ourselves as a people. As you can find in the works of that generation, it continues to inspire some of us, if not many of us.

ALT: Can you name specifically anyone whose works from that generation specifically speaks to you? Or who inspired you that you have a deeper connection with?

KA: I could name individuals like Kofi Awoonor, who did what I was trying to do, what I should have started doing in the first place. It will be unfair to stop with just one or two names because I have already indicated the kind of inspiration I got from other people of his generation. But there is a whole movement in my creative career where my greatest inspiration came from the creators of the African Diaspora. There was a powerful influence from Langston Hughes, Kamau Brathwaite, from Rene Depestre of Haiti, and Abdias do Nascimento of Brazil through translation. The African-American tradition also influenced me. I could recite several of Langston Hughes' poems as a young creator-teacher and I inflicted them on all my students. So it is a widening slide, like dropping a stone in a pool; the circles expand and expand.

ALT: Thank you so much. We are just curious. You have an album produced alongside a collection of poems and you decided to do some folk songs in your mother tongue. When you went into doing this, how did your family take it, seeing that they couldn't understand you originally when you did it in English?

KA: Let me tell you something that I hope will nail it down. My father did not take care of me. It was my mother's youngest brother who, when I dropped out of school at a certain point, took me under his care, taught me how to weave kente cloth, and insisted that I must go to school. That uncle happened to be an incredible composer as well and a master drummer. And the impact of his song compositions and performances in my life and work is immeasurable. I finally produced a CD of my first poems in *Ewe* and started singing some of the songs for my people. This is one of the CDs of my songs in *Ewe*. When the recording of the second one was ready, my uncle came to visit me in Accra and that evening I bought him a bottle of beer and asked him to sit down. I put the CD on and left the room. I could hear him laughing clapping and full of excitement. When the thing ended, I went in and sat down with him. He looked at me and said, 'It is now that I know that your going to school was a good thing. I can see how great you can be. Some of the things in those poems even I could not have thought of saying them like that in our own language. You have taken the tradition and you are enriching it. I am glad I sent you to school, but it is only today that I can see what a great opportunity it can be, that you came back to your tradition and added something to it – the benefit of going to school' (Kodzovi Anyidoho).

ALT: So, what is the present state of *Ewe* poetry today?

KA: Unfortunately, not as healthy as I would like it to be.

ALT: Is it because the traditional ones are gone and something has disappeared?

KA: There is a lot of reticence. The tradition has been 'hijacked' by the church. The songs that used to move me, coming from the inner core of my people's culture have been replaced by Biblical ones. Most of the songs in Ewe now are in bits and pieces of Biblical texts. …some of the best lovers of Highlife music I used to know are Nigerians, not Ghanaians.

ALT: Let's follow up on your collections, the accompaniment and all. What do you say is the relationship between performed poetry and poetry in print?

KA: As a follow-up on the CD cassette recording of my poetry and its impact, it was clear to me that some of that could be valuable when I published this book *Praise Song* for *The Land*. It came out with a CD. Later, *The Place We Call Home* also came out with CD recordings.

ALT: This was even before the digital era. What inspired you to do that at the time?

KA: When I did the *Ewe* CDs, there was a program on Ghana Television called 'Adult Education in *Ewe*'. The producer and host Yaoga Amuzu invited me for a chat. He wanted me to share with people my research on some of the traditional composers like Henoga Vinoko Akpalu, the greatest of the composers whose work had tremendous effect on Kofi Awoonor, myself, and countless others. So, I shared my knowledge about the power of *Ewe* traditional poetry as in the voice of Akpalu and others. At the end of it, he noted that I had said a lot of wonderful things about Akpalu and my grandfather, about how they enriched the *Ewe* traditional poetry. He then wanted to know my generation's contribution towards the enrichment of the *Ewe* oral tradition. So I shared a few of my poems on the TV program. As I was performing, and

ALT Interview with Professor Kofi Anyidoho **123**

I have to emphasize, 'Performing' because I was not reading, I could tell that the recording crew in the studio became very energized. The camera operator got carried away. I could hear the director shouting at him, 'Look into the camera, look into the camera'. He was so fascinated; he was looking at me instead of the camera. The performance was broadcast. Later, I travelled home and in one of the neighbouring markets, Anloga, I went to buy Sabala (a particular variety of onions). The woman raised her head to give me the onions, looked at my face and shouted **Ghananya!** – the title of one of the poems that were broadcast – and then she proceeded to recite almost the whole poem. This woman had never been to school. She was playing back chunks of my poetry, which she had heard just once on TV. Then, I went back to school. The next Monday, a young man, a messenger who worked in the bindery of Balme Library was waiting for me at my door. He said, 'Prof those poems, can you share them with us?' I mentioned that they were going to be published soon. 'You mean to put them in a book?' I said. 'Yes.' He said, 'Prof, wouldn't that hide it from us. People like me who cannot read? Why don't you record them for us?' So in fact, when I finished the recording and launched it, I invited that young man. He was the one who got the first copy.

ALT: This is '*The Praise Song for the Lion*'?

KA: No, this is the recording of my poems in Ewe. *Ghananya*

ALT: One is struck by the title of your collection '*Praise Song for The Land*'. It corresponds with Elizabeth Alexander's American poem read at the 'Obama Presidential Inauguration' talking about '*The Praise Song for the Lion*' for the day. Did you see that as an echo of your poem?

KA: When you put it that way, you suggest that I know her work as well as you do, but I wouldn't like to even assume that. I rather like to believe that the creative impulse goes around.

ALT: Let's return to this Ewe Poetry. You are such a powerful, influential voice in African poetry. It goes beyond Ghana, West Africa, and the continent. Listening to you and thinking about that moment when your family says 'everyone else seems to be enjoying what you are doing, but we don't have access to what you are doing'. Then you began writing in Ewe and recording your poetry. There is this unprompted reaction from younger viewers who are interested in the language of African literature, especially literature in the indigenous languages; how would you like to engage with this big question that we always ask – What is the best language for representing African literature? What is the most effective language to deploy to represent African culture, sensibility and aesthetics?

KA: I try not to be dogmatic about it. When I set out on the journey of writing some of my works in Ewe, part of that came from Kofi Awoonor who said to me 'Don't ever send me a note in English again. You have to write to me in Ewe and I will do so too.' It is not an 'either or situation'. My sister sold things in the market in Accra for many years; she didn't speak English; she didn't speak dominant languages in the market. However, when it became critical, she managed a word or two in English. However, the important thing for me is your best creative work normally can be done in your own language and as a student of literary history/comparative literatures, I know that the best work created in any language will always eventually reach the world through translation.

ALT: Let's come back again to '*Praise Song for The Land*'. You dedicated it to all the people 'I call my people, ancestral voices'. Who are they?

KA: It was deliberately framed so. I could have just said to my ancestors. They are not the only people who are my people. I have already told you how I have been influenced by other people from different parts of the African world, but we have to go beyond that. In my newly published collection of poems in Ewe, I acknowledged all the people I've mentioned. But I also point out that those people who have been my teachers deserve part of the praise, not only my teachers, but look at all the time you invested into the study of English, …Shakespeare, etc. They also deserve to be acknowledged. I also appreciate my direct family members, the larger African people and the Diaspora community. I must acknowledge how much the Diaspora has become part of my consciousness. Similarly, you sitting here today (referring to the ALT Editor, Prof. Emenyonu), when I see you, I can't believe that it is the same person. You remember the Calabar days, when you organized the Calabar conferences – ICAEL an annual conference that held in the first week of May and was well known world-wide?

ALT: We would like to ask you a question about Transafrican, Transdiaspora in African literature. What has happened to literature in the continent?

KA: In my own career, you all know about that moment in our history in Ghana when it looked like everything had fallen into pieces. What sustained me as a creative person, a scholar, a teacher during that period was what was happening in Nigeria. Every year, I had opportunity to visit Nigeria either once or twice. It could be Ibadan; it could be Calabar, Lagos. Most of my colleagues back home were too busy looking for ways of escape, trying to get their passports and try their luck elsewhere. Then what happened to us in Ghana earlier also happened in Nigeria. All my Nigerian colleagues of the late seveties through the mid-eighties, most of them are now here in the US and elsewhere. So that's the unfortunate development, but we don't have to lament, because there is always a good thing that can come out of so-called bad situations. Would we have preferred it that you all stayed in Nigeria or is it not better that you found your way out against the odds and establish new lines of work which have become beneficial to all of us today both at home and here in the Diaspora? At a certain point in our lives, I was as familiar with some of what was going on in Nigeria, who the new crop of writers were; and there was what was going on in Kenya, South Africa, Tanzania, Uganda. Today, that's not happening much anymore. I'll be presenting a paper here on a panel tomorrow on the work of Tade Ipadeola. I was invited out of the blue in 2013 to serve as the international consultant for the 'Nigerian Prize in Literature (Poetry)' and I received the final slot of the poetry collections. I was embarrassed to discover that yes, I knew one of the three short-listed poets – Ogochukwu Promise – but the other two, I hadn't even heard their names. I started reading their work and I was excited. I saw the anchor of myself, a professor of African literature, but I hadn't even heard about these incredible writers next door. It is still possible for us to improve remarkably. At the award ceremony in Lagos, Nigeria, when Ipadeola was announced winner that evening, he said he was going to use most of the prize-money, $100,000, to establish something in honour of Kofi Awoonor, who had just been killed in a terrorist attack in Nairobi, an acknowledgment of how much impact Awoonor may have had on him. But that direct thing is no longer happening and I feel sad about it. Poetry is alive in our various countries; however, the young generations have gone away from books into spoken word artistry. I thought those I knew in Ghana were doing great till I visited Togo on a particular occasion and saw a group of four young artists break into the hall and start performing incredible spoken word poetry in Ewe, English, and French and I was amazed. I wish some of my people in Ghana were there to see what was happening. As far as I can tell, those guys have beaten them to it. And I know some of that is happening in South Africa and Uganda.

ALT: The difference between spoken-word and written poetry has to be done canonically. How do we preserve that?

KA: It is supposedly new, but that was what my grandfather and my mother did. We are the ones who are going to play catch-up, but with an important advantage that we can now do it in our own languages, on the local platforms as well as on a wider platform and even internationally.

ALT: You call the new crop of poets, young generation, so, what is your specific message to them?

KA: My message to them is simple. We value what our oral traditions stand for, but we also regret the fact that we have no record of them once the performance is over. Today, it doesn't have to be that way anymore. You must try to be a spoken-word artist as well as a published writer. That's my challenge to them.

ALT (Iquo Diana Abasi): From your position, it does seem that all young poets are spoken-word poets. I want us to make that distinction. There are spoken-word poets, performers, and writers. I'm also a spoken-word poet. I also do performance and write, and there are many young poets like me. Some have the challenge of their inability to write their poems on paper and have it appreciated.

KA: I also insist that they do it as much in their own languages as in English. For example, last year I had the privilege of being selected as the winner of the Republic of Serbia's Highest Award for Lifetime Achievement in Poetry. What they call the 'Golden Key of Smederevo Award' and part of the reason I discovered when I went there was the awareness that I was doing poetry both in English and in Ewe. I don't know whether Professor Milena Vladic Jovanov is here. She is in one of the panels to present a paper on my work. She was chair of the search committee and played a key role in my selection for the award. At the awards ceremony, I performed many poems in English and Ewe, but in the end, the audience asked me to repeat a particular poem in its Ewe original. Here is a book of my selected poems specially published for the occasion, *Twin Brother*. It is a bilingual collection in English and Serbian, edited by Prof. Milena Vladic Jovanov, who also did the translations.

ALT: Who are the publishers?

KA: The festival organization that awarded me the prize. So, for the people who do not understand my language, they made it clear that of all the poems I shared with them, the ones that they enjoyed most were the ones in my own language. It is a remarkable observation. The same thing happened at the national level; I gave a reading two months ago in Ghana. At the end of it, the poem that they asked me to repeat was the one in Ewe. Well, most of the people in the audience were not from my area. That tells you something: you can only sell with confidence what is truly yours.

ALT: Some people were nudging you to name names, but there's a name that has popped up quite a few times, this evening: Kofi Awoonor, you mentioned him. There was a reference to the commitment you both made to write to each other in Ewe. We know that in 2015, you had published '*The Promise of Hope*', which was a collection of selected poems that you edited of Kofi Awoonor, coming right after his demise. He went to Nairobi because the work was about to be launched and published. What do you think of his place in African poetry?

KA: There is no doubt in my mind that he was highly revered. He was generous with his creativity, generous in relationships. He was as close to the Nigerian colleagues of his generation, sometimes even more than he was with colleagues in Ghana, sometime because of politics. His legacy as an intellectual creative colleague as far as I am concerned in Ghana is in a class of its own. Fortunately, towards the end of his life, I invited him to the English Department where he joined me in the training of young creative writers, some of whom since then have matured and would always acknowledge both of us as those who made it possible for them and it's important that we should never forget people like that.

ALT: What is the state of poetry in Ghana today?

KA: The state of poetry in Ghana is moving in various directions. There are a few people I know who are doing well. One of them has written a paper on my work for presentation at this conference. He was in a creative writing club and in English. There is a whole majority, male and female, who are going places as spoken-word artists. The best among them include Nana Asaase and Chief Moomen, now full-time professional spoken-word artists, drawing large audiences on all kinds of stages and platforms in a way we of our generation never dreamed of.

ALT: Thank you very much. You have made us very proud. This particular year's African Literature Association Conference is one that is going to be difficult to forget.

Interview with *Kwame Dawes*

KADIJA GEORGE

Kwame Dawes was born in Ghana to a Ghanaian mother and Jamaican father, novelist and poet Neville Dawes, who was born in Nigeria. He spent his formative years in Jamaica, describing himself as 'completely Pan-African'. Equally, he is 'completely a poet'. His life, he says, makes no sense if poetry is not part of it, something reflected in his founding of the African Poetry Book Fund in 2014. With the nurturing of poets at its core, the strands to the organisation are: a classic series, critical poetry series, translation series, research on mechanisms to distribute poetry in Africa, and archiving content on African poetry to form a hub for African poetics, housed at the University of Nebraska, where Dawes teaches. APBF celebrates its tenth anniversary with the publication of *The Anthology of Contemporary African Poetry* by the University of Nebraska Press. Dawes has been contracted by Gale to produce a two-volume *Dictionary of Literary Biography* on African Poets.

Kwame Dawes: The APBF began when Chris Abani and I were in southern Africa in 2011 as part of a tour of African poets with 'Poetry Africa', touring South Africa, Malawi and Zimbabwe. It was exciting and had a number of people from Senegal, South Africa... like Lebo Mashile and T. J. Dema. We were touched by how much good poetry we were listening to. We asked T. J. and Lebo about work they had published. Lebo had already published a couple of books, but it had been a few years since she had had anything out, but we thought their work should be available abroad. So, the idea began with us thinking, how can we make this happen? Both Chris and I had been involved in other initiatives independently. I'd been working in South Carolina and Jamaica, publishing first Caribbean and then South Carolonian poets. I had developed a model of collaborating with publishing houses. I convinced them that we would underwrite the production costs if they were willing to publish the works so that they would not lose money as there is always anxiety about losing money publishing poetry.

128

Interview with Kwame Dawes **129**

The goal was that over time they would slowly start to acquire and take over the costs, so we decided to start out by trying to partner APBF with other publishers. We realised that the reason why African poets were not being published was because editors [outside Africa] did not know what to do with African poetry, they would either get anxious that they had no context to assess it, or they just didn't know that there were poets in Africa. It was as ridiculous as that. This was the model we floated around to a number of places. Initially, Slapering Hol Press agreed to work with us, and finally, the University of Nebraska Press agreed to do the chapbooks as a series.

I was being awarded the Barnes and Noble 'Writers for Writers Award' presented at the Poets & Writers' annual gala in New York when I met Laura Sillerman. Because we had the plan, I announced it when I said thank you for the award… 'but what I need is money because I have this great idea…', and after the event, this is almost like legend, this woman walks up to me who I never knew, and said how much do you need? And I just said, we could do with $50k and she said, 'Okay, you got it. I'll get that for you.' Then she said, 'here is my card, call me tomorrow.' She walks off and I look at the back of the card and it says, 'I'm not drunk, this is serious.' This started a relationship with philanthropists Laura Sillerman and her husband who gave us $50k a year for two years. This is what we used to start supplementing the cost of the publications.

After a while we got some funding from the university and individual donors. The editorial team is an amazing team of people like Bernardine Evaristo, Aracelis Girmay, Gabeba Baderoon, Mathew Shenoda, Chris Abani, John Keene, Phillippa Yaa de Villiers, and myself. That team has been doing this for the last eight years. Everything that is published goes through that team, they review it, discuss it and University of Nebraska said, as you have such high calibre people, we'll treat that board as the editorial board.

The idea has generated a Mellon grant of $750,000 and a major grant from The Poetry Foundation of $350,000; the Mellon grant is wrapping up now, a digital humanities project and so with all the arms – the translation series, the critical series, a classic series, the libraries – we've done quite a bit of work and maintained it. The numbers are remarkable as we've published about 180 African poets in less than 10 years.

Kadija George: So you've published enough for a generation or more?

KD: Absolutely. In the 40 years of Heinemann, their total number of titles was about 386, with very little poetry at all.[1] Two things I think

---

1 Khadija Nguanya Koroma, 'Women and the Heinemann African Writers'

130 *Kadija George*

that have accelerated this process, is a good strategy, the APBF board as a team with the technology. We've never actually physically met; we've done it all online. We've had one Zoom meeting, otherwise it is just email, exchanging and having robust discussions. Tech has been remarkable and the association with the university where we have access to a great deal of students who have come into our PhD programme as writers from Africa, have become part of our research programme for the various projects that we do. I get excited about what has been achieved so far, the quality of the work and the work we are publishing is stunning and we've made a concerted effort to celebrate African art on all the covers.

KG: Have you achieved what you expected to have achieved at your 10 year anniversary?

KD: I think we have done more than we expected, but I must say that when we look back at the initial plan, pretty much all of these steps have been followed. We haven't veered away from our expectations, and they have been incremental. We have exceeded our expectations – I say this because we couldn't anticipate the number of people submitting work; we couldn't anticipate what the prizes would do. When we started the Sillerman Prize, which is a first book prize, Bernardine [Evaristo] in the UK, independent of what we were doing, started the Brunel Prize at the same time, so having her on board and us starting to work together, we couldn't have anticipated that but that was transformative and now we've taken over the Brunel prize and doing it as the Evaristo Prize. That combination has allowed us to generate a tremendous amount of interest. We said we wanted to publish four or five titles a year and we are now up to five or six. From the beginning, we wanted to do translation work, but it's taken a while and now we are starting to generate a lot of translation work. We've been translating for about five years, some French, for example with Tanella Boni [Ivorian poet], but also from indigenous languages, in Swahili and so on. An area that we knew from the beginning we had to do but which we couldn't build immediately was a critical series that looks at the work we are publishing. We started that series with Matthew Shenoda leading it.[2]

---

series. (PhD, University of Leicester, 2023). In her Introduction, Koroma states 360 titles. She notes that their first poetry anthology, *Poems of Black Africa*, by Wole Soyinka in 1975 was published 13 years after HAWS was founded. Its 346 poems includes only two poems written by one woman, Noemia de Sousa. A notable comparison to the number of African women poets published by APBF.

2   Adil Babikir, *The Beauty Hunters: Sudanese Bedouin Poetry, Evolution and Impact*, Nebraska University Press, 2023. The first book published in the

Interview with Kwame Dawes **131**

He started about three years ago and I've started to publish work that responds to it so I would say the vision is solid and clear. So few poets were being published and had so little access to publications. Of our senior poets across Africa, there were none who had collective works. Since then [2014], we've published Okara, Awoonor, Ama Ata Aidoo, and Kgositsile. We've been steadily publishing these collective works by the major African poets, but I think the greatest impact that was intended was not that we would become a publishing entity. I never envisaged us becoming a publishing house per se and you can see that the way we have designed it was not to become a publishing house but to partner with publishers, to generate in the UK, the US, and in Africa the interest in African poetry.

We did a survey and called editors and said, 'what do you know about African poetry?' To a person they said, 'well we can think of novelists, we can't think of poets,' and that told me that with that absence of any kind of knowledge and even if you Googled it at the time, you were seeing stuff that was 20–30 years old, nothing contemporary. None of the major publishers, Oxford, Cambridge, Norton's, Bedford/ St. Martin's, none of them have done an anthology of African poets. It's shocking![3]

When you think about what was said, what needs to happen is that we need to flood the market with books of poetry. We knew that the quality would be there because we'd seen it, and soon, what we knew would happen is that publishers would start publishing and almost to a fault, all the chapbook writers that we published within a year or two, are now with a major publisher; with Copper Canyon, with Graywolf, and they are getting picked up as they have a calling card. Now there is a wave – it is not a faddish wave – it's a wave that says, 'now there is a knowledge base for this work.' This is intentional. What I didn't anticipate is, many of the poets who we published are getting offers and interest from other places, yet insisting that they come back to us. They want APBF to publish them, when I ask why, they say, 'We are forming a family here,' so it's very telling. Part of it is the editorial attention that they get, which they still can't get from the major places, and I think they like the idea of the freedom it gives them to move back and forth. So, people like Romeo Oriogun, Saddiq Dzukogi,

---

'On African Poetry' series.

3 Heinemann's later poetry anthologies were, Adewale Maja-Pierce, ed., *The Heinemann Book of African Poetry in English* (African Writers Series) Heinemann, African Writers Series (1990); K.L. Goodwin, *Understanding African Poetry: A study of ten poets*, London, 1982; Frank and Stella Chipasula, *The Heinemann Book of African Women's Poetry* (African Writers Series), London, 1995.

132 *Kadija George*

all of these people keep coming back to us. Others like Safia Elhilo, are being published in major places, and Warsan [Shire] blew up of course with *Lemonade*.[4]

But it's a tough model because I still have to find subvention costs, a few thousand dollars for each book that we publish. I'm committed to that; I don't have a problem underwriting African poetry. Underwriting poetry, I think is valid, but I think eventually, publishers are trusting that there is a real body of work.

KG: The fact that you went to major publishers and asked them what they think about African poetry, and they didn't know anything, do you think that is part of the historic belief that major publishers in Britain in the 50s/60s made a conscious decision that they would publish fiction, but they would not publish poetry?[5]

KD: I think there are really interesting philosophical and economic reasons why African poetry has had so tragically little attention over the years, but I think that is changing.

One of the things that I'm preparing is a series of lectures on African poetry and the work we are doing. I wanted to look into Heinemann as Heinemann is really pivotal.[6]

Heinemann published, Chinua Achebe's *Things Fall Apart* before they had anything to do with Africa, but it wasn't selling; it certainly wasn't selling in Africa, so Heinemann decided to form a distribution mechanism in Africa, essentially, to sell *Things Fall Apart*. They came up with an idea which we are thinking a lot about because we are doing a major research project on book distribution.

KG: It is interesting as well, that you have done that comparison with Heinemann as APBF is in some ways like a reflection of what the Heinemann series was. What do you want it to be? Or would you rather not be compared to Heinemann?[7]

---

4   Safia Elhilo's latest poetry collection is *Girls That Never Die*, Penguin Random House, 2022. Warsan Shire's latest collection is *Bless the Daughter Raised by a Voice in Her Head*, Chatto & Windus, 2022.

5   Caroline Davis, *Creating Postcolonial Literature: African Writers and British Publishers*, Palgrave Macmillan, 2013.

6   Since the announcement in 2003 that Heinemann African Writers Series would not be publishing further titles, it has been relaunched twice. In 2023, Head of Zeus relaunched 100 of the classic titles as the Apollo Africa list.

7   Kadija Sesay, 'Does Anyone Miss Heinemann African Writers Series?' *Journal of African Literature* (2006).

KD: I think it must be compared to Heinemann because of what we can learn from Heinemann and also the work we decide to do, to what is a colonial reckoning. We are publishing from outside of Africa, so there is the danger of falling into this colonial pattern. One of the things we do to fight that is the dominance of our leadership and the outfit is run by Africans, we've been very committed to that, but the other thing is that we have to recognize the control that Heinemann could assert was because they came in during colonialism, so they had readymade access to the relationship between the UK and these African countries.[8] Those channels are completely gone so we know that we can't get into the education game in the same way except country by country, so then the question is, what distribution is in Africa currently? How does poetry move and our research is looking at poetry. How are poetry books published in Africa, published out of Africa by Africans? How are these books distributed?[9] We interviewed hundreds of people writers, editors, festival directors, booksellers – we've been interviewing people from Egypt to South Africa to get a picture of it and we've got some beautiful useful reports.

A global approach [to distribution] may not work, it has to be a localised arrangement. It is harder to manage that arrangement because every one of these things have to function in a certain way, but increasingly, my sense is, I can't think we've concluded exactly what the mechanism is. We started with Amalion Publishing in Senegal and that has worked relatively well. They thought they could do all of West Africa, but it hasn't worked out that way, so they get Senegal, they might get Nigeria because the director is Nigerian [Sulaiman Adebowale], so it helps but the problem of course is that these individual publishers are trying to make their own money, but we are using a completely nonprofit mechanism. Our writers get 20% of royalties for the first thousand copies that they sell to give them a strong kickstart and then after that they get seven per cent, which is really decent. Publishers in other places will not do that but we are not-for-profit and they are for profit so how do we work in ways that could benefit them? It is a big question that we're still trying to answer and then we ask ourselves,

---

8   Kadijattu George, 'Black British Publishers and Pan-Africanism: 1960–1980' (PhD, University of Brighton-England, 2022). British book publishers continued to benefit from their colonial relationships as it moved to one of neo-colonialism, supported by The British Council.

9   Olayinka Adekola, Jacob Anderson, Joel Cabrita, Katlo Gasewagae, Bena Habtamu, Brittany Linuus, Bary Miggot, Michelle Ng, Anita Too and Kyle Wang, eds., *ImprintAfrica: Conversations with African Women Publishers*, Huza Press, 2024.

134   *Kadija George*

are there booksellers that publishers will trust – this is one of the problems – publishers don't trust the booksellers in Africa because they say, well you know, you can send the books and then the books don't sell, they never send them back.

So, the question, is do we develop a fund, that will underwrite all of those fields, in other words, we'll say to the publishers, send them, if you lose, we will underwrite that cost and we will work with the distribution in Africa. Penguin said they won't do it anymore. If we can recreate trust with booksellers, especially for festivals for example, that might be a way for poetry books, but we don't know so these are the things that we are trying to test out to see whether they will work. South Africans don't necessarily trust sending books to Nigeria, for instance, for the same reasons. South Africa has a lot of poetry small presses that are fairly successful, but they do not distribute outside of southern Africa. So again, if you want anything from South Africa, you have to go through Amazon.

KG: I don't know if the poetry presses are using – you know Zukiswa [Wanner] set up a WhatsApp distribution system.[10]

KD: I think so, and there are a number of – even though they don't do a lot of poetry – there are a number of outfits in the UK. If you Google book distribution in Africa, there are about three companies in the UK. The good news is because we are focused on poetry, it allows us to make a clear and specific kind of investigation, the results of which will affect all genres but the focus on the poetry allows it to be manageable about who we ask, who we talk to and what is happening, but it's the big frontier for us to understand.

KG: Distribution is key. It's about ownership and the power of that, so if we don't control it, it's never going to happen, so I think if people see you can get a handle on it for poetry, they will be so surprised, they will want to follow and see how the model works.

Can you talk about the successes and achievements of APBF – what has been a challenge that you didn't expect?

KD: One of the big challenges was funding. Because of the structure, which requires me to find funding to subvent costs also finding funding to pay for permissions. When we are doing these collections, we have to get permissions and we have to find the money for it. We've

10 The Book Fam Africa collective receives a discount with DHL in more than 40 countries to send books to other African countries. It has also been useful as a platform to find translators which enables co-publishing.

Interview with Kwame Dawes **135**

surmounted that challenge, but we still need a secure endowment or something like that, that would allow us to continue to function. Our grant writing mechanism was also a challenge, but we increased the team of people who can work on that area, so we've been doing very well on grant writing. The projects like translation are very interesting because when you want to lead the process and say, 'look we want more indigenous work,' you have to start commissioning and commissioning requires you to find funding to pay people to do the translation.

KG: In, the next 10 years, where are you hoping to be? Funding is probably always going to be a challenge, but apart from that?

KD: It will be, but I don't worry about the funding because I think the brand has created a lot of good will and also funding as you know, is a strategy. Succession is very important to us, and I think we built it into the system of the editorial team. I'm senior, Chris is senior, although at this point, we still have some years, but you know we have people like Matthew, John, all of these people who remain interested in it. I think one of the things we are developing is how to secure the APBF's function and role for the future so that it continues adapting to what the need is. Our first situation was absence – a complete absence of work on African poetry, even contemporary African poetry.

We are starting to fix that. One of the fascinating realities is, in the work that we've been doing, on archiving African poetry and creating a hub of African poetry, one of the interesting 'discoveries' has been the hunt that many studies have been done on African poetry throughout Africa by PhD and Masters' students. These theses never moved towards publication because no-one was interested in publishing African poetry. We've started to look at some of these theses and they are brilliant, innovative stuff, work on indigenous voices and how they engage with the contemporary space, work on gender, performatives, and so on. We don't have to be forcing a new creation of material, there is stuff that is there.

You know there is something violent about the silencing of Black voices through the structures of publishing and that to me is something that people don't really understand. People think ok, they are just not writing the work, *i nah true*. These people have PhD's of their work. Many of them finished their Master's and went on to do other things. Not even the journals would take it and this is good work… really important work and work that is close to the ground. They did field studies, recordings, from the 50s and the 60s, up till now, so even if all we do is start cataloguing it and summarising it for researchers to be able to access it, then we're good.

136 *Kadija George*

KG: In terms of the poets that you've published, are there any of them who've come from that first stage, from the Brunel to Sillerman to Glenna Luschei Prize?

KD: The Brunel structure is that it identifies a longlist. That longlist becomes useful for us for the chapbook series, so we use that longlist because what we do with the chapbooks series is that every year we put together lists through recommendations. We send off requests all over Africa and then we take even the Brunel shortlist and we put it into a pool and identify 60–70 poets who we write to and say, 'you have two weeks to send us a chapbook.' Then from that pool, we identify for the Sillerman prize. We tell the judges, there are two things to look for, one, the winner, two, anybody you see whose work might not be quite ready, but there's a chapbook in there somewhere. We tag it, we take that and we then approach them for a chapbook. From that 60, we end up with 13 or 14; so we publish from a wide reach. A lot of the people we publish in chapbooks many of them came out of the Brunel Prize, similarly, the Sillerman winners tend to be people who have already entered the Brunel, so there is a symbiotic kind of relationship between all of these things that date it, so we didn't want to make it a funnel because someone maybe out of that funnel, and we still want to be able to consider their work.

KG: In terms of the work, what have you, the team noticed regionally, with the writers that you publish? Have there been similarities you've noticed whether it be style or themes?

KD: There's a recent, article of a study of contemporary African poetry emerging looking at these younger poets, and they made a proposition that said well, is this work, really African or how is it influenced by the West, so there are these kinds of questions and I welcome them.[11] But this is a question that of course we've been looking at that and very interested in it but one of the key things that Chris [Abani] and I talk about is, we're not going to dictate what people write about, we are going to try and let the writing tell us where African poetry is, where Nigerian poetry is. We knew that what would happen is poets are like everybody else, they want to be published, they want to know what is being published and whether they can get on it somehow, that's human

---

11 Chibueze Darlington Anuonye, 'Facebook Writers: The Emergence of a New Generation of Nigerian Poets' *Research in African Literature*, May 2024. Anuonye uses Harry Garuba's 'strategic intervention' as a theoretic framework to classify a fourth generation of Nigerian poets.

Interview with Kwame Dawes **137**

and we don't have a problem with that. But poets are also people who have to understand writing is about where their soul is, where their heart is, what is their passion, and what is driving them, what resonates with them. They are human, they are responding to things. Africa is not a static place, influences from inside and outside continue and the work is going to reflect that, but what I'm seeing is in many of these poets, they have confidence now that they have a home where they can get published, they are no longer imitative, they are now wrestling with what does it mean to be a Muslim poet in Minna, northern Nigeria who also has a Hausa background that goes back to a long literary tradition, poetic tradition, and then there is a strong Islamic influence, how do I know my family, my voice, my ancestry in that space? I'm seeing poets wrestling with that to create fresh, challenging, complex work, work that they would not have risked if they did not have an assurance that somebody was listening, that there is a space for it, so I am completely at ease with poets who are imitative. If it is just slavish imitation, it's going to be bad poetry.

So, we are asking ourselves, what is fresh and interesting; what is new and what is dynamic and how are they talking to each other, so several things are happening. There are poets saying, 'let me look out the window, let me see what my world is doing,' and they are writing in that space, that is what I think poets should be. Poets are listening to each other now they have access, so a poet in Ghana can read Clifton Chicagua in Kenya and say, 'wow, I love that style, let me see how I can…', and they are reading each other. How do we know this? They are crediting, they are writing epigraphs; it's wonderful!

So, I'm not worried because I think the poets are being free to be true. The women are blowing up this space because now they are saying, what is woman's body in Africa today in that poetics? How do I write that body, how do I deal with my language, my languages and I'm writing in English but how do I deal with my languages? The work is reflecting all of that kind of thing. I want the critics, the scholars to start asking what has emerged? Our job is to take what is in there and say, 'here it is.'

KG: Where are you not getting poetry from?

KD: Not enough from East Africa. I think people have to understand how populations spread. People say there are so many Nigerian poets and so I say, 'do you know the population of Nigeria relative to the rest of Africa?' If that wasn't happening, then there would be a problem.

So, there is a lot of Nigerian work; we get a lot of South African work, but not a lot because South Africa has a fairly robust publishing

138 *Kadija George*

mechanism and, for years, it was very Afrikaans but they are publishing more Black African writers now, so I don't think the imbalance is that crazy. Part of it is language; Somalia has one of the greatest poetic traditions in the world but it's in Somali and so we are now working with the Library of Congress to translate a lot of Somali work. We have started to identify, and we are getting some like Warsan [Shire] who are Somali writing in English who are dominating, but I'm satisfied where we are getting work from. Smaller countries where things are difficult, like the Congo, we're trying to generate more work; places like Rwanda, Botswana, these are smaller markets and smaller spaces where we are not getting as much work from as we would hope, but I think all of it still makes sense because where the tradition is longer, in West Africa, it's likely that those mechanisms would work. Where it's French [for example] it has to be translated so we are not going to get that, we're reflective of the English-speaking world.

KG: One of the aspects I think which is still a struggle, which may be less in places like South Africa, is the editorial factor of working with new writers. For example, if they are not getting to send you their work, or even if they are and you say, oh this is interesting but the work is still not there, how can poets be assisted on the continent where they have obviously got this love of poetry whether it is in English or whether it is in a mixture of languages, how do we get the editors in there?

KD: The way we've encouraged it is that our writers who we publish are mentoring. For a long time, we were not getting anything out of Liberia for instance and Patricia Jabbah Wesley then asked to do an anthology of Liberian poetry, and asked if we would publish it. She went to Liberia, and she started writing workshops and she's been back and forth with these young writers. Now we are getting a lot of really strong work out of Liberia, really boots on the ground. We can't do it, but when our writers are saying we are going to do it, they now have a message which says, if you get your work to a point, there is somewhere we can send it and there are different stages of that development. That's one of the things that is important, so whenever I go anywhere in Africa, I always have a gathering of poets, whether it's Ghana, Kenya, or so on, I ask, 'What are the challenges, what are the needs, how can we help your publishing world?' This is the way of the APBF and whenever we have been able to do that, that has made a difference because we trust that poets and their ambition will drive this process.

(Re)Echoing a Collective Trauma in Nigerian Poetry: An Interview with Kehinde Akano

ADEWUYI AREMU AYODEJI

Introduction

A poet, playwright, essayist, and journalist, Kehinde Akano was born in Shao in Moro Local Government Area of Kwara State, Nigeria in 1970. He graduated from Obafemi Awolowo University, Ile-Ife with a Bachelor's degree in English Education in 1994. He studied at the University of Ilorin, Ilorin between 2002 and 2012 for his Master's degree and PhD in Literature-in-English. A member of the Editorial Board of the *State Mobilizer*, a quarterly publication of the Kwara State Directorate of National Orientation Agency and Carrot Publishers, Kehinde Akano is also the Project Director for the Millennium Initiatives on Social Values (MISSAVs), a nongovernmental organization. His poems have appeared in *Symphony of Harmony*, a collection of poems published by the Association of Nigerian Authors (ANA), Kwara State Chapter. As part of his service to his community, Akano has served as the secretary of the Shao Awonga Forum and Moro Progressive Movement. Akano currently teaches courses in African Literature at Kwara State University, Malete, where he is the Director of the Centre for Affiliation and Linkages. He lives in Ilorin, Nigeria. To date, Akano has published four literary works, *Songs of Awon Gaga* (2014), *Invoking the Emirate Spirit* (2014), *Emirate Blues and Home Resistance* (2019) and *Pajepolobi* (2021) – three poetry collections and one play. He was the winner of the Association of Nigerian Authors (ANA) Prize for Poetry for his poetry collection *Emirate Blues and Home Resistance* and a second runner-up for the ANA Prize for Drama for his first play, *Pajepolobi*, in 2021.

In this interview, Kehinde Akano avers that the thematic preoccupation of his work is the exigency for the abolition of feudalism (emirate system) in his local government area and in Nigeria as a whole. He maintains that his poetry is primarily contrived as a response to the emirate system imposed on the people of Moro Local Government Area of Kwara State, Nigeria. He argues that feudalism

139

140   *Adewuyi Aremu Ayodeji*

is not just a collective trauma for his people, but that it is the bane of socio-political development in Nigeria. Akano reveals that what gives his work much relevance is his ability to re-echo the collective trauma through a literary medium and, at the same time, synchronize it with the ensuing underdevelopment in his immediate environment and Nigeria at large. Commenting on his use of local or traditional aesthetics, Akano emphasizes that all the material for his work is sourced from his community and identifies the goddess of Awon as his poetic muse.

Adewuyi Ayodeji: Let me start off by congratulating you on your award as the 2021 ANA Poet of the Year. I believe that portends a remarkable development in your writing career. What do you have to say about that?

Kehinde Akano: Thank you. Ordinarily… in this season when creativity is not that valued, when there is a poor reading culture, when hundreds of thousands of creative works – whether standard or substandard – are being churned out on a daily basis, one should relish being celebrated. The fact remains that it becomes difficult to know which author to or not to celebrate in our time. So, for emerging authors like me, literary prizes from reputable organizations such as the Association of Nigerian Authors, which was founded by the great Chinua Achebe, which has played host to several authors in Nigeria and recently celebrated its 40th anniversary, can only encourage us to continue writing. And apart from the LNG Literary Prize, which is usually called African Nobel Prize and considered one of the 10 richest and most prestigious awards in the world, ANA literary award is one of the best on the continent, not just in Nigeria. So, finding me worthy of the award gives me the joy that I'm being celebrated by a reputable organization like ANA. These days when we write, we can hardly distinguish the standard from the substandard, but when your work goes out there for competition in ANA and it is found worthy of the first position, that gives you leverage and confidence that you have come of age. Because if your work could undergo such a review or screening by a panel of literary scholars and professors, that is a kind of authoritative stamping of your work. That's a positive censorship… that your style of writing, your aesthetics, your grammar are in line with the set literary standard. On a lighter note, even among your colleagues in the department, who hitherto couldn't show any overt interest in your work whether by giving it critical review or analysis, such an authoritative judgement takes care of any doubt or bickering anybody might have against your work. In a nutshell, I am happy I won the prize.

An Interview with Kehinde Akano **141**

AA: Talking about the acceptance of your work after winning the award, is there any significant upsurge in the level of acceptance of your work?

KA: One thing which has become a new yardstick for measuring the success or popularity of literary works and writers nowadays is the internet. The award has exposed my work to the internet in some ways. One of such is the wide coverage of the event by major (online) newspapers in the country. Another is the acknowledgement of the award by the University of Ilorin in her monthly bulletin, with the caption: 'An Alumnus of Unilorin Wins ANA Award'. The award was also well celebrated in my school's annual magazine. More so, early this year, I think, the Kwara State chapter of ANA dedicated a reading session for the celebration of the award. As a matter of fact, not until I won the award did I discover that no writer from the Kwara State chapter had won it before. Even among my colleagues, the narrative has changed – the comments are now more of applause of my work. We now have people recommending my works to their students in schools other than mine, KWASU. The acceptance, although gradual, is significant and greatly appreciated.

AA: It is good to hear that, because nothing makes a writer happier than a wide readership of his/her work. Now to business proper. You have written four literary works – all collections of poems except for the last, *Pajepolobi*, which is a drama text. So, let's start with the one that won the ANA prize, *Emirate Blues*. I have read it and I find it artistically and thematically rich. Compared to your previous collections, there is this theme of emirate system peculiar to your poetry. For instance, you have one titled *Invoking the Emirate Spirit* while this one is *Emirate Blues*. Any connection, or what is it with this emirate theme you have sustained in your poetry?

KA: Every writer has a muse or an inspiring environment. Nigeria is our fatherland and remains the constituency of most Nigerian writers. But, then, there are other sub-constituencies which demonstrate the kind of political rigmarole which Nigeria is known for. Quite a number of authors have picked Nigeria as a whole from the macro to the micro. For example, Niyi Osundare, in his *The Eye of the Earth*, *Songs of the Marketplace* and *Village Voices*, captures more of the macro Nigeria, yet his local sentiments about his hometown and Yoruba culture clearly manifest. So also does Tanure Ojaide address the general Nigerian situation in his poetry collections such as *The Fate of Vultures*, *Waiting for the Hatching of a Cockerel* and *I Want to Dance*, but not without first locating the micro Niger Delta in the discussion. In my case, I am

142   *Adewuyi Aremu Ayodeji*

inspired by the system of government called emirate practised in my environment. I am inspired by it because it is a system alien to my culture and it is anti-human as far as my people are concerned. We have always rejected it, but having been long entrenched, we are still battling with it. So, I try to operate from the micro level of the Nigerian nation. I try to dwell on what affects my people and, consequently, Nigeria as a whole – that is emirate, feudal system. My second collection was *Invoking the Emirate Spirit* and the third was *Emirate Blues*. The recurrence of the emirate subject in my poetry is a way of emphasizing the practice I so much hate, and to enable me drive home my position in reaction to emirate system as it pervades my local environment.

AA: And your reaction, even as revealed in *Emirate Blues*, indicates you are not alone in this struggle. In other words, you are only trying to chronicle or, somehow, rehash a community's struggle for freedom in your writing.

KA: Yes.

AA: Across your collections of poetry, you present emirate system as a collective trauma for your people. That is, the system renders them traumatized. Could you expatiate on this?

KA: Thanks for your use of this apt expression – collective trauma. Emirate system is truly a collective trauma for my people. And not just for my people, the bane of Nigerian development is feudalism, but it is unfortunate that we experience the crudest form of it in my part of the country. Talk to anybody in Moro or Kwara, they will tell you how pervasive, oppressive, anti-human, retrogressive and slavish the system is. And it is the majority that bears the brunt. What I do in my work as the mouthpiece of the majority is to synchronize this collective trauma with the ensuing underdevelopment in my area specifically and in my country generally. I try to chronicle and expose the evils of the common virus called emirate system in my books so that the age-long contention could go beyond oral complaints from my people. What I have done is not new to anybody; it is just the medium of echoing and re-echoing it that gives my work some relevance. I am just chorusing what others are saying using the literary platform to globalize it. And the ANA prize has begun to aid this globalization of our collective trauma.

AA: In your poem, 'Their Magaji's Cali-Fate', featured in *Emirate Blues*, you make a comparison of Sokoto Emirate and Ilorin Emirate. You write: 'This is their Magaji's Cali-Fate/The emirate for the Beyeribe/Not a prototype of Sokoto/Where Father Kuka and the Sultan exchange pleasantries'. You try to portray Sokoto Emirate as far less oppressive

An Interview with Kehinde Akano **143**

than Ilorin Emirate. Of course religion, Islam, comes to play in your comparison. The big question is: are you not already 'Islamizing' the whole issue of emirate system? Or, let me put it this way: how do you aim to make a balance in your work between emirate system as a feature of Islam and emirate as a political system vis-à-vis the trauma it has caused your people?

KA: As far as Nigeria is concerned, emirate system originated from the Sokoto Caliphate. The question is: how come it is better practised in Sokoto? First, in Sokoto, emirate system is based largely on religious activities… ethnic-bound, and practised in a relatively homogeneous cultural environment. That is not the case in Ilorin Emirate where the impostors are culturally and ethnically different from the people on whom the system is imposed. Second, this pertains to the issue of conquest. The Fulani of Sokoto today may have culturally transformed from the Fulani who conquered Sokoto because, for instance, they now speak more Hausa than the Fulfulde language in the State. Meaning that there is some kind of cultural integration. Do we have that in Kwara? No! Here, we have an alien socio-political practice in an environment with diverse cultural norms and religions. In Sokoto, the system might not have been challenged because of the seemingly ethnic-cum-religious homogeneity of the people. In Kwara, the environment is not conducive for the practice – it is being forced on the people. In Sokoto, there is a kind of democratized system of emirate – a hybrid of sort, partly feudal, partly democratic. Under the Sultan, the local chiefs are fairly well treated, which is incomparable with the way community chiefs and Obas are lowly treated in Ilorin Emirate. So, the two emirate systems are two poles apart. Now to the second part of your question. It appears that emirate system grew out of a religious practice, but that is not actually the case. It is for the purpose of easy administration of the practice that it is tied to Islam. With that religious affinity or affiliation, the impostors of the system could indulge in oppression in the name of Islam whereas Islam does not teach oppression. Therefore, there is a clear distinction between emirate system and Islam. The two are lumped together in order for the impostors to perfect oppression of others using religion as a shield. Again, the emirate system here differs from Sokoto's because, here, the impostors profane the name of the Prophet by doing the opposite of what they openly preach. In Sokoto, we know them for what they do and that is why, as I point out in one of the poems in *Emirate Blues*, Matthew Kuka could stay there and practise his Christianity freely. Do the emirate lords in my area want to claim to be holier than the Sultan? How come emirate system becomes more brutal in a place that copied it from Sokoto?

144 *Adewuyi Aremu Ayodeji*

AA: With the way you talk, blunt and daring, which is hardly different from the way you write, can one just label you a revolutionary? Then you could also let us know who your literary influences are.

KA: Being a revolutionary... I think writing is a calling and more or less a crusade. You must have a reason for writing. Just like pastors and Imams want to win souls, so also does a writer want to ensure equity, justice and positive change. But how you achieve your aim as a writer depends on your approach – whether peaceful or violent. This marks you out as a Marxist or revolutionary. While I cannot claim to be a Marxist or revolutionary, my own purpose of writing is to effect attitudinal change in human society. Let justice reign! Sincerely, I can't pin down my literary influence to a single writer; I have a roll call of influences. Any visionary writer who speaks to the conscience of oppressors is my role model. In this category are Wole Soyinka, Niyi Osundare, Tanure Ojaide and Olu Obafemi. These writers address socio-political rots in our society of which feudalism is crucial. In that wise, I can say I am following in their footsteps.

AA: Let me take it up from there. One common feature of all the four African writers you just mentioned is the use of traditional elements in their works. Likewise, you employ a lot of traditional elements in your work. Chief among them is allusion. You always allude to legends and mythical figures. In your *Song of Awongaga*, you particularly draw on a goddess called Awon. Could you talk about that?

KA: Yes, you are right. Every African writer is covertly or overtly indebted to oral tradition. We borrow from our oral traditions either by omission or commission, transposition, revalidation or authentication. We all go back to our traditions at the level of myths, proverbs, narratives or satires. This is not peculiar to African writers alone... even the great Shakespeare borrowed extensively from the English tradition to... adopt in his numerous classical plays. Having said that, you can see local aesthetics in my works. One of such mythical or mystic influences is Awongaga – a river goddess whose name is synonymous with my town, Shao. Awon is a composite character with a multiplicity of meanings in my town. Awon is a river goddess and there is a river called Awon in Shao. My community is also famous for Awon festival which is a festival of mass wedding. So, the influence of Awon on my people is so massive that you cannot separate Awon from Shao and vice versa. As a native of that culturally endowed ancient town, one is unwaveringly identified with Awon; one cannot but refer to Awon either as a river or a goddess. I think that is why Awon has tremendous influence on my work too. Comparatively speaking, Awon is to my work what Olosunta is to Niyi Osundare's, or what water is to Tanure Ojaide's.

AA: What an interesting comparison there! As we are drawing close, we need to talk about *Pajepolobi* too – your only play. Interestingly, it was the second runner-up in the 2021 ANA Prize for Drama. As regards your use of local aesthetics, the play is about a legend, Pajepolobi, whose traditional mode of activism is modernly emulated by his son, Ologunde. In all, you scheme a blend of the old and the modern. What's the inspiration for that play?

KA: You will note that *Pajepolobi* is a clear departure from my usual feudal theme. It is a clear departure in capturing a more national or global issue of governance, yet the material or the creative impulse is sourced locally. In fact, all the material for all my works is sourced from my community. Just like you said, the play is about a legend, Taiwo Omobimpe Pajepolobi, who also had a masquerade by the same name. The man and his masquerade remain inseparable because of the feats he was able to achieve through the masquerade in his life time. The creative ingenuity I have brought into the material is to create a parallel between past and modernity. Even before the introduction of modern democracy or nationhood, it was not as if African communities were devoid of oppression, injustice and social vices. But the oppressors and these inimical traditional systems of government were confronted by certain people, who, in modern parlance, are called activists. Taiwo Omobimpe was one of such people who used traditional means or mystic powers to tackle wicked people and promote harmony, peace and freedom. In modern times, activists protest openly, talk to the press and carry placards. I have created a parallel between Pajepolobi's traditional activism and Ologunde Labala's modern mode of activism. You now have in your hands two eras… making a comparison between how it was done then and how it is being done now. In the end, it is left for the reader to decide whether there are correlations between traditional and modern modes of activism.

AA: Trying to draw a curtain on this interview, I think we should do it on a lighter note. When writing a new work, say a poem, does your first line or sentence often remain in that position when you are done?

KA: You are asking whether the line I start with in a new poem ends up being the first line.

AA: Exactly my question.

KA: I would say yes and no. You know why?

AA: No.

KA: For me, creativity is more of perspiration than inspiration, but both work hand in hand. For instance, I have a play in the press and

146 *Adewuyi Aremu Ayodeji*

I'm working on two collections of poems. The first line in a collection may not be the first in that collection. However, I equate the first line or sentence with the first drop of the muse and it's that inspiring sentence that keeps you going. Usually, that first line or sentence inspires me to write more poems and contrive the title. For that reason, the line or sentence is better retained until the work is completed. You become possessed by it and that drives you to write further. You want to hold on to it as it serves as an ignition key that helps.

AA: Thank you very much for your time. I have had a good time talking with you. I hope we can have a time like this in the future to discuss your forthcoming works and more. Thanks again.

KA: It is my pleasure.

Tributes

Ama Ata Aidoo: Ghana's Literary Treasure
A Tribute to Ama Ata Aidoo (23 March 1940 – 31 May 2023)

ROSE A. SACKEYFIO

Africa, the diaspora, and the world mourn the passing of Ama Ata Aidoo as a celebrated feminist and author of a distinguished array of pathbreaking literary works. As one of the godmothers of postcolonial African fiction, her dramatic works, novels, short fiction, poetry, essays, and literary criticism are landmarks of women's entrance onto the literary stage alongside iconic male writers during the mid-twentieth century. Through her creative artistry, Ama Ata Aidoo became a voice for African women to interrogate the complexities of the postcolonial landscape from a female perspective. Her literary style draws upon African oral traditions and a combination of prose and poetry. Her literary corpus conveys clear-sighted vision, critique, and thematic focus on compelling issues of women's identity, tradition and modernity, cultural norms and expectations, the relationship between Ghana and the diaspora, and the incongruent trajectories of post-independence Ghana. Ama Ata Aidoo joined the ancestors on 31 May 2023, and her loss will be felt for generations throughout Africa and the world. Her literary works will live on as classics that represent women's unsilenced voices of resistance to oppressive experiences, and the expression of their selfhood and identity.

For over 20 years, my research, scholarship, and teaching have explored the literature of African women writers, including Aidoo's work, to highlight their experiences in society and to celebrate their remarkable contributions to women's and gender studies through literary expression. At the African Literature Association Conference in 2012, I was honoured to meet Ama Ata Aidoo, and this event marked the beginning of a rewarding friendship that developed through visits to her home each time I visited Ghana. I experienced warm hospitality, laughter, and a rich exchange of ideas about Ghana and the diaspora, women and gender, and literature, among other compelling topics. In

Ama Ata Aidoo: Ghana's Literary Treasure **149**

her presence, I never felt like an outsider to Ghana or to Africa because of her welcoming spirit, generosity, and kindness. Her groundbreaking dramatic work, *Dilemma of a Ghost*, resonates deeply with me because it is the first literary text by an African writer that examines the historical connections between Ghana/Africa and the diaspora. The ideas explored in the work are just as timely and important in the global age as they were in the mid-twentieth century, if not more so. The relationship between Ghana/Africa and the diaspora is 'charged', as stated by Ama Ata Aidoo in the documentary, *The Art of Ama Ata Aidoo* (2014), and I commend her for exploring a sensitive issue that has not completely healed between Ghanaians/Africans and their brothers and sisters in the diaspora. The ending of the play conveys a powerful message of acceptance and the potential for understanding among Ghanaians and the displaced Africans of the diaspora.

I will always cherish the memory of our friendship as well as her insightful perspectives on contemporary women's issues that shape the lives of Ghanaian and African women. In the early years of my career as a literary scholar, her fiction inspired my scholarly engagement with the portrayal of African women characters by female authors as well as my approach to feminist inspired African texts through critical analysis of her novel *Changes: A Love Story*, the short story collection *No Sweetness Here*, and the play *Anowa*. Through my analysis of these and other texts, I explored the ways in which African women writers use their creative artistry to reconfigure the complexities of women's identities and their role in society.

Ama Ata Aidoo was born on 23 March1940, in southern Ghana, to a royal family among the Fante ethnic community. Encouraged by her father to pursue Western education, she was fortunate to win a scholarship to Wesley Girl's High School, where she developed her interest in writing. She won a short story competition sponsored by the *Daily Graphic* called 'To Us a Child is Born'. After completing secondary school, she attended the University of Ghana at Legon, where she majored in English Literature. While at the University she participated in the Ghana Drama Studio and published her first play, *Dilemma of a Ghost*, in 1965. Her teaching career began in 1970 and lasted for over a decade at the University of Cape Coast, but the unfavourable political climate in the country failed to nurture her creative talent. In 1982, she was appointed Minister of Education by the then head of state, J. J. Rawlings. She resigned from her position in less than two years and migrated to Zimbabwe, where she resumed writing and teaching. In 1991, she founded the New York-based Organization of Women

150 Rose A. Sackeyfio

Writers of Africa with poet Jayne Cortez, and in 1994, she helped to create the Women's World Organization for Rights Development and Literature to support women's access to publishing. In 2000, Ama Ata Aidoo established the Mbassem Foundation to support African women writers. She subsequently taught in the United States at the University of Richmond and at Brown University until her retirement in 2012. Her works have received critical acclaim and robust scholarly engagement by scholars, writers, and literary critics. Among these are *The Art of Ama Ata Aidoo: Polylectics and Reading Against Neocolonialism* (1994), *Emerging Perspectives on Ama Ata Aidoo* (1999), *Essays in Honor of Ama Ata Aidoo at 70: a Reader in African Cultural Studies* (2012), and the documentary film *The Art of Ama Ata Aidoo*: (2014).

As a groundbreaking dramatic work, the publication of *Dilemma of a Ghost* broke barriers for African women writers in a male-dominated field. The play examines interlocking themes of the tensions between Ghana and her diaspora, tradition and modernity, the past and the present, and the cultural collisions that explode familial harmony. The publication of her second play, *Anowa*, in 1970 confirmed her talent as gifted storyteller of compelling messages to Ghanaians and to the African world. Aidoo's powerful play conveys her commitment to unveil uncomfortable truths by examining the trauma of slavery through a gendered lens. The setting of *Anowa* is nineteenth-century colonial Ghana where feminist themes emerge through the actions of the female protagonist. Anowa rebels against parental authority and the traditional roles for women by marrying a man her family has rejected, resulting in tragic outcomes.

As a pioneering literary figure, Aidoo reconfigured the image of African women within a male-dominated canon in African literature during the mid-1960s. Her novels *Our Sister Killjoy: or Reflections of a Black- Eyed Squint* (1977) and *Changes: A Love Story* (1999) disrupted stereotypical portrayals of African women that were common in male-authored African texts written during the twentieth century. In both novels, Aidoo crafted female protagonists who were strong, intelligent, and outspoken as a form of 'writing back' to reclaim women's voices from the margins to centre stage in the African literary world. Important themes that resonate in both works include feminist critique of gender dynamics, and post-independence ruptures in Ghana. In the iconic novel, *Our Sister Killjoy: or Reflections of a Black-Eyed Squint*, Aidoo's literary imagination brought to life the finely sketched character of Sissie, the 'black-eyed squint', whose perceptions express the clear-eyed vision of a former colonial subject who describes the unseemly transformations of Ghana's colonial past. The term 'black-eyed squint' is a metaphorical signifier of Sissie's gaze that captures the spatio-temporal nexus of Ghana and Africa's encounter with the West. Through a skilfully woven tapestry of poetry and prose, Sissie's observations in Europe interrogate the psychological impact of colonization on her fellow Africans and the confluence of gendered expectations at home and abroad.

In the novel *Changes: A Love Story* (1991) and the short story collection *No Sweetness Here* (1970) Ama Ata Aidoo's critical voice presents paradoxical outcomes for women characters as they respond to patriarchy, urbanization, and the conflicting demands of modernity in the colonial and postcolonial landscape of Ghana. *Changes* was awarded the Commonwealth Writer's Prize for Africa in 1992, and it skilfully examines the complexities of Ghanaian women's difficult choices and responsibility for one's destiny in life. Aidoo interrogates the extent to which a woman who follows her own path ends up better off than the woman who bends to the status quo through obedience to conventional norms for women in society. The stories in *No Sweetness Here* portray Ghanaian women faced with choices that challenge cultural roles and expectations as well as the realities of the modern world of social flux and changing identities. *Diplomatic Pounds* was published in 2012, and the stories resonate contemporary diaspora themes of transnationalism, cultural hybridity, and African women's identity in modern urban settings.

In her role as an outspoken voice for women, Aidoo articulated the impact of social, economic, and political forces on the lives of African women. In the 1998 essay 'The African Woman Today', Aidoo affirmed that she is a feminist and insisted that: 'every woman and every man should be a feminist'. She asserts that, 'on the whole, African traditional societies seem to have been at odds with themselves as to what exactly to do with women. For although some of them appeared to doubt gender and biology as bases for judging women, in the end they all used gender and biology to judge women's capabilities'. This dilemma lies at the crux of Aidoo's feminist sentiments expressed in her writing and underscore the pressing need for social transformation to achieve women's equality. Aidoo's unapologetic feminism animated her women characters, who are strong, resourceful, and self-directed as they navigate tradition and modernity, gender dynamics, and the exigencies of nationhood in post-independence Africa.

152 *Rose A. Sackeyfio*

Aidoo's literary corpus is recognized as foundational in African Anglophone Writing, and Feminist Literature, within a postcolonial framework that spans decades of the twentieth and twenty-first centuries. As a consummate storyteller, Aidoo's prolific writings capture the transformative energies of Ghanaian and African women's lives through strong willed and self-driven women characters that exhibit agency and autonomy in the search for happiness and success.

Her poetry collections include *Someone Talking to Sometime* (1985), *Birds and Other Poems* (1987), *An Angry Letter in January and Other Poems* (1992), and *After the Ceremonies: New and Selected Poems* (2017). Like many African writers in the past and the present, Aidoo's literary style draws heavily upon African oral traditions and a combination of prose and poetry.

Ama Ata Aidoo's poetic voice infuses feminist critique in the sharp tones that permeate her 1992 poem, 'An Angry Letter in January': where she 'writes back' to race, class, and gender barriers erected by the white, male power structure. The letter is addressed to a Bank Manager who has rejected her request for a loan. The narrative voice asserts that 'I have been happy being me: an African, a woman and a writer. Just take your racism, your sexism, your pragmatism off me'.

The beauty of the poem transcends the narrator's anger to convey the power of her African identity, self-worth, and dignity. The poem illustrates the ways in which Aidoo's women characters speak with one voice against patriarchal structures and gender roles in society. Ama Ata Aidoo emphasizes the role of the African writer when she boldly asserts: 'For us Africans, literature must serve a purpose: to expose, embarrass, and fight corruption and authoritarianism. It is understandable why the African artist is utilitarian'.

Literary scholars, writers, and critics acknowledge her contribution to literature that continues to inspire many contemporary African female authors to re-envision the image of women in their fictional works. Aidoo's oeuvre represents feminist synergy to achieve her vision of social transformation to empower women in society. Ama Ata Aidoo's legacy may be seen in the outpouring of African literature in the twenty-first century by women authors who now dominate the field, and their fictional works herald dramatic changes in the trajectory of the African novel in the global age. A new generation of leading women writers from Africa owe their inspiration to Ama Ata Aidoo and other pioneers like Flora Nwapa, Buchi Emecheta, and Mariama Ba, who broke barriers for women as literary godmothers of feminist expression and innovative ways of telling the African story. Aidoo's writing firmly establishes her role as a ground-breaking literary figure through her portrayal of dynamic African women who redefine their identities in society. Ghana and the world have lost a commanding presence on the literary stage, and her works will live on as cherished classics in African and world literature.

I Mourn Ama Ata Aidoo, the Author of 'A Woman must be Foolish for a Marriage to Work, though a bad Marriage Destroys the Soul'

A Tribute to Ama Ata Aidoo (23 March 1940 – 31 May 2023)

ALEXANDER OPICHO

During my childhood days in Bungoma District, Western Kenya, we had a socially conspicuous neighbour. He was a tall brown man in his late thirties. He had over eight hundred native cows and five granaries permanently filled to the roof with maize, millet, sorghum, pumpkin, and calabash. This neighbour of ours also had three enviable, bustling, short wives, over twelve giant pots for brewing beer, and over ten acres of sugar fields for commercial purpose. What made our neighbour more conspicuous was that he never had any sandals; he was always walking bare-foot in a grime-ridden, brown, pull-neck, home-made-sweater hanging over an ever-black long trouser folded back to the knees of his legs. Our neighbour was showy with his style of picking a screw of snuff from a giant and ever-filled tobacco-horn; he showed off more with his style of inserting the tobacco in his ample nostrils without sneezing. Our neighbour had an unwavering schedule of having the three meals of the day from his mother's house before his eating circuit that began at the first wife's and then down to the third wife's. Our neighbour's name was Wanyonyi (born during planting season). By then his mother was over 90 years old; her name was Akombe. So, people stole the opportunity behind his back to refer to him as Wanyonyi Akombe. A pique to his overtly patriarchal manners. When Akombe died, Wanyonyi wailed and wept at his mother's graveside for five hours every evening for 10 years. It was a source of childish amusement.

Later on I also came to learn that Chairman Mao Tse Tung mourned at his mother's grave-side for 30 months. While on the cross and a few

154

I Mourn Ama Ata Aidoo   **155**

hours shy of his death, Jesus Christ also beckoned John, his disciple, to take care of Mary (mother of Jesus). Those of us who are familiar with Islam are aware that the deepest loss to the Prophet Mohamed (SWS) was the death of his mother.

Ergo, I will not escape the moral duty to stand on the exemplary shoulders of the above giants to mourn Mama Ama Ata Aidoo. I will mourn her for the rest of my life. She was not my biological mother. But she is the mother of my intellectual audacity, sense of maverick position in literature, and unflagging sense of chauvinism for female education. She died at the age of 81, on 31 May 2023.

Born in Ghana eight decades ago, Ama Ata Aidoo maintained an unbroken literary momentum; she published intellectually incisive novels, farcical-cum-tragi-comic plays, informative short stories, spell-binding children's books, and poetry. Beyond books, her literary talks were full of bravura; she spoke the truth to capital. In one of her speeches, available on YouTube, she cautioned the Western capitalist machinery to stop their traditional culture of double speak about the Anthropocene – Ebola, HIV, Tuberculosis, Asthma, COVID-19, to mention but a few. During her life, she was outspoken in support of female education all over the world; she was always aglow with feminist fire that broke through the fissures of patriarchal rocks to illuminate feminist consciousness to the generations of African women writers ranging from Chimamanda Ngozi Adichie, Doreen Baingana, Helen Oyeyemi, Sefi Atta, Taiye Selasi, and NoViolet Bulawayo, without forgetting to mention Susan Nalukwe Kiguli, Emma Dabiri, and other daughters of Africa who dedicated their whole lives to being crusaders for human rights through the praxis of feminist ideology.

Ama Ata Aidoo's father was an advocate of female education; he went against the zeitgeist of his time to send Ama Ata to the Wesley Girls' High School in Cape Coast from 1961 to 1964. When she was in Form Three, the headmistress asked her what she planned to do with her future. Aidoo replied that she wanted to be a poet. 'Poetry doesn't feed anyone, Christine', the teacher told her. Nevertheless, she bought Aidoo an Olivetti typewriter to encourage her literary pursuits. A few months later, Aidoo spotted a pair of pink shoes in a store. Wanting to buy them but lacking the cash, she decided to enter a Christmas short story contest sponsored by the local newspaper, *The Daily Graphic*. She wrote her entry in longhand and sent it in. On the twenty-fourth of December of the same year, Ama Ata was in her mother's kitchen; when she opened the centre page of a stray, old newspaper, she saw her name. This is how she got the money, of course from her first

156 *Alexander Opicho*

publication. Ama Ata used the money to buy the coveted pink shoes. She was only 18 years old at the time.

While she was a junior university student, she wrote her first play, *The Dilemma of a Ghost*, about a Ghanaian man who returns from a sojourn in the United States with an African-American wife, much to his family's dismay. The play, initially staged in 1965, was published the following year, making Aidoo the first published African woman dramatist. These are the efforts you cannot come by easily among the TikTok-toting university students in our present times.

Aidoo wrote *Anowa*, a play based upon an old Ghanaian legend and concerning the African slave trade, an issue which she insists African writers continue to ignore. The play continues to resonate with global anti-slavery consciousness; it was performed in 2012 by a multicultural cast at the University of California at Santa Barbara.

Ama Ata Aidoo's first novel, *Our Sister Killjoy (1977)*, was inspired by her sojourn in Europe, which looked like a rehearsal for going to heaven for most of Africans of her time. Sissie, the protagonist in the novel, is disappointed by what she finds in London and Germany. She is further confused by the sexual overtures of her German friend, Marija. Aidoo says that she has been attacked by both conservative Ghanaians for presenting same-sex relations in her work, and by lesbians for not exploring the issue more fully. She insists that her portrayal of Sissie is not a judgment, but a reflection of her own naïveté as a young woman in Europe. This was sometimes before she was appointed Ghana's Minister of Education in 1982. She used her ministerial position to help female teachers earn respect. However, Aidoo was frustrated by her inability to effect change and by her desire to write; she left the ministerial post after only 18 months and went back to writing.

The texture of literary bravura is palpable in Aidoo's unabashedly feminist disposition and inclusive literary socialization that echoes with cultural rights of non-binary sexualities, women in general, and mothers and daughters in particular by having them figure prominently in her work. This is hardly surprising as Aidoo got the idea for her first play from a story told by her mother and was herself the single mother of a daughter. This virtue appears across the range of her works; in *Choosing*, the writer-turned-teacher-turned-trader frequently asks her mother for advice, although she doesn't always follow it. In *Outfoxed*, she recounts a contentious mother-daughter relationship. Esaaba, believing that she is finally in a position to win her mother's respect, travels to visit her only to find that she has died, seemingly timing her death to spite her daughter.

Ama Ata Aidoo was eco-friendly in practice through her *antinatalist* family values. She only had one child, a daughter. A position which she defended by arguing that, 'I didn't think much of myself as a mother in practical terms. Even with my one daughter, I've always felt that I was not able to give her as much of my time and attention as I considered necessary. So having another child or more children was simply out of the question.' However, in 2000, Aidoo established Mbaasem, meaning *Women's Words,* a foundation dedicated to promoting the work of Ghanaian and African women writers.

Ama Ata Aidoo was not writing for money. One day she won a literary prize worth thousands of dollars, but the prize presenter failed to pronounce Aidoo's name correctly; Aidoo rejected the prize in public and walked away. She was a great soldier who crusaded for the dignity of the African image. Yes, she was not alone in the struggle. There were also Mariama Ba of Senegal and Flora Nwapa and Buchi Emecheta, both from Nigeria. It is the struggle that was also supported by the heroic Naawal El Saadawi, the author of *Woman at Point Zero*, from Egypt, and many others, like Nadine Gordimer, Doris Lessing, Grace Ogot, Maya Angelou, and Toni Morrison. However, Ama Ata Aidoo stood out for her multiple talents in the spoken word, long prose, plays, poetry, and fierce activism for human rights.

Personally, I respect her latest literary efforts in her short story *No Sweetness Here.* This story, which was recently read to the public in London by Chimamanda Ngozi Adichie at the Guardian Books Podcast festival, has Mad! Mad! Mad literary flavor, unique intellectual depth, sharp witticism, radical feminism, iconoclasticism, deconstructivism, determinism, fatalism, sensationalism, cosmopolitanism, spotless-humanism, and matchless capacity to paint the angst of human despair in the abyss of existentialism. It is in this story that Ama Ata Aidoo comes out to say that, 'as if globalized patriarchal value systems have socialized a fallacy that women must accept to be foolish in order to survive in a marriage', but how long will they be foolish? She condemns this fallacy by arguing that bad marriages destroy the soul.

I fully agree: it is very true there is no sweetness in a marriage that requires a woman to accept being foolish even if she is not. Long Life, dear Mama! Ama Ata Aidoo.

Literary Supplement

Three Poems

KOFI ANYIDOHO

A Memorial for KAMAU BRATHWAITE
An Africa – Africa Diaspora Dialogue
[Bridgetown, Barbados. May 14, 2022]

PanAfrican AirWays   our DreamAirline:
Five Hours Direct Accra-BridgeTown
to Sao Paulo and San Salvador Brazil
or StopOvers to Sister CaribIslands
to Havana in Armpit of the BuffaloBull

But
Devious Logic of Geography
made Furious by Storms
of Crooked Colonial History
put me back on BritishAirways
took me up up North
to Proud Imperial London
then down down South
across Unending Moaning Waves
to your Coral Island Home in CaribSeas
Wishing and Hoping Somehow to Find
your long arms stretched out in Warm Embrace.
I have Lingered So Long to Redeem
a Promise of Coming Home to Bajan
in the Midst of History's Hurricanes.

Kamau   SoulBrother-Mentor   Pathfinder
You who Walked Tall in HowlingStorms
Ancestral as a god sent by Odomankoma
to Re-Humanize our World with WORDS
with Unfolding Imagination Fueled
by Unfailing AncestralMemory.

160

You who once asked for **Words**
to Guide our Feet on Slippery Slopes
in a Wounded World of So Much **Hurt**.

From The Hilton Barbados Resort
through Bridgetown's Somber
Streets with no Billboards
to Surrounding Open Fields
Green with Hints of a Paradise
Lost to Nostalgia & Endless Longing
Our Brother David Comissiong
Drove with Steady Thoughtful Care
to your Final Place of Rest
from a Long & Immensely Fruitful Life.

Below your Familiar Sacred Name
Your Date of Birth   of Death
Your Beloved Grieving Beverly
Immortalized You with Words of Love Eternal:
DEATH LEAVES A HEARTACHE NO ONE CAN HEAL
LOVE LEAVES A MEMORY NO ONE CAN STEAL.

I stood behind your modest Granite HeadStone
Head Bowed   Eyes Gently Closed
Listened with a Pain and a Joy in my Heart
As David Brought Back to Life
Those Haunting Lines from **Negus**
Your Quintessential Poem of Hope

> *I*
> *must be given words to shape my name*
> *to the syllables of trees*

> *I*
> *must be given words to refashion futures*
> *like a healer's hands…*

Kamau   PathFinder & ForeRunner
You who Reclaimed our Past
from Tombs of Lost Histories
You who Revived our Present
from Wombs of DreamStories
You who Planted your Left Foot
Firm in Bajan's Coral Stone
Rooted your Right Foot

Deep in Africa's Tellurian Soil
Arms Shaped Wide and Firm to Brace
StormTime across The Middle Passage.

Kamau   Kamau   Kamau
You Bridged our Fractured Souls
with the Healer's Soothing Words
You Healed our Fumbling Futures
in Countless BreathingSoundings
of your Voice   your Word   your Song
You Gave us Back our Lost Compass
to New Fiestas of Our SoulsHarvest.

Armed with the Urgent Clarity
of Your Mission Your Vision
I return
I return now
from your HomeLand in Bajan
to your HeartLand in Ghana
I Carry Back to Our Ancestors
The Love and Memory
of One of their Great Beloved Sons
Snatched Away by ThunderStorms
Brought Back Home by Hurricanes
Returned to Bajan Riding Atlantic's
Waves & HarmattanDust WesterlyWinds
Weaving Calypsos into Dance&Words
That Tame the Rage in the Heart
of ThunderStorms and Hurricanes

KAMAU BRATHWAITE Now For Ever at REST at PEACE in Gentle
   Arms of Asaase Yaa.

For Willie Keorapetse Kgositsile

Takyiwaa Manuh   Akilagpa Sawyerr
Two Comrades from Your Exile Days in Dar
Shared the News of Your Farewell Call.

Willie   Keorapetse Kgositsile
SongBird of Liberation Dreams
They Say you Caught the MidNight Freedom Train
at the Final Stop in SophiaTown

Three Poems   **163**

Homeward Bound.   No More Stops Along the Way.

The Nation Stood Still
to Wave You Home in Solemn Gratitude
Memories of You So Long Ensnared in
Struggles Deeper than All Our Troubled Seas.

I Recall Our First Meeting
in Chicago's Wailing Winter Winds
your One-Time Exile Home in Babylon
You took me in with an Embrace
Wider and Warmer than Old Friendships.

The Vista from Your Windows Was Amazing!

I Thought of Nat Nakasa   and of Donny Hathaway.
I Shook my Head in Memorial Fear of Dizzy Heights.

You wondered how come I couldn't put away
more than one small can of Budweiser.

I OverHeard you Whisper to YourSelf :
        God Knows I've Taken This Watery Stuff
        Enough to Last Through Three Life Times.

And Oh!   How I Worried you Might
Never See Soweto Again in This Life Time.
Somehow   You Survived.
You Survived Your Exile Years

Came Back Home to Old Comrades
You Thought You'd Never See Again.

Came Back Home to Lay Your Exile Tears
to Rest Among the Graves of Old Warriors

Share Your Dreams of LiberationTime
with a Generation Too Young to Know
the Taste of Blood from Bitter Battle Days

Bitter Bleeding Battles Fought So Long
Over a Nation Torn Apart Between
HerSelf   and   TheColours of HerSkin.

Oh! Willie   Keorapetse Kgositsile
Old SongBird of Liberation Dreams

May Cross-Rhythms of Jazz&Blues
Ride You Slow & Ride You Gently Home

164   *Kofi Anyidoho*

to RainBows in Celestial Splendour Hues
Standing Guard for You at HeavensGate.

A Song for Nyidevu
for Afetsi, who survived to Tell

They say the Panther Died in his Sleep
But not without a Leap.
The Hippo Drowned in a Pool of Blood
But with a Gentle Smile on his Face.

So you took Death by the Hand
Brought Him Home
to a Harvest of Ancestral Songs.
You took down his Battle Dress
gave him a Gown of Flames
wrapped in Laughter's Tender Care
You removed the Thunder from His Voice
the Lightning from His Eyes.

You Placed a RainBow on His Face.

You Explained to Death
How and Why He must be Brave
Turn His Back upon the Grave
So the Children in their Sleep
May Dream the Future
Filled with Hope   The Promise of Hope.

From Freedom to Free Doom

ADEMOLA ADESOLA

The people abandon the oases of reason.
For their strange love of easy answers,
they lurch from freedom to free doom.

The denizens seek the rare miracle of water becoming wine.
For their preposterous thirst for solutions made easy,
they gallop from freedom to free doom.

The compatriots deride knowledge and learning.
For their gnawing embrace of ignorance and superficiality,
they cavort from freedom to free doom.

The 'citizens' pledge themselves to philistinism.
For their ruinous affection for all things ephemeral,
they gambol from freedom to free doom.

The 'patriots' applaud the ritual of specious change.
For their uncanny docility and weird gullibility,
they pirouette from freedom to free doom.

The habitués of holy grounds soak themselves in the intoxicants of
    religiosity.
For their unhelpful escapism and tactless denial,
they wander from freedom to free doom.

The inhabitants of the arid land conform to unfreedom.
For their incomprehensible belief in falsehood,
they sashay from freedom to free doom.

To The Memory Of Aunty Toriomo

RACHEL OLUWAFISAYO ALUKO

Last night Jennifer lost the grip
On home, family, marriage, and kitchen
"I'm leaving this marriage," she said to me
With dreary wet eyes; a brazen look
I hushed her into a quick silence
A frantic glance at her and behind
"You know she won't give you the chance-
To leave your children and kitchen."
"Who?"
"Aunty Toriomo, of course"
Jenny's laughter gave me the shivers
Is she running mad?
Depression, I know, is rife in her marriage
It triggers madness… but God forbid!
"She died some years back, just before I got married."
"Who?"
Aunty Toriomo of course!
A new wave of shivers at the news,
Aunty Toriomo died and I never knew
A popular dame of exceptional virtue
Gone in silence, and all too soon!
Mixed feelings
Resignation to fate
Girlfriend leaving
Reversing the faith
Gone are the days of aunty Toriomo
A woman of great wisdom-
Skilled in keeping mothers with their men.
Once upon a time she lived
My aunt, I think, she ought to be
Unsure how the family tie binds us

To The Memory Of Aunty Toriomo   167

But she's a relation for sure
As she seldom leaves our house
Though heard of often; never seen
A dexterous woman- resolving couples' fights
She must be mother's dear sister of younger years
Mother never stopped singing her praises
"I remained in this marriage with him- just because of Toriomo"
Though not social, but full of impact
Often mentioned, but never seen
I guess she's challenged- deaf or maimed
Not sure of her case
A name more visible than the being
That night I say, quite young but sharp
Noise prevailed in our quarters as usual
Couple's fight!
Iya'Beji was having her turn
At calling husbandman useless.
Women dragged her into our home
Mother leading the procession to aunty
Broken lips
Tattered blouse
A raving woman describes her best…
Wait a minute-
She knows the name
Toriomo; my dear sweet aunt.
Mama Aduke, mama Akwudo
Mallama Bello, Iyawo Pastor Richard
Leading women in our quarters
All married to useless men
Defied the hurdles of marriage, persevering with much resilience
All because of mother's sister-
Toriomo; my dear sweet aunt.
Growing with children of our quarters
Different times bequeath our rising
Days of playing with dolls and balls
Gift of fathers from UTC
Festive seasons to show off dresses
Bought by fathers at Kingsway Stores
New school years to more fees
When fathers are paid at work by government
Eating daily
Growing steadily
Fathers paying bills in anger

Fighting couples
A common scenario
Baggage out
Baggage in
Boxes thrown and strewn about
Toriomo once and always prevailed
Waters now have passed under the bridge
Some years before I started this story
Eggs; now hens, or cocks they say
Now I know my dear sweet aunt!
Toriomo-
But gone too soon!

I Swallow Fufu

JEROME MASAMAKA

Belch grrrrhh… on a gulp of light soup
Smack with me
on a mouthful of smooth morsels
Lump lump my fingers stuck
Lump again the soft mound…

I swallow fufu, slurp with me
The strong aroma of goat soup

wafting, lingering,
the scent of stubborn goat
arguing in pepper soup.
Boiled yam pounded into a mash
with plantain and cassava adhering
the blended portion

Meanwhile soup is sizzling

scoped and poured
The flooded bowl is steaming

Broth of meat, zesty and red
garnished with avia leaf
and pebbles of green shito
floating
around jutting rib bones
and the oily tenderloin

Prayer is hasty
with one eye open
spying a snooping fly
and the neighbourhood kids…

It doesn't take long in a weekend chop-bar
with low toned Amakye Dede

No dancing when asanka arrives
Heads bent low, a short praise
to the ancestral soil and the women
We shall bury all arguments.

I swallow fufu, smack with me
Let's belch on grasscutter soup
and smile to the good old days
before the coup
and famine tore our land.

Two Poems

MARINUS YONG

No Door, No Roof

Destitute, the miscreants that have no home
Are wont to move and always roam.
They comb the streets and search for meals
Which they can eat and pay no bills.

Before the sun shows its smiling face
They're off to the highways in a rapid race
To mind and man and mend the bus
Amidst the fights and fumes and fuss.

Some sell all that there is to hold
Running and rushing after cars that hoot
In hope and wish their wares are sold
And ensure the date's wretched food.

As the red sun dims and brings the moon
They head back where they have no roof
In limps and hobbles to tend their wound
Acquired from fights and fuss and goof.

They have no door that they can lock
And sleep just where they count the stars.
You find them there near every block
Nursing new wounds on scary scars.

Bowls for Alms

The teeming kids who throng the streets
Are armed always with bowls for alms
They mill around with daring feats
To assuage their hunger with ulcer balms.

172 Marinus Yong

They move in droves in dirty robes
That tell the world of wanted care
Eluding them from thieves of votes
Whose alms to them are very rare.

Now they are told to go indoors
And lock their doors
Against the adversity
They cannot see.

Now they are told to keep clean hands
And split at once their clustered bands
In fear of he they cannot see
Like a little bee on the crown's dim lee.

Now they are told to always disguise
With a blinding device
That keeps at bay
The crown's foray.

They wonder why you talk of doors
When they have never needed one
As they don't even know your flaws
Have nursed and nurtured their pinching want.

They wonder why you mix hands and clean
When you know they have never seen soap
Since their unknown mothers had to wean
And dump them on the streets to try and cope.

They wonder why they should hide the face
To give what they can't see a violent chase.
They laugh at you and stretch their bowl
So you keep as one their body and soul.

Two Poems

VICTOR TEMITOPE ALABI

No peace

You gave him no peace.
You will have no peace!

As you sit, on the seat, he upon sat,
And you walk in the shoes he once walked!

thE bEst tEachEr

It has once been said.
'Tis best to have experience,
But many have died,
Trying to have experience.

I say this,
Learn from **examples**…
Examples set by others.
Learn from the **experience**…
Of others,
And at a distance,
Learn from deep **explanations**…
Doing deep **explorations**!

As I Watched Her Dying

ERNEST EMENYONU

Nne, Nne, Nne, I called,
Hoping she would hear and answer me
She who had given me suck
Fed, carried, and pampered me
Who would never say nay to me
Nor nay to my demands and requests
She now I endearingly called Nne,
And lo, she is past hearing my voice
My mother, my mother, my mother.

Foolish tears, coward's sword,
Can't you do more than women and children?
Foolish tears, let me alone
I have more profound things to say and do
And this running nose, be man and retrain thyself

Here she lies dying and you eyes and nose
Pester me with petty occupations
My mother, my only mother, my beloved mother
One and only,
Never more shall I look upon a woman
And say, Nne, Nnem Nkika

Now you tears, idle foolish tears,
Have your way, if that's the way
The only way to bid her eternal farewell
Fall like the dew, and pour like the rain
And my mother, my mother,
You know I love you
I had given gold and silver
Lots of fortune and precious pearls
To have you always
But I am mortal, so are my efforts.

Short Stories

The Mysterious Examination Paper

IFEOMA OKOYE

It was ten minutes past midnight, and Mrs Ezebabayemi, a widow for many years, was still wide awake. She was sitting on her bed and had been trying unsuccessfully for hours to solve a big problem. It had surfaced as she left her office the day before to go home. She had been, for three years now, the Head of the Department of General Studies at Divem University, many miles away from where she lived. She had not wanted the post and had pleaded in vain with the Vice Chancellor of the University to give the job to one of the lecturers who had wanted it and had canvassed for it.

'Don't tell me how to do my job, Mrs Ezebabayemi', the Vice Chancellor had said to her in a commanding tone. That was three years before.

Mrs Ezebabayemi, still greatly bothered by her problem, left her bedroom and walked into a small, adjacent room which she used as an office. Under her worktable were sealed packages of question papers for the GS103 Examination scheduled for 2pm that day. The university was many miles away from where she lived, and it took her more than one hour to get there in her eight-year-old car. She sat down on an old stool, rested her head on her worktable and was soon lost in thought. She had never had this type of problem before.

The problem had surfaced as she left her office and was walking along the veranda of a large classroom block to the car park. That was many hours before, yet she had not been able to find a solution. Her reputation was greatly at risk, and she might even lose her job if the problem was allowed to come to light because many fingers would be pointing at her as the culprit. She must, therefore, find a way to deal with the problem.

She heaved a loud sigh, rested her head on the table and was soon lost in thought. She had done everything within her power to safeguard the examination paper. She had watched the secretary type the question paper, produce the number required, package them

176

The Mysterious Examination Paper   177

securely in large envelopes and load the envelopes in her car boot. All these to make sure that the examination questions were safe.

An hour later, an idea popped into her head. She opened one of the bundles of the GS 103 Examination Question Paper and began to go through the questions again. There were twenty questions altogether for the examination, and after each question were five suggested answers labelled A, B, C, D, E. The students were to decide which of the five given answers was the correct answer for the question and then write that letter as the answer to the question.

As usual she had done everything possible to make sure that, apart from the lecturer who taught the course, only she and her secretary had seen the contents of the examination paper. She had, as usual, watched the secretary type the question paper, produce the number required, put them in large envelopes, seal the envelopes securely and put them in the boot of her car.

Although she had done everything possible to secure the GS103 examination paper, something she had heard concerning the paper had jolted her. The incident had kept telling her that something about the GS 103 Examination scheduled for the next day was amiss and was going to destroy her name if not quickly dealt with. It was this feeling that had kept her awake throughout the night. 'I must leave for work early enough to be able to carry out this plan', she told herself after she had worked out how to deal with the problem.

By six in the morning, she was ready to drive to the university with the package of the examination paper securely locked in the boot of her car. She phoned her secretary to tell him that she would be in the office earlier than usual.

'Please be in the Department by seven o'clock', she pleaded with him. 'I have something very important and urgent for you to do for me before the GS103 examination at 2pm.'

'Are you all right, Madam?' her secretary asked.

'Yes, I am, Edwin.'

'You sound em, em, em, I don't know how to put it.'

'I am all right, Edwin. It's just overwork. Organising an examination for hundreds of students from different departments is not that easy for me.'

'I know it isn't, Madam, but you are doing it very well. Much better than the Head of Department before you.'

'Thanks, Edwin. You're doing your work very well too, and that is helping me a lot. You're trustworthy, helpful, and respectful, and you're making my work much easier for me. I will be in the office soon.'

178 *Ifeoma Okoye*

'Thank you, Madam. Safe journey, Madam. I will be there before you arrive.'

'Thanks, Edwin. See you later.'

A few minutes later, Mrs Ezebabayemi, loaded the GS103 examination question papers in the boot of her car and locked the boot. After being awake throughout the night, she was too tired to drive to the university, but she had no option. She wished again that she could afford to employ a driver, but as a widow with two children in the university, that was unthinkable. That was one of the major reasons she did not want the post of HEAD OF DEPARTMENT that had been forced on her. With this post, she was expected to be at the university five days in a week at least, and she had no option but to drive herself each time.

She went into her car, locked the doors for safety, and said a short prayer as she always did before driving. But the car hissed and hissed and refused to start.

'Oh God, why are all these happening to me?' she cried out aloud. 'What have I done to deserve all these difficult problems facing me? Why is this car misbehaving today of all days?'

She placed her head on the steering and did her best to control her tears. A few minutes later, she calmed herself and took her phone from her handbag.

'Oh God, let the car mechanic be available', she cried out.

She came out of her car and locked the car. She checked to make sure she had locked the boot and walked briskly out of the compound. The car mechanic's workshop was within walking distance. But what if he were away from his workplace or if he were too busy to help her? She prayed as she walked to the mechanic's workshop.

The car mechanic was in his old car and was about to drive out of his workshop.

'Stop, please stop', she yelled at him and walked quickly to his car.

The mechanic stopped, but he did not switch off the engine of his old Volkswagen car. 'What's the problem, Madam?' he asked. 'You're looking very worried?'

'My car won't start, and I've an important examination to deal with today. I need to get to the university early enough to organise the exam, and I have a big problem to solve before the exam.'

'Take it easy, Madam,' the mechanic said. 'I'm going to the car parts shop to buy some car parts to service an important customer's car. And I don't want to disappoint him. He's one of my best customers, if not the best. He pays me well, and I don't want to disappoint him and have him look for another mechanic.'

The Mysterious Examination Paper 179

'I understand, but please help me', she pleaded. 'I've a very difficult problem to solve, and I must get to the office early enough to try to solve the problem. My job is at stake and my good name too. I don't want to lose any of these. Please help me. Pl-ea-se.'

'All right, Madam', the mechanic said gently. 'Come into my car, and let's go to where your car is. You must have a big problem. I can see something like tears in your eyes.'

'Thank you very much. You're very helpful, very hardworking. And you've been very good to me.'

'And you are an honest and hardworking Madam. Let's go.'

It was now eleven o'clock, and Mrs Ezebabayemi was on her way to the university. She had only a few hours to get to the university and get the GS103 Examination Question Paper ready before 2pm when the examination was scheduled to start. She also had to stop at the university bookshop to buy cyclostyling material for reproducing the examination question paper.

As she expected, there were many policemen and policewomen on the road searching all the vehicles to make sure that there were no guns or ammunition or any other dangerous materials hidden inside the vehicles. The searching of many vehicles and the arguments with the vehicle owners and drivers delayed her badly, and so also did the stop at the university bookshop to buy cyclostyling paper, printing ink, and reams of paper for producing the question paper.

Fortunately, her secretary, Edwin, was already in her office in the Department waiting for her to arrive.

'Thank you, Edwin, for being here on time', she said to him as she walked into the office.

'I promised you I would, Madam.'

'But some people don't keep their promise.'

'You are good to me. Indeed, to all of us working here. I will be very unhappy if I disappoint you.'

'I am very sorry, Edwin, you're going to have to retype the GS103 question paper and produce the number required before the time scheduled for the exam. And you don't have much time. The examination starts at 2pm, you remember. The distribution of the question paper will take a lot of time because of the number of students taking the examination.'

'Madam, did I make some grievous mistakes in the one I typed yesterday? Or was the mistake made during the production?'

'No, Edwin,' said Mrs. Ezebabayemi. 'What I'm being forced to do has nothing to do with you. You're very good at your job, very careful, very trustworthy, and very respectful. I'm very proud of you, Edwin.

180 *Ifeoma Okoye*

You won't know how many Heads of Department have tried to take you from me. I'll tell you later what brought about all that I'm trying to do now. We don't have the time for me to explain things to you now. And, please Edwin, be very careful with your typing. There'll be no time for me to correct mistakes.'

'I will, Madam. Trust me.'

'Of course, I trust you, Edwin. Indeed, I do.'

'Thank you, Madam. You're different from many lecturers in many ways. I am happy that I am posted to this department to work with you.'

'I am happy with you working here, Edwin,' she said. And she was indeed, for she was very sure that he was not the one who had caused the big problem she had been trying to solve since the day before. She prayed that her planned solution to the problem would work well and save her good name. 'A good name is better than money', was the English translation of her first name, and she had been trying to live up to the name.

The GS103 examination started as scheduled. The large hall was filled up with students. The invigilators were punctual, and so were the students. Mrs Ezebabayemi noticed that the three students she heard discussing the examination questions the day before were sitting close together. They were shaking their heads as if in disbelief and were whispering to one another. She was tempted to change their seats so that they would not sit close to one another. On second thought, she felt that their plan had been shattered and there was nothing else they could do.

A few minutes after the beginning of the examination, the lecturer who taught the course walked into the examination hall. He spotted Mrs Ezebabayemi and walked straight to where she was standing and watching the three students.

'Good afternoon, Madam', he said. 'How is the examination going?'

'Very well, I believe,' Mrs Ezebabayemi said.

'Can I have a copy of the exam paper, Madam?' asked the lecturer.

'Of course,' Mrs Ezebabayemi said, handing him a copy of the question paper from the bundle of paper in her hand.

She kept her eyes on him as he began to go through the question paper. Suddenly, he frowned and began to shake his head violently.

'Madam', he began, still shaking his head, 'this is not the question paper I submitted to you.'

'It is', Mrs Ezebabayemi said in a low voice, looking around to see whether anybody else was listening to them. 'And please lower your voice. Some students are already disturbed and are listening to us.'

The Mysterious Examination Paper **181**

'This is not the question paper I submitted to you, Madam', the lecturer said angrily, spelling out the words.

'It is.'

'It is not my paper', the lecturer said. 'I am very sure of that, Madam. What have you done to the question paper I submitted to you? I am very sure, Madam, that this is not the exam paper I submitted to you.'

Mrs Ezebabayemi lowered her voice. 'Your questions are all intact. I did not tamper with them. What I did was to reshuffle the numbering of the questions.'

'Why did you tamper with my questions, Madam?

'I'm sure you know why I did that. You leaked the question paper to some of your students.'

'I did not.'

'Yes, you did.'

'Can you prove that I did?'

'Of course I can prove it. I heard three of your students discussing the very questions you submitted to me. They were alone in the classroom.'

'What about your secretary? Couldn't he have done it?'

'No.'

'How are you sure he didn't?

'Because as usual I watched him throughout the production of the question paper to make sure that he could not leak the questions, even though I know he is very trustworthy. And the only way to deal with what you did with your paper was to reshuffle the numbering of the questions. I did not add a letter to your questions. I did not delete any. I knew the students would come with just a list of the numbers of the questions and the letters that indicate the answers.'

The GS103 lecturer's jaw dropped. He did not say a word.

'When a person is guilty, the person's jaw drops', Mrs Ezebabayemi quoted a proverb of her people to the lecturer. 'Many people become tongue-tied when their lie is discovered', she explained the proverb to the lecturer.

The lecturer looked at her with devilish eyes, turned abruptly, and stalked angrily towards the entrance of the hall without saying another word.

Mrs Ezebabayemi's face brightened. She kept her eyes on the lecturer until he was out of the examination hall. She looked steadily at the ceiling of the examination hall and heaved a sigh of relief.

The Ignored

MATRIDA PHIRI

Emmanuel Chakazamba's father is a rich man. He owns a countrywide real estate company dealing with private and commercial properties. His mother runs a beauty salon, of international standards, in the heart of the elite Kabulonga Township of Lusaka. The family lives in Ibex Hill in a six-bedroom house, which boasts vast, well-kept grounds, a swimming pool and several detached guest quarters. They have four expensive cars. Life should have been good for Emmanuel, an only child, but it is not. He is thirteen years old and in Grade 8 at the Elton White Technical School, an elite school for the cream of society. His father gives him everything a child could ever want, yet he is not happy.

'I never have enough sleep', Emmanuel confided in his friend Kondwani. 'My parents fight all the time. When Dad comes home, mum will start calling him names that are insulting, and he reciprocates by hitting her or calling her horrible names too. I only sleep in the early hours of the morning when their voices are hoarse and they are too tired to continue... I hate my home.'

Kondwani was shocked.

The two boys were leaving the school premises. Emmanuel, who had to wait for his father's driver, was walking his friend to the bus stop.

'But what do they fight about?'

'According to my mother, my father has a mistress.'

'What!' Kondwani exclaimed.

'It is that bad, my friend', Emmanuel sobbed.

Kondwani hugged his friend in silence.

A bus pulled up. Kondwani let go of his friend with a sad little wave.

When Emmanuel got home, he felt a longing for his sister Precious. Forcing himself to think of other things, he went upstairs to his room.

'I hope tonight I will be able to sleep a little.' Sighing, he sat on

The Ignored   **183**

the bed. He recalled how his parents often blamed each other for his sister's death. Filled with sadness, the boy fell asleep.

The sound of a car woke him up. Emmanuel scrambled to the door and flung it open, watching as his father walked hurriedly towards the house. His step faltered when he saw Emmanuel standing in the doorway.

'How was school?' Strange, his father never asked him about school.

'School was fine, Dad. Why are you home so early?' the boy asked.

'I feel tired.' His father was looking down.

Emmanuel followed his father into the house.

'Dad, can I speak to you about something?' Emmanuel always found engaging his father in conversation a very daunting task.

'Sure, son, what is it?' He gestured for Emmanuel to sit while he remained standing.

'Something wrong?' His father frowned.

'I would like to go to boarding school,' Emmanuel stated, startling his father, who jerked forward.

'What is wrong with your school?' He could not believe this.

'My school is fine, but I fail to sleep enough at home.'

Emmanuel's father sat down. He had never realized this. What could he say when…

His thoughts were interrupted by the sound of the gate. He turned to his son, 'Go to your room, son.

Emmanuel wanted to protest. Why should he to go to his room? But the look on his father's face scared him. He ran upstairs to his room. The front door opened.

'I beat up your mistress, you adulterous man!'

His mother's angry voice floated up. The tone of it had Emmanuel's heart thumping. This would be a bad day.

'Let's discuss this outside,' his father said quietly.

'There is nothing to discuss,' she snapped. 'This is the limit for me. How could you cheat on me, Jonathan? I am leaving.' Emmanuel shivered. Mum wanted to leave? What would life be like without her?

'Marjorie, I do not want the boy to hear this!' Emmanuel hoped his mother would acquiesce for his sake, but she screamed even louder.

'You never thought of him when you were committing adultery! You impregnated her as if Emmanuel is not good enough for you.' Her voice rose in a screaming shrill, 'Let Emmy know that you and your harlot are expecting twins!'

Even as Emmanuel tried to digest the fact that his father was having children elsewhere, he heard the first slap.

184 *Matrida Phiri*

'The woman is not pregnant!'

The rage in his father's voice was alarming. Emmanuel moved to the top of the stairway. He heard his mother scream in pain even as she picked up the statue of the Hindu elephant god Ganesh. She brandished it threateningly in front of his father's face.

'Your harlot told me that you are expecting twins who are intended to replace my beloved Precious! How do you think I feel?' Before his father could think of something to say, the statue landed square on his face. Emmanuel saw blood spurt out from his nostrils, and crimson stains appeared on his snow-white shirt. He ran down the stairs as he saw his mother lift the statue again.

'Mum, leave him alone, you will kill him.'

She looked fleetingly at him and struck again. His father staggered and almost fell. There was blood on the side of his face. Emmanuel watched helplessly as his father grabbed both his mother's wrists forcing her to drop the statue. It crashed to the floor with a loud clang. He then clenched his fists and rained blows at her. She screamed with pain as the onslaught continued. The boy had never witnessed a fight this ugly before. He ran to his father and tugged at his shirt.

'Stop it, Dad!' He was weeping as he ran to the front door, calling out to Silas.

'Uncle Silas! Please come quickly.'

Silas was already standing outside the door but scared to involve himself lest he lose his job. The boy took his hand and pulled him into the house.

'Please do something, Uncle.' Emmanuel pleaded.

His father continued to hit his mother. Silas went to kneel beside his employer. 'Please, sir, stop.' His mild tone got through. The man moved away from his wife. He wiped blood off his face with the cuff of his shirt.

'Bring a clean towel and some water son. We need to clean your mother and take her to the hospital.' He sounded weary.

'But you also need to be cleaned up, Dad. Your face is all bloody too!' Emmanuel started crying again. What wrong had he done for him to have such parents? It was hard to even look at them.

'Go do as I say.'

'Yes, Sir.' Emmanuel ran off.

Silas cleared his throat.

'I think home remedies would be better. Going to the hospital might attract unnecessary attention, Sir.'

The Ignored 185

Emmanuel's father understood what he meant. 'I guess you are right, Silas. Please get me the first aid box from the kitchen. I will do what I can.'

Silas politely bowed his head and headed for the kitchen. Sighing heavily, he reached for the first aid box, grabbed some ice and the roll of paper towel. He rushed back to the living room.

'Thank you, Silas,' His employer said.

Kneeling beside his wife, Emmanuel's father attended to her. He carried his wife upstairs and tucked her into bed before attending to himself and taking a bath. Afterwards he cooked dinner with his swollen face. It was the strangest night Emmanuel had ever experienced.

'What are you preparing, Dad?' He was genuinely curious.

'I am making spaghetti with meatballs.' His father smiled slightly, his face looking funny with all the little Band-Aids on his bruised face. The meal was delicious, and the two of them ate it together on the floor of his parents' bedroom. Emmanuel's mother had not stirred yet. When he was done eating, Emmanuel sat on his mother's bed and held her hand. His father had gone back to the kitchen to clean up. His mother suddenly opened her eyes and looked intently at him. The boy was startled.

'Emmy, my son,' she muttered weakly. 'Why Am I in bed?'

'Mother, you are awake!' Emmanuel smiled widely at her. He could not understand why she was asking him such a question. Did she not remember the fight? If so, then Emmanuel did not want to be the one to tell her why she was in bed. Let his father come and deal with this awkwardness himself. After all, he caused it, didn't he?

Emmanuel looked down at the floor, praying that his father would soon appear. He was out of his depth here. Just then, as if in answer to his unspoken prayer, his father walked into the room. From his sudden change of expression, it was evident that he expected a barrage of words from his wife, but when none came, he looked at his son with confusion.

'What happened to me?' The question was directed at Emmanuel's father in a quiet and confused tone. His wife did not remember what happened? He thanked his lucky stars, hoping she would never remember. But even as he was thinking these happy thoughts, realization was slowly dawning on his wife's face. An angry expression came over her beautiful face. She attempted to sit up but fell back against the pillows. Emmanuel stood up from the bed. His mother, he realized, had remembered. He hoped another fight would not start.

'Emmanuel, bring me a glass of water please', his mother said.

'I will get it, Emmanuel.' His father stopped him.

'I said Emmanuel!' his mother snapped. 'I could never drink anything you touch, you monster. You want to poison me?'

Emmanuel rushed out of the bedroom to get the water, glad to leave the room.

'I want a divorce.' Emmanuel's mother looked at her husband.

A deathly silence followed her statement. Emmanuel's father did not know what to say. He knew that whatever he said would provoke a screaming response. Better to just sit this storm out and pray his wife gradually calmed down.

Emmanuel walked in with a glass of cold water. He offered it to his mother quietly.

'Thank you.' She did not look up at him. She took a long drink of the water, sighed and said to the boy, 'Your father and I are getting divorced. He is marrying a new wife.'

Emmanuel looked at his father with horrified eyes. His father looked back at him without saying anything. The boy took this to mean this was true.

'Dad, is it true?'

'No, son.'

The boy wanted to believe his father, but what if his mother was right? What would he do?

'It is true', his mother said slowly in a subdued voice. It seemed as though all the fight had drained out of her. Emmanuel felt the tears gather in his eyes even as his mother continued explaining.

'I received an anonymous note at the office the other day telling me that your father was having an affair with a young woman! I did not want to judge your father unheard. So, I visited the woman's house using the directions given in the note.'

Emmanuel looked accusingly at his father. He felt terribly betrayed.

'Do you know what happened when I got there?'

Emmanuel turned his attention back to his mother.

'I did not knock but turned the handle of the door and walked in! You should have seen the look on your father's face as he turned from kissing the woman to see me in the doorway!'

'No!' Emmanuel screamed.

'Go to your room,' Emmanuel heard his father say quietly to him. He was so glad to leave the room. He flung himself on his bed and cried his heart out. Eventually, he fell into a deep dreamless sleep.

Silas had to sprinkle cold water on Emmanuel's face the next morning in order to get him to wake up. The boy was still exhausted.

The Ignored **187**

'Please let me just sleep; I can't go to school today', he implored Silas, who would not hear of it.

'You have to go, Emmanuel. Talking and laughing with your friends will help lighten your mood.'

'I guess you are right. I will get up. Have you seen my mother?'

'Yes.' Silas did not expand on that.

'How is she?' the boy asked.

'She looks alright to me. You should not worry; everything will be okay. It is normal for couples to have differences now and then.'

'You have a mistress, Uncle Silas?' Emmanuel asked.

'No, I do not think God would approve of that.' Silas was a very devout man raised in the Baptist faith. He had a wife and three small children. He often told Emmanuel that his life revolved around God, his wife and his children. He lived for nothing else. Emmanuel could not understand why his father could not just love his mother the way Silas loved his wife? He could not see what made the two men different.

Emmanuel got ready for school. He felt very tired and wished this was a Saturday instead of Friday. Yawning widely, he packed his books and headed for the door. Emmanuel could not go without seeing his parents, so, walking rapidly towards their bedroom door, he knocked.

'Good morning, Emmy.' His mother's voice greeted him. It sounded quite normal but a little sad.

'Good morning, Mummy. How are you feeling?'

'Don't worry about me, son. I feel fine. You run along, and I will see you later.' Her cheerful chatter sounded forced, but Emmanuel was happy that she was not angry anymore.

'Do you have everything you need?' His father asked from downstairs. He was carrying a pillow and a light blanket. Obviously, he had spent the night in the guest bedroom downstairs. Emmanuel felt the tears welling up, but he wiped them angrily away.

'Yes, Dad. I have everything. I will be off now. Enjoy your day.'

'Have a good day, son.'

Uncle Zulu glanced at him before starting the car, but the boy kept his face averted. He did not want him to see his sleep-deprived eyes. They drove for almost ten minutes before Uncle Zulu asked quietly, 'Everything okay?'

'Yes.' He still did not look at Uncle Zulu.

There was silence in the car until they got to the school gate. Uncle Zulu stopped the car and looked at the boy. Emmanuel had fallen asleep with his mouth open. This was not the first time this had happened, on the twenty-five-minute drive to school. Uncle Zulu's heart broke with sadness. He could not understand why the boy's parents were not seeing what they were doing to their son. He wished he could just drive the boy back home so he could sleep. Silas had told him what had transpired the previous day back at the house between his employer and his wife. The couple lived such a terribly unhappy life. Uncle Zulu sighed. He reached his hand and gently nudged the boy awake.

'Emmanuel, we are at the school. Fight hard. Do not sleep in class today.'

The boy nodded, wearily opened the door and stepped out. He had firmly refused for Uncle Zulu to be getting out of the car to open the door for him. He was not some royalty or government top-ranking official, Emmanuel stubbornly asserted. Uncle Zulu loved the boy for his humble disposition, so different from the spoiled rich kids he came into contact nowadays. He smiled widely at the boy, hoping to cheer him up a little, and waved his hand.

Emmanuel's first subject that morning was History, and their teacher announced that they would be having a test. He could not believe it! Today was the worst day for a test for him. He was in such a terrible state and was dying to close his eyes and sleep. Someone nudged him on the shoulder. It was his friend Kondwani. Emmanuel was delighted.

'What happened to you, Kondwani? I have been looking for you all over! Were you late?'

'Yes, my friend.' Kondwani had sat at the desk behind Emmanuel since the term began, and because the door of the classroom was at the back of the room, he had walked in without his friend seeing him.

'What happened to you, Emmanuel? You look terrible.' The words came out in a fierce whisper.

'There was hell at home last night.' No use hiding anything from his friend now.

'I will explain to you at break time. It was terrible, Kondwani!' Emmanuel was almost in tears.

The teacher noticed them talking.

'What is going on there at the back, Kondwani and Emmanuel? Do you want to be disqualified from taking the test?'

'Sorry, Sir,' Kondwani mumbled quickly before the teacher could notice the haggard look on Emmanuel's face.

Five minutes later the test started. Emmanuel's eyelids were so heavy he was having problems keeping them open. He tried to force himself to stay awake, but the room appeared to be going round and round. Should he perhaps ask the teacher for permission to go out? But that

The Ignored   **189**

would be unacceptable. He had already seen the question paper, and the teacher would think that he was going to consult his books for the answers. It was better to just sit still and continue battling the sleep that was fast overpowering him. He began to hear the angry voices of his mother and father raised in anger. Their faces were beginning to manifest in front of his eyes, zooming in and out of focus. The boy desperately tried rubbing his eyes to make the images go away, but nothing was working. Emmanuel thought he was going to lose his senses. What could he do? He felt the pen fall from his fingers and heard it hit the floor. He bent over to retrieve it, and his head made contact with the desk. At that point everything swung out of focus, and his world went black.

Everything was quiet in the class until suddenly sounds of loud, deep snoring were heard. The teacher could not believe it! Was someone actually sleeping in his class? His eyes roamed the classroom until they rested on Emmanuel's head, cradled in the crook of his arm, fast asleep. Alarmed, Mr. Simwanza walked over to Emmanuel and gently shook him.

'Hey, Emmanuel, wake up! Are you sick?'

The boy mumbled something and went back to sleep. Amid laughter and disbelief, the whole class was now watching.

'Emmanuel!' The teacher shook again.

Startled, Emmanuel sat up and looked around him. He seemed dazed and disoriented.

'You are in class, writing a test', the teacher explained.

'I do not think that I will manage to write today, Sir. I do not feel well.' Emmanuel indeed looked sick.

'You should not have attended school then. Should we call your father or mother?'

'No, Sir. I will call Uncle Zulu to come. All I need is sleep.'

'Alright then. Collect all your belongings.'

'Thank you, Sir.'

Soon Uncle Zulu was at the school, concern written all over his face. Emmanuel was soundly sleeping in the secretary's office.

'Emmanuel', Uncle Zulu shook him awake. 'Let me take you home. Are you feeling any pain?'

'No, Uncle Zulu. I just need to sleep. I can't remember the last time that I slept properly.'

The secretary waved at him.

'Go get some rest, dear. We will see you soon!'

Emmanuel waved back and walked out.

190 *Matrida Phiri*

Jonathan Chakazamba, Emmanuel's father, was on his way to a meeting at the Civic Centre when his phone rang. He noticed that it was his son's school calling, and fraught with worry, he picked up the call.

'Is everything okay?'

'Yes. The issue is not a serious one but we need to have a meeting with you and your wife at your earliest convenience.' Emmanuel's father recognized the Head Master's voice.

'What happened?'

'Your son slept through a history test. We are deeply concerned, Sir.'

'I will speak to my wife and get back to you this afternoon.' Emmanuel's father hated himself even as he responded to the Head Master. All this was his fault, and he knew it. He had created a house for his son but not a home.

Emmanuel was getting out of the car outside their gate when he saw his father arriving also. He was surprised and alarmed. Maybe his father was not feeling well after all; the blow he received to the head from the idol had been very hard. He waved to Uncle Zulu as he drove off and stood waiting for his dad to pull up beside him. The gate was already wide open because Silas had seen his father arrive too. His father stopped the car and got out. 'Son, are you alright?' Before Emmanuel could respond, his father enfolded him in a bear hug. The boy was amazed. 'Are you sick, Dad?'

His father tried to speak, but he could not. Tears were now falling freely from his eyes, and he did nothing to stop them. Let the boy see how sorry he was. Emmanuel had never seen his father so emotional. He took his son's backpack and, still holding his hand tightly, started walking towards the house.

'You are leaving the car outside?' Silas politely asked him.

'O, the car! I totally forgot. Let me drive it in.'

Still holding his son, he retraced his steps to the car, opened the passenger door for Emmanuel and then went round to get into the driver's seat. He was behaving as if he could not let the boy out of his sight. They drove into the yard and stopped at the front door.

'Let us go inside and see how your mom is doing.' Emmanuel merely nodded. This was all so overwhelmingly new to him. Love was not demonstrated anymore in his home, and this from his father felt strange and awkward but nice. He smiled and followed his father inside. His mother was sitting in one of the recliners, reading. Emmanuel had never known his mother to like TV except international news and occasionally the local news.

'How are you feeling Marjorie?' Jonathan greeted his wife quietly.

'What do you expect, Jonathan. I am doing well.' Her reply was

The Ignored   **191**

sarcastic but without the angry sting of the previous night. She noticed her son then, and she struggled to stand, to go to him. Emmanuel walked over to her and embraced her.

'Why are you back so early from school?' she glanced at her husband inquiringly.

'It is a long story', Emmanuel's father replied. 'I will tell you everything, but Emmanuel needs to go to bed right now.' The boy nodded vigorously and took off. Let them talk; after all, it was their fault.

Emmanuel's mother went back to the recliner and closed her eyes. She had no intention of talking to her husband.

'I am so sorry, Marjorie, for the way I have been behaving since our daughter died. I was so much in pain that I did not know how to handle it. In seeking a remedy for my pain, I allowed myself to fall into temptation, and before I knew it, I was in too deep.'

He paused to give time to his wife to say something, anything, but she was silent. He did not have the courage to look at her face. He was scared of what he might find there. Since his wife was not saying anything, he soldiered on.

'My relationship with the woman in Chawama was a mistake. I was drunk the night I met her, barely three days after we buried Precious. I needed something with which to dull the pain and the alcohol seemed like a good idea. I had no idea that it would land me in so much trouble, and when I started the affair with Mwaka, it was purely as a remedy for pain. However, she was so cunning that I imagined myself in love with her. I know for sure that she is not pregnant, and I will never forgive her for deceiving you the way she has done. I want to give you my solemn word that I will end this foolishness and come back home. I can't bear to see you and Emmanuel in so much pain.' He moved closer to his wife's chair and lifted up his face to look at her. Her eyes were closed. He had to do what he had to do to make this right. He fell on his knees in front of her, as the tears began to fall.

'Let me tell you what else I am guilty of, Marjorie. Today our son was sleeping in class while his class mates wrote a test. Efforts by the teacher to make him wake up and start writing failed. He was too drowsy to even comprehend what the teacher was saying. The Head Master called me. He wants to meet with us as soon as possible. He is concerned about our son's welfare. That is the reason why I had to cancel my morning's meeting to come and talk with you.' Emmanuel's father's voice broke with the intense emotion he was feeling. But at last, his wife opened her eyes wide with shock and looked at him.

'It has come to this?' she asked sorrowfully. 'What have we done to our son, Jonathan?'

192 *Matrida Phiri*

'Yes, it has come to this. I have made our son suffer so much that he is the laughing stock of his class and his school. After thinking about this on the way home, I realized how sleep deprived the boy is. He never gets the full eight hours or more of sleep that he should because we fight all the time until way after midnight. The head of the school sounded really angry at me. This is wholly my fault. I admit it, and I promise to do what I can to change everything.' He took his wife's hands in his and was surprised that she did not draw away.

'I know I do not deserve it, but can you please find it within you to forgive me?'

'Jonathan, we will discuss this later, but can we rush to the school now?'

Her husband stood up and helped her up.

The ride to the school was quiet but comfortable. Both of them were deep in thought.

The meeting with the Head Master was short. He wanted to know why their son was sleeping in class. Was he ill? Emmanuel's mother left the talking to her husband.

'There have been certain circumstances that hindered Emmanuel from getting enough sleep. We shall do right by him from today onwards. I promise you this without any hesitation. He will have the rest he deserves every night.' The man was sincerely contrite, and the Head Master could see that, and although he could not understand what the parent had meant by 'certain circumstances', he knew that it must be a sensitive matter. He had no wish to pry into their private family issues if they did not want to share. But he needed to make one thing clear in order to reinforce the voluntarily given assurance.

'If he sleeps in class again or pays someone to do his homework for him again, we will have no choice but to consider suspending him.'

Emmanuel's mother gasped. 'He pays others to do homework for him?'

'Of course. How else can he get it done? He is always drowsy. When I went to investigate this matter in the class, learners there came out to confess that many times, he has had to pay them to do his homework for him or to explain things he is unable to understand in class because of his drowsy state. Frankly, all his friends are worried about him. He is such a friendly and humble little guy. I just hope that we will not witness another snoring incident in the middle of a class test.'

Both parents were looking at the floor, unable to lock eyes with the Head Master.

'We promise to make the necessary changes to improve his performance in class', Emmanuel's father mumbled sheepishly.

'OK, that is settled then.' The Head Master smiled at them both. 'Thank you for taking the time to meet with me at such short notice.'

'Thank you,' they both answered simultaneously and stood up.

On the way home, Emmanuel's parents were both silently crying.

'How could we not see what we were doing to the boy, Jonathan? Our poor son had no one to turn to, and even when he lost his sister, we were too buried in our own grief to realize that he needed us. I wonder what he really thinks of us', Emmanuel's mother lamented.

'He obviously hates us,' her husband said, shaking his head. 'I only hope that it is not too late to right this grievous wrong.'

When they reached home and Emmanuel's father had parked the car, they both sat in the car without doing anything and without speaking.

Finally, Emmanuel's mother said to her husband. 'Are you sure that continuing with this marriage is what you want, and are you also sure that you are not expecting twins with your mistress?'

'As of today, Marjorie, there is no mistress, and there certainly are no twins. The stupid, illiterate fool was lying to you! I am begging you to forgive me, and let us give assurance to our son that we shall be happy as a family again, the way we were when Precious was alive. I am sure her soul was grieved by my behaviour. I am so ashamed of myself. Will you please forgive me, Marjorie?'

His wife suddenly reached out and held both his hands in hers. She squeezed them gently.

'It is okay. Let us turn over a new leaf and give our son the life he deserves.'

The following morning was a Saturday. Emmanuel woke up at 7 o'clock. He had slept for twelve hours straight. Silas made breakfast for him.

Emmanuel was just finishing his breakfast when he heard both his parents coming down the stairs. He could not believe that they were speaking to each other normally. When they noticed him at the kitchen table, there was a short awkward silence, and then Silas came to the rescue.

'What can I prepare for you, Boss and Madam?'

'I will have black coffee and plain toast, please', his father said

'I will have the same, Silas.' His mother smiled at him. Emmanuel could not understand why the two were not mad at him for sleeping in class. And when had this reconciliation taken place? He smiled at both his parents and picked up his empty plate and glass. He dropped the items into the sink.

'Would you like some more food or perhaps orange juice?' Silas addressed the boy politely.

'No thank you, Uncle Silas. I am stuffed.'

He was about to withdraw into the living room when his father addressed him.

'Please sit down, son, we need to talk.'

Here it comes, Emmanuel thought, sitting down. He hoped it would be brief.

When his father begun to talk, the boy thought he was not hearing right, 'I want to apologize to you, my son, for my behaviour in this house since the time your sister, Precious, left us.' He paused and then continued. 'I have no excuse for the suffering I have caused you and your mother by straying from my home. I know that it is entirely my fault, because if I had not gotten myself entangled with another woman, I would not have been fighting with your mother all the time, thereby depriving you of a quiet and peaceful environment in which to rest and sleep. I cannot apologize enough for this. Please forgive me, my son.' He waited for his son to say something, but the boy was so overwhelmed with joy that tears were already falling from his eyes. Emmanuel remembered Kondwani his friend telling him that he had been praying for him; for his life to get better. God must have heard his prayers. His father started to speak again.

'I also want to assure you that I have ended the foolish relationship I had with the woman in Chawama Compound. She and I are not expecting any children. Everything she said to your mother was a blatant lie. I want us to live happily as a family again. I regret that it had to take the recent ugly events in this family to make me realize just how much I treasure and need you and your mother. All we have is each other, and we must not take this good thing we have going for granted. From now on, my life will revolve around the two of you.'

Emmanuel stood up and put his arms around his father.

'Thank you, Dad! I will do my best to be a good son to you and Mummy, and I will improve on my school work.'

'Thank you for your forgiveness, son. Your mother and I had a meeting with the Head Master at your school, and we admitted before him that it was our fault that you never get to rest and sleep adequately. We gave him our word that from now on things will be different.' Emmanuel disengaged himself from his father and went to his mother, whom he held tightly. He was so happy that he had gotten his parents back.

Reviews

196   *Reviews*

Irene Salami-Agunloye, ed. Retelling History:
Restaging African Women in Drama and Film
Nonfiction, Women Studies, Theatre and Film Studies
Paperback – 795 pages. Ibadan, Oyo State, Nigeria: Kraft Books Limited, 2022
ISBN: 978-978-918-543-6

Irene Salami-Agunloye, dramatist, Professor of African Theatre and Film Studies, and Director of the Centre for Gender and Women's Studies at the University of Jos, Nigeria, has taken on the monumental task of unravelling the way African feminist aesthetics engage historical memory, ritual, and creative force in order to empower African women, through resistance strategies of performance in drama and film. Salami-Agunloye assembles formidable essays from scholars and artists that explore African heroines who unleash singular voices to drive their own empowerment.

The book attempts to correct the historical record, which too often relegates the depiction of women on stage and screen to subservient roles, while challenging male-dominated dramaturgy in a rich tapestry of heroines from across the African continent. Out from the yoke of male annals, Queen Idia and Yaa Asentewaa (West Africa), Mekatilili (East Africa), Queen Nzaigha (Central Africa), Cleopatra (North Africa), Carlota (enslaved in Cuba), Queen Nanny (enslaved in Jamaica), and Nehanda (Southern Africa) are among the heroines that spring forth as ferocious females in the text. Divided into nine sections, the anthology explores a number of perspectives on *who gets to tell the story*. In 795 pages, 55 essays portray the sweeping role of African women in aspects of precolonial, colonial, and postcolonial societies. The essays rip apart male hegemony as women traverse through patriarchal landscapes designed to ignore their independent social and political arenas. Unfortunately, space does not allow a discussion of 55 essays; therefore, selected papers in each of the nine sections will be highlighted.

Section One (12 essays) focuses on 'African Women, Power, Politics, and Leadership'. Essays by Umaru Tsaku Hussaini and Issac B. Lar document the importance of revisiting courageous women of the past in literature. Tsaku showcases Veronique Tadjo's *Queen Poko*, a retelling of an ancient Akan myth surrounding Abraha Poko, who sacrifices her infant son to save her people and appease the gods of the land. Queen Poko serves as a model for displaying the attributes of a virtuous leader, in this case a woman, who places the collective good of her people before the child she loves more than herself. Issac B. Lar's

Reviews **197**

essay, 'The Feminist Quest for Political Leadership and its Realisation in Irene Salami-Agunloye's *More than Dancing*', considers how the playwright, in 2003, broke open the glass ceiling, albeit imaginarily, by creating a protagonist, Professor Nona Odaro, who emerges as the first female president of Nigeria. In crafting female characters that are archetypes of all sections of society, Salami-Agunloye's drama shows women harmoniously engaging in the political process for the betterment of their nation.

Section Two (6 essays) considers 'African Warrior Queens'. Rose Sackeyfio explores female leadership in Salami-Agunloye's historical drama, *Idia, The Warrior Queen of Benin*. Sackeyfio maintains that the playwright constructs Idia, surrounded by indecisive male leaders, as a fearless warrior who moves into action and triumphantly defends the Benin kingdom in the sixteenth century, as an example of female political agency in a traditional African culture. Ellison Domkap reflects on how Queen Kambasa of Bonny, in *More Than Dancing* (also by Salami-Agunloye), serves as a model of female leadership to inspire the protagonist, Nona Odaro, as she rises to the top of Nigeria's political sphere.

Section Three (6 essays) delves into 'African Women in Myth and Legend'. Elizabeth Idoko champions the altruistic sacrifices of Moremi in 'The Courageous Woman: A Study of Segun Ajayi's *Moremi, the Courageous Queen*'. The play is based on the myth of Princess Moremi, who calls upon the river goddess, Esinminrin, to help her save the Oduduwa people from the frightening Igboboro raiders. The goddess agrees to help her, demanding she sacrifice her only son, Oluorogbo, if successful and, without hesitation, Moremi allows herself to be captured. While living among the Igboboro, she unravels the secret of their invincible war attire, which is nothing more than bamboo and grass, and after escaping back to Ile-Ife reveals the truth to her people. Idoko argues that Moremi stands as a symbol of true bravery during war, as she sped into action to save her people with no thought of the price she would be forced to pay. Victor Anyagu considers metaphysical consciousness as the masculine gods, Ogun and Sango, and the feminine goddess, Oya, emerge from the ancestral realms into a modern play in his critique, 'The Gods at War: A Feminist Discourse of Akinwumi Isola's *Belly Bellows*'. Anyagu discusses the way Isola uses the Yoruba cosmos to drive the dramatic conflict of the play as Ogun and Sango vie for Oya's affection, and stressed the way this goddess fights oppression and injustice against women in the metaphysical sphere.

198 *Reviews*

Section Four (3 essays) addresses 'African Women: Martyrdom and Sacrifice'. James Dung provides a dramatic appraisal of sacrifice, martyrdom, and death in Salami-Agunloye's youth play, *The Queen Who Gave Her Life*. Dung uses the storyline of Iden, the wife of Oba Ewapke of Benin, who agrees to be buried alive in order to save the throne of her husband, as a symbol to further discuss self-serving traditional institutions and the countless Nigerian female activists, past and present, sacrificing for equity and justice.

Section Five (4 essays) focuses on 'Violence Against Women'. Isaac Lar focuses on Salami-Agunloye's *The Queen Sisters*, a historical drama set in the fifteenth-century Benin Empire. The play explores two young wives of Oba Ewaure, Ubi and her half-sister Ewere. Ubi, denied agency, refuses to take on the docile role of a wife in the harem, which leads to a whirlwind of vicious disruption in the palace, while Ewere is exalted for calm acquiescence to every command of the Oba. When Ubi is banished for 'bedwetting' and condemned as evil, the patriarchal social order is restored, which, according to Lar, is the focus of the playwright's dramatic premise, that the public sphere has far too long been closed to women.

Section Six (7 essays) emphasizes 'African Women Resisting Colonialism'. Iniobong I. Uko targets the grass roots effort of Opobo women to revolt against repressive colonial taxation policies in her essay, 'Drama as History: Female Heroism in Effiong Johnson's drama, *Not Without Bones*'. Uko examines the way Johnson uses the 1929 women's uprising in southern-eastern Nigeria as the backdrop for a play, in which the colonial government imposes heavy taxation on the people. Men flee and are imprisoned, leaving women as the sole supporters of their families with little hope until a group of disenfranchised market women, led by the protagonist Ekaiban, march across the land destroying colonial power structures. Although many women are shot and imprisoned, the Opobo men, inspired by the courage of their women, ultimately join the revolt to restore their land. Uko suggests that modern women can also benefit from the collective solidarity of these fearless women to empower their own political and social mobility. Salami-Agunyole offers a fascinating account of the revolt led by an enslaved woman in 'Challenging the Master, Resisting Slavery: The 1843 "Carlota War"'. Carlota, an enslaved Yoruba woman, led an armed resistance, machete in hand, at the Triumvirato Sugarmill in Matanzas Province, Cuba against the brutal and inhumane conditions on the sugar plantation. For over a year, the fearless insurgents wreaked havoc on the enslavers, until captured by the Spanish, and Carlota suffered martyrdom in 1844, when her body was brutally ripped apart by horses.

Section Seven (7 essays) highlights 'African Women and Postcolonial Struggles'. Nesther Nachafiya Alu highlights the political activist, Gambo Sawaba, in her article, 'Reconstruction of Heroic Life and History in Irene Salami-Agunloye's *More Than Dancing: A Study of Gambo Sawaba*'. Alu contends that including the Nigerian women's rights activist and politician, Gambo Sawaba, in the play serves as a window to help inspire the way a woman from an impoverished background, with little education, is able to serve her political party and people with a steadfast commitment to justice and equity.

Section Eight (7 essays) concentrates on 'Restaging African Heroines in Film'. Samuel Igomu and Yaki D. Musa exalt the bravery of Yaa Asantewaa in 'The Brave and Gallant Women of African History: A Feminist Analysis of Yaa Asantewaa in Hezekiah Lewis' Short Film, *Warrior Queen*'. Igomu and Musa applaud the rare inclusion of an African warrior queen as the basis for a film that recreates a historical account of the Asante Queen Mother's refusal to relinquish the Golden Stool to the colonial government and then commanding the Asante nation army in the 1900 war against the British. Although the Asante were defeated and Yaa Asantewaa exiled to the Seychelles Islands, her unflinching bravery kept the Golden Stool from the British. The authors conclude that film can be a great vehicle to preserve the legacy of African heroines. Salami-Agunloye draws on Roy T. Anderson's documentary, 'Queen Nanny Legendary Maroon Chieftainess', to discuss the ever-present role of armed resistance to enslavement, in the captivating story of the Jamaican Windward Maroons, led by Queen Nanny in the 1730s. The filmmaker, in a synthesis of re-enactments, interviews with maroon descendants, and historians, brings the folklore and oral history surrounding Nanny, who appears as a guerrilla spirit guide in the film, into view. In 1975 Queen Nanny was proclaimed a National Heroine by the Jamaican government. Salami-Agunyole's next essay, 'Breaking the Glass Ceiling in Africa: Ellen Johnson Sirleaf, Heroine of Modern Africa', offers a tribute to the twenty-fourth president of Liberia (2006–2018), the first female president of an African nation. In 2011, Sirleaf received the Nobel Prize for Peace.

Section Nine (2 essays) targets 'Music in Women's Historical Drama'. The anthology concludes with Emmanuel Imasekhoevbo Aimiuwu's essay, which emphasizes the role of music in every aspect of African traditional societies and the integration of music and drama throughout the history of performance. Showcasing Salami-Agunyole's

200   *Reviews*

The Queen Sisters, Aimiuwu demonstrates the way the playwright adeptly employed music and songs in her historical drama in order to spotlight elements of the culturally rich ancient Benin Kingdom.

At times, *Retelling History: Restaging African Women in Drama and Film* is a thinly veiled celebration of the editor's work. Of the 55 articles, 11 are composed by the editor, and 14 by academics discussing her work. The text falls short of its premise, as promised by Salami-Agunloye in the Introduction: '*this book brings together thoughts and knowledge of global intellectuals and scholars*' (xli); when in fact, it focuses almost exclusively on scholars and artists residing in Nigeria, who composed 53 of the articles (two articles are written by African scholars teaching in the United States). Twenty-eight of the articles, which include the 11 written by Salami-Agunloye, are constructed by academics at the University of Jos, where the editor holds tenure. The glaring omission of any discourse on the heroic dramatists, Zulu Sofola, Ama Ata Aidoo, and Osonye Tess Onwueme, arguably the forerunners of African feminist drama, and inclusion of essays on the role of women in the plays of Wole Soyinka and Femi Osofisan (their male contemporaries), is disappointing. Although I champion this pioneering anthology, if an opportunity arises for a second edition, the text will benefit from a professional editor to objectively review the material so that it receives the attention it deserves on the international stage.

CAROLYN NUR WISTRAND
Dillard University
New Orleans, Louisiana, USA

Chika Unigwe, *The Middle Daughter*
DZANC BOOKS, Ann Arbor, 2023, 310 pages. $26.95. ISBN: 9781950539468
Hardback

The Middle Daughter (2023) is Chika Unigwe's fourth novel and illustrates her mastery as a gifted storyteller of fictional works that garner critical acclaim. The author's skill resonates with the talent she displays in her second novel, *On Black Sisters' Street* (2011), which won the highly coveted Nigeria Prize for Literature in 2012. Through her creative artistry, Unigwe narrates African stories in new and compelling ways in the global age of transformation in Nigeria, Africa, and the world.

The Middle Daughter takes readers into the world of a vulnerable young woman whose downward spiral is a path toward liberation and selfhood. At the centre of the novel is Nani, a sheltered middle daughter whose coming-of-age experience is a tangled web of emotional trauma, loss, family conflict, and physical abuse. The work unfolds the *bildungsroman* of womanhood that reconfigures the identity of the protagonist amidst the upside-down realities of contemporary Nigerian life.

Skilfully crafted in a mosaic of interlocking themes, the novel unpacks moral decay, patriarchy, religious hypocrisy, generational conflict, and local and global tensions that incite family discord. Unigwe revisits the myth of Hades and Persephone, which is refashioned to suggest the need for renewed family values that bind loved ones and guide them away from dangerous elements in society. The family is the most important and foundational institution in society and in *The Middle Daughter* almost a character in its own right. As a mirror of society, the five-member family is unbalanced, deteriorating, and fractured from within. The novel is set against the background of Enugu, where most of the events take place, as well as Atlanta, Georgia, in America. The deeply troubled family is a microcosm of Nigeria's woes that have beset the nation since independence in 1962. The existence of social, economic, and political travail wreaks havoc from centre to periphery in the nation as moral corruption rips a hole in the fabric of society.

The work is divided into three parts that move back and forth in time to form a spatio-temporal nexus narrated from multiple perspectives. *The Middle Daughter* is thus a polyphonic rendering of a family torn asunder with the middle daughter at the centre. Unigwe's narrative punctuates pivotal events in the work through the voices of the Chorus, as another infusion of Greek literature. The book opens in the present, in 2014, and swiftly captivates readers through vivid prose in English and Igbo. Like many African writers, Unigwe' style conveys oral traditions that unfold the neatly paced events that engulf the world of the protagonist.

As a mirror of the Nigerian landscape and the African world, local and global factors fuel the American dreams of success for the women in Nani's family. In chapters that shift the action from multiple perspectives, Unigwe artfully presents ideas and behaviours that describe cultural hybridity amidst the oddities of American life. The novel sheds light on immigrant experiences as Nigerians learn to navigate and reconstruct their identities within Western spaces.

202 Reviews

Nani and her sisters are groomed for professional careers in America that will elevate their status as Nigerians living abroad in the future. Nani's elder sister makes it to university in America only to die tragically in a car accident. The loss of her sister leaves a deep scar in Nani's fragile psyche that never heals because of time and distance, generational conflict, and teenage angst. Unigwe illustrates the ways in which American dreams may turn into nightmares that haunt people's lives at home and abroad. Although foreign spaces present exciting opportunities for success, transnational landscapes may harbour unseen dangers for unwary Nigerian immigrants. Splintered family relations further divide Nani's family between Enugu and Atlanta as a site of escape to America as the 'land of the free'.

Unlike most African novels that chronicle women's experiences, the father figure in *The Middle Daughter* represents the moral centre of Nani's world, and when he dies her spirit is broken. As the middle daughter, Nani is thrown off centre, and her emotional development marks her painful path to selfhood. These traumatic events set the stage for rebellion, confusion, and sadly, vulnerability to predatory and dangerous influences that lurk beyond her sheltered world. She falls prey to an itinerant preacher who is the proverbial wolf in sheep's clothing. Propelled by loneliness, naïveté, and youthful daring, Nani makes unwise choices that lead to unfavourable outcomes. Through the experience of sexual assault, entrapment, and her downward spiral into an abusive marriage, Unigwe unfurls the dark underbelly of religious hypocrisy and moral corruption that occurs in the post-independence landscape of Nigeria.

Feminist themes emerge through Nani's gradual awakening to self-worth and autonomy, although on the surface Nani appears helpless with little or no agency. Readers may be frustrated over the amount of abuse Nani suffers in her marriage because she cannot part with her children. Unigwe examines the psychological trauma of an oppressed woman who eventually recovers the will to survive by fighting back and carefully plotting her escape. Like other feminist writers who empower women characters, Unigwe infuses themes of sisterhood to illustrate the collective power of women to subvert patriarchy and to reclaim their lives. Women characters in Nani's fractured life protect her as she begins a new chapter in her future at the end of the novel.

Patriarchy looms large in *The Middle Daughter*, and the only positive male character is the protagonist's father, who is nurturing and protective of his daughter. Sadly, religious hypocrisy and the fanaticism of Nani's husband subjugate her through violence and coercion. At one point in the novel, Nani is no longer locked in their home

Reviews **203**

because her husband knows she will never leave. His punitive abuse of Nani is derived from twisted Christian principles that resonate in Chimamanda Ngozi Adichie's Papa Eugene in *Purple Hibiscus* (2003) and the religious fervour of Prophet Revelations Bitchington Mborro in NoViolet Bulawayo's *We Need New Names* (2013). Appropriately, women characters help to uproot him from Nani's life, and he ends up locked away from society forever.

Mother-daughter conflict fuels intergenerational ruptures that significantly influence Nani's estrangement from her family throughout much of the novel. Nani's mother is also devastated by the untimely death of the family patriarch, although she becomes wealthy by opening a maternity clinic that is actually the site of a 'baby factory'. Like many contemporary African writers, Unigwe draws attention to prevailing ills in society, and unfortunately, Nigeria has experienced an increase in baby factories and child harvesting as part of the trafficking industry in the global age. Gender norms and the stigma of infertility spark the growth of these unwholesome practices in Nigeria. To evade the police, Nani's mother and sister flee to America, but Nani refuses to join them because of moral outrage over her mother's illicit business. Ironically, rejection of the American dream offers Nani the opportunity for personal growth, financial independence, and autonomy as her new identity emerges at the end of the novel. The decision to reject America supports the idea that Nigerians and other Africans can create alternative and viable futures within local settings through their own agency and determination.

Through a gendered perspective, *The Middle Daughter* expertly unfolds a young woman's journey to empowerment. Readers follow her obstacle-strewn path to overcome the tragic loss of loved ones, emotional and physical abuse, poverty, and shame. As a writer of feminist literature, Chika Unigwe has woven a powerful tale of a woman's transformation from victimhood to an independent woman with a promising future. Narrated from multiple perspectives, the novel takes a critical look at Nigeria in the global age to interrogate new issues of postcolonial disjuncture such as religious fanaticism, ill-gotten wealth, and moral corruption. The novel examines the ways in which the loss of loved ones may destroy peoples' dreams and distort the lives of those left behind. Patriarchy will always be a compelling theme in African literature written by women because gender inequality is a glaring reality in Nigeria and throughout the world in the global age. *The Middle Daughter* leaves readers wondering whether generational fissures will be healed in ways that restore familial bonds. A subtle message of the work suggests that stronger families may

204 *Reviews*

influence societal and national issues that determine social, economic, and political outcomes for Nigerians in the twenty-first century.

ROSE SACKEYFIO
Winston-Salem State University
North Carolina, USA

Ọmófọ́lábọ̀, Àjàyí Ṣóyinká and Naana Banyiwa Horne (Eds.), *IMMIGRANT VOICES IN SHORT STORIES: Health and Wellbeing of African Immigrants in Transnational and Transformative Encounters & Spaces*
Goldline and Jacobs Publishing, Milwaukee, WI 2013, 213pp ISBN 978-193-859-853-1
paperback

Writing on a collection of short stories is a tricky journey. One runs the risk of scattering summaries on the pathways and leaving the depth unattended. However, the task of picking a particular story and writing on it, while skipping the others creates a chance of leaving things unsaid. Nonetheless, this conflict, albeit to some degree, is resolved when the stories are all connected in their different forms and styles. Mostly when they are themed around an idea, it feels like telling one of the stories is a link to the others. This fact notwithstanding, all the stories in the anthology have been briefly reviewed below as they all offer unique perspectives to the common theme they share.

Immigrant Voices in Short Stories: Health and Wellbeing of African Immigrants in Transnational and Transformative Encounters and Spaces, edited by Àjàyí Ṣóyinká Ọmófọ́lábọ̀ and Naana Banyiwa Horne, is a collection of 16 short stories centred on the theme of migration. Two stories each are told by distinguished scholars and accomplished story writers like Akachi Adimora-Ezeigbo, Ada Uzoamaka Azodo, H. Oby Okolocha, and Temi Adeaga, amongst others. The setting of the tales is fairly topical, considering the account of the devastating effect of the coronavirus in some of the stories. More interesting is the depth of the stories, which shows the complexities in the migration narrative. This follows the claim by Fatemeh Pourjafari and Abdolali Vahidpour in 'Migration Literature: A Theoretical Perspective' that:

> Creative or imaginative literature has a power to reflect complex and ambiguous realities that make it a far more plausible representation of human feelings and understandings than many of the branches of

scientific researches. In migration, above all topics, the levels of ambivalence, of hybridization and plurality, of shifting identities and transnationalism are perhaps greater than in many other aspects of life. (679)

The foci the duo refer to above can be seen in several of the stories in the anthology, and they follow the condition that writers like Samuel Selvon in The *Lonely Londoners* and Buchi Emecheta in *Second Class Citizens* have shown in their fictions.

The first story in the anthology opens the readers to the reality of the life of Africans abroad, and the 'kind' of issues that lead to their migration. H. Oby Okolocha's 'Kunta: The Area Gentleman' is a story that opens itself to diverse tales of the experiences of Africans abroad and the sort of stereotypes that trail them. The opening sentence sets the tempo for what is to come: 'Huddled in faded, bulky autumn clothes, Kunta stood still at the T-shaped Liberty junction, his newspaper clutched in his left hand' (13). This shows the faded personality of migrants, here-in, shifted to the clothes using transfer-epithet. It is significant to note the loneliness that comes with living outside of one's home, a loneliness that is accompanied by a loss of identity, and this is shown in Kunta's initial change of his identity from Okotie to Kunta.

'The Promise of Coro-Covid' is another story by H. Oby Okolocha. It is a thought-provoking story set during a wedding reception, highlighting the impact of COVID-19 on gatherings and human behaviour. It explores the conflict between safety rules and the desire for normalcy, as well as the complexities of faith, societal expectations, and generational differences. The story encourages reflection on choices during the pandemic.

Akachi Adimora-Ezeigbo's 'The Dove's Revenge' is a captivating story about Yemisi, who discovers her husband's unfaithfulness. It's a tale of relationships, betrayal, and resilience, set in Nigeria and London. Yemisi's journey is emotionally gripping, and the characters are well-drawn. The story explores love, trust, and deceit, making it a thought-provoking read. It leaves some questions open, making you think about the characters' choices. Overall, it's a powerful story about human strength in the face of betrayal and challenges. By contrast, her short story, 'One Frontliner is Enough', is a heartwarming story about Matilda, a former frontliner, dealing with the challenges of the COVID-19 pandemic. It explores her fears, caring for her mother, and financial struggles. Matilda's decision to quit her job reflects the difficult choices essential workers faced. Her unexpected friendship with Bessie shows the power of human connection during tough times. The story touches on social inequality and the resilience of individuals, highlighting unity and strength during the pandemic.

206   *Reviews*

Ada Uzoamaka Azodo's 'Mother Ruminates on Natural Existence' is a poignant and complex narrative that delves into the life of an aging mother, interweaving real-life experiences with dream sequences. The story revolves around Mother's struggles with aging, health issues, and difficult decisions, highlighting her significant friendship with Leticia. This story is distinctive in its experimental blend of storytelling, contemplation, and societal commentary, which can be challenging for some readers. The dream sequences and scientific details may require multiple readings for full comprehension. Ultimately, it is a thought-provoking tale that prompts reflection on life, family, and the passage of time, evoking a mix of emotions and contemplation.

'Under the Oak Trees', on the other hand, is a charming story about three friends navigating the challenges of the COVID-19 pandemic. The narrative blends philosophy, folklore, and humor, offering insightful reflections on the global crisis. The engaging storytelling style and the friends' discussions make the characters relatable. The story covers various pandemic-related topics, including fears and conversations about treatments and vaccines. Overall, it conveys a message of hope and the strength of friendship during tough times.

Another central story in the collection is the narrative of Pede Hollist's 'Mami Wata', which interrogates the issues of cultural conflicts in 'what-is-what' at home and the changes abroad in the life of a migrant. While Hollist's story is greatly satiric in projecting the way male migrants think, she does it with a narrative pattern that rather investigates the subconscious desire of the African in the face of a changing society that differs from the world they knew back home. In essence, it's an emotionally deep narrative that sheds light on cultural and family challenges.

Her 'Renaissance Spillover' is a story that delves into the complexities of human relationships and the impact of societal changes on individuals. Set in Sierra Leone, the narrative follows the lives of ordinary people as they navigate the challenges of post-war reconstruction and cultural transformation. Hollist's storytelling is richly layered, beautifully capturing the nuances of human emotions and the interplay of tradition and modernity. The characters are vividly portrayed, with their struggles and triumphs resonating with readers. 'Renaissance Spillover' is a powerful exploration of identity, resilience, and the enduring nature of the human spirit.

Tomi Adeaga's 'Resilience' is an inspiring and heartwarming story about Mamie, a determined woman who got an education despite societal norms. It highlights the power of determination and the enduring value of education. The story reveals Mamie's challenges and successes, offering insights into cultural changes and the evolving role of women during her time. Tomi Adeaga skillfully tells Mamie's journey, underlining the importance of education for those facing obstacles. Whether you're looking for personal empowerment, a historical account of cultural shifts, or a touching tale of unwavering commitment to learning, 'Resilience' is a compelling read that delivers on all fronts. 'Spreading Our Wings with Zoom' is another enchanting story by Tomi Adeaga that explores the Global African Women Association's annual conferences. It talks about how these gatherings affect women from different backgrounds, celebrating the accomplishments of African women and discussing the challenges they face.

Ọmófọlábọ̀ Àjàyí Ṣóyinká's 'The Repairman' is a story that blends suspense, humour, and cultural insights. It's about a surprising visit from a repairman who turns out to be quite intriguing. It explores how people from different cultures perceive each other, especially during a pandemic. The story touches on themes like feeling alone, missing the past, and wanting to connect with others. Her 'Peace Has Come, Peace Is Here' is a powerful and emotionally charged story that follows Abimi, a humanitarian worker, and Mide, a young girl who has suffered greatly due to conflict. The narrative explores themes of resilience, trauma, and healing in the face of adversity. It sheds light on the experiences of child soldiers and war victims, revealing the profound impact of conflict on their lives. This stirring and heart-wrenching story offers a unique perspective on the human toll of war and the search for peace and recovery in its aftermath.

M'bha Kamara's short story is about Kekura, a young Sierra Leonean facing personal struggles and civil war. The story explores themes of love, tradition, and the clash between old and new ways of thinking. It takes unexpected turns, raising questions about masculinity and societal norms. The narrative captures life's complexities in the face of adversity and prompts readers to reflect on personal choices and family dynamics. Overall, it offers a unique perspective on life in Sierra Leone during a turbulent period and the universal struggles of the human experience. It's a captivating and thought-provoking read that explores personal desires and societal expectations.

Kamara's 'Never Enough', on the other hand, is about Ishmael, an African immigrant in the US facing challenges supporting his family, especially his father in Sierra Leone, who constantly needs money. It delves into the struggle of meeting family obligations and cultural expectations. The story follows Ishmael's life, from his past to his

208   *Reviews*

marriage and the difficulties of sending money home amid Sierra Leone's civil war. It highlights the pressures immigrants feel to support their families back home and the sacrifices they make. The emotional ending reveals how endless demands can impact an individual. Overall, 'Never Enough' is a moving exploration of family dynamics and cultural identity, making it an exciting read.

Naana Banyiwa Horne's 'When Life Comes Knocking' is a touching story about the strong friendship between Esi and Hathor. They face many challenges together, especially when Hathor gets sick. The story shows how they support each other through tough times and celebrate each other's successes. The characters appear real, but the story could be a bit shorter. In the end, it's a moving story about friendship and strength, giving us a close look at these two amazing women. The last story in the collection, also by Horne, 'Just Another Sweltering Day in the Tropics', is a great story about students at St. Jude Catholic Preparatory School in Accra, Ghana. It tells us about the lives of five best friends, Gyasiwaa, Efua, Amua, Abba, and Tawia. The story is full of life, and it shows readers the students' interests and school activities. It also makes us laugh with the Writers' Club activities. The story is easy to read and keeps readers interested. It's a lovely story that reminds us of the fun of being a child, having good friends, and trying to get better.

The anthology paints the objective reality of migration and what people face. The stories are well delivered and still project factual issues. As A. Walton Litz notes in the introductory section to *The Scribner Quarto of Modern Literature*, 'part of the power of the short story has been its ability to assimilate many characteristics of the novel while maintaining a certain purity of form' (2). The stories in this anthology exhibit this virtue and more.

REFERENCES

Litz, A. Walton. Ed. *The Scribner Quarto of Modern Literature*. Charles Scribner's Sons. 1978.

Pourjafari, Fatemeh and Abdolali Vahidpour. 'Migration Literature: A Theoretical Perspective'.in *The Dawn Journal*. vol. 3, no. 1, January–June 2014. https://thedawnjournal.in/wp-content/uploads/2013/12/2-Fatemeh-Pourjafari.pdf

ELIZABETH ONOGWU
University of Nigeria
Nsukka, Nigeria

Reviews **209**

Yaw Agawu-kakraba , *The Restless Crucible*
Lemont, Berlin, Mt.Nittany Press, 2022. Paperback, 342 pages. ISBN 978-1-63233-328-5

The Restless Crucible re-enacts the narrative of the Transatlantic Slave Trade and slavery that happened in parts of West Africa and Brazil during the eighteenth century. The novel is in two parts and revolves around the central character, Pedro de Barbosa, and a major character, Queen Ena Sunu. Part I focuses on the passage of Pedro from innocence to experience through his tortuous childhood and adolescent experiences. These experiences are represented as convoluted choices and engagements that he must as a matter of necessity take in order to truly live and thrive in a world bereft of any moral compass.

Part II captures Queen Ena Sunu's childhood days and the contribution of her environment in shaping her mindset and launching her into her campaign against gender inequality and the slave trade. This part then connects the careers of Pedro de Barbosa, a slave dealer, and Queen Ena Sunu, an advocate of human freedom, and examines how they strategize to achieve their different goals.

A popular adage has it that 'The same boiling water that softens the potato hardens the egg. It's not the circumstances; it's what you are made of.' Pedro de Barbosa's experience of slavery and racial discrimination make him categorize humans into two groups: the oppressor and the oppressed. In order to escape being oppressed, he must strive to join the league of the oppressors at all costs. His observations of the Catholic Church's endorsement of racial discrimination and hypocrisy through its involvement in the slave trade erode Pedro's regard for the church and any form of moral considerations in his search for freedom and power. Therefore, to attain the position of a *senhor,* he blends together blackmailing, double-dealing, murder, physical strength, diplomacy, spying, and intelligence to earn the political and economic power that qualify him to become a slave dealer. Through his activities and those of other slave dealers, the text reveals the tensions, intrigue, and power-play that go into the gaining and entrenchment of political power.

While Pedro de Barbosa's fight for independence and freedom is self-centred, Queen Ena Sunu's outlook is selfless. She observes that a majority of the important decisions in her life and in the lives of other women are made by the men in their lives, and interrogates this unequal treatment of women. As the wife of King Gesa, she is offered as a kola to her husband's guest, Prince Dozan, from another kingdom. 'You must regard yourself as lucky the king chose you to share the Dahomey people's property with the Quidah Kingdom' (195). 'So that

210 *Reviews*

was who she was! A piece of property, Queen Ena Sunu thought. Hers was a body they hauled away without her approval, as her father had done' (195). She equally frowns at the law forbidding female soldiers from marrying or having sexual partners, while their male counterparts enjoy the pleasure of intimacy and family friendship and bonding. She dismantles this unfair treatment with the assistance of the female military leadership. In addition, through her alliance with the female military soldiers and her adult sons, she works to abolish slavery in her kingdom and in the surrounding kingdoms. It is her fight for the eradication of slavery that births her encounter with Pedro de Barbosa and the ultimate abolishment of slavery and the slave trade in her kingdom and in the surrounding kingdoms.

The text is relevant in today's world for numerous reasons. One, it suggests that interactions between the oppressive economic and political structures of societies and humans can lead to rebellions and many forms of violence that impede society's growth. Pedro's choice of perpetuating slavery and oppression arises out of the lack of better options at the initial stage. Two, the text observes that the road to independence and freedom is knotty and requires decisions and actions that lack moral considerations. Pedro's strategies and those of Queen Ena Sunu are the same. However, the difference lies in the end of one: enslavement, and the other: freedom and the abolition of slave trade.

Three, the text continues the conversations on gender inequality and racial discrimination, which consolidate difference at various levels and contribute massively to the tensions and war between various peoples, ethnic groups, and several nations to date. Finally, it draws attention to the challenge of modern day slavery in the world and how human beings still subtly consolidate structures that inflict physical and psychological pain on their fellow beings, regardless of the colossal evolution and development of human societies and various societies' claim of civilization. The novel is a must-read for all because of the diverse concerns that it raises, which will certainly resonate with people of all ages and cultures.

NONYE CHINYERE AHUMIBE
Imo State University
Nigeria

Reviews **211**

Kofi Anyidoho, *SeedTIME*
DAkpabli and Associates, 2022, Accra, 222 pages, 978-998-890-223-0

Reviewing *SeedTIME: Selected Poems I*, Kofi Anyidoho's latest collection of poems, is like walking down memory lane, a stroll through time and space in reverse order, re-engaging with familiar poetic narratives – from the mundane to the esoteric, from the temporal to the cosmic – about people and places, landmarks and lifetimes; about history, geography and politics; about despair and hope; about the human condition and, above all, about home and all the cultural and ancestral memories they carry. These memories and the voices we hear span half a century but are still as vibrant and evocative as they were distilled into an impressive and timeless repertory of poems, songs and dance-drama in the beginning of time, through a succession of collections, each with a unique thrust and literary craftsmanship, by a poet who, perhaps, needs no introduction.

SeedTIME is a compilation of selections of Anyidoho's poems from five of his collections: *Ancestral Logic & Caribbean Blues, Earth Child, A Harvest of Our Dreams, Elegy for the Revolution* and *Brain Surgery*. The volume offers the reader a one-stop opportunity to savour the selected poems from fresh perspectives and to relive the experiences and ideas that inspired their composition. What makes the reissue of these selections important is that the human memory is short, predisposed to induced or selective amnesia. Most Ghanaians, and followers of Ghana's political history, have taken for granted the country's present constitutional order and the musical chair dance of political actors since 1992. But, before the current 'calm', there was the 'storm' – the so-called 'revolutionary years'. *A Harvest of Our Dreams* and *Elegy for the Revolution* bring back those turbulent years, complete with the haunting, sarcastic and parodic images and metaphors that capture the period and jolt us into a new state of consciousness. 'Radio Revolution', a poem from *Elegy for the Revolution* (from the 'Soul in Birthwaters' sequence), unwinds the clock back to those days when our sleep would be stampeded and truncated by a brief serenade of martial music on Radio Ghana, followed by the roar of a military voice announcing the overthrow of a sitting government, military or civilian: 'Again this dawn our Radio/broke off the vital end of sleep... Revolution!... Devolution!... Resolution!' The same can be said of *Ancestral Logic & Caribbean Blues*, a collection that chronicles the multiple dimensions of the trans-Atlantic Slave Trade, the African Diaspora and its eternal and spiritual connections with continental

212 Reviews

Africa, and the celebration of Africa's survival spirit across history. In 'Havana Soul', the poet is overwhelmed by the sights and sounds that ignite his sense of African history in Cuba, a Caribbean island which Fidel Castro once described as 'part of Africa':

So I made the ultimate connection
Between two lifetimes set apart
By a final death of old mythologies...

Mythologies that set his memory 'ablaze with sparks and fireflies'. Thus, like wine, the older these poems and songs get, the more potent and relevant they are, and the more they connect us with our world and our place in it, in all its dynamism and cross-generational, cross-cultural and cross-linguistic configurations. By inference, even time cannot nudge these poems into oblivion, nor dim their appeal, as both message and art. This is reinforced by the fact that some of Anyidoho's poems, including some in *SeedTIME*, have been translated into many languages including French, Spanish, Italian, Chinese, Bengali, Korean, Slavonic, Turkish, Serbian, etc.; not to mention those captured on CD, or those brought to life from time to time through performative renditions in Ghana, Republic of Togo and across the world.

As one engages with the selected poems from one segment to another – from *Ancestral Logic* to *Brain Surgery* – the old Anyidoho the poet we know re-emerges with renewed vigour speaking to us, in even stronger cadences, through the same poetic mediums that have established him firmly on the world stage. In the same vein, the same old poems, like 'Agbenoxevi', 'Awoyo', 'Fertility Game', 'Earth Child', 'A Harvest of Our Dreams', 'Brain Surgery', 'Elegy for the Revolution', 'Mythmaker', 'SeedTime', 'Desert Storm' (a commentary on the US invasion of Iraq in 1992, and which also helps us to draw parallels between that event and today's Russia-Ukraine war) and 'Do not give too much of your love to me' and 'They Hunt the Night' (which have been West African Examinations Council (WAEC) selected poems for secondary schools for a number of years), and others, take on fresh urgency and provoke in the reader the same sensibilities that have drawn us to the poet and his works over the years.

SeedTIME also opens our eyes to certain issues that have characterized our appreciation of writers and their works in mainstream society and institutions, particularly condescending attitudes to the creative and performing arts. In his author's note, Anyidoho recalls how, against formidable hurdles, he had to combine producing creative works with the high demands of his core occupation as a scholar, researcher and

Reviews **213**

lecturer to earn upward mobility in academia. He laments the 'kind of devious academic bias against creative excellence in such disciplines as poetry, music, dance, and drama', which he contends 'is still a cherished tradition in our institutions of "higher learning"'. However, the redeeming grace in all this is that:

> Fortunately, though, the creative impulse is something of an incurable gift. Whether appreciated and rewarded or ignored and vilified, it does not easily disappear or despair. That's why I will always regret the many poems I could have written but never did because I was too busy writing academic papers. It is why I am relieved that no matter how long my occupation as a scholar takes me away to conferences and peer reviewed journals, **I will always come back to my preoccupation as a poet, as a singer. You cannot take song away from the singer or the singer away from the song** (my emphasis).

These emphatic and defiant statements by the poet undergird the putting together of his many poems in English, Ewe and those in translation in other world languages, which, thankfully, have been condensed into *SeedTIME*.

From all indications, *SeedTIME* is designed to be part of a series. This is only the first volume. We cannot wait for the sequels. Although the poet has acknowledged publishers he has worked with over the years, I must add that the contribution of the publishers of *SeedTIME*, DAkpabli and Associates, to this volume of Anyidoho's poems cannot be overstated. The poems are cast in reader-friendly font size and style and attractively typeset on off-white paper. The book cover, featuring a seed sprouting from rich brown earth against a green background, reminds us of Chinua Achebe's *Morning Yet on Creation Day* – that, it is only 'seed time' yet.

MAWULI ADJEI
University of Ghana
Legon, Ghana

214 *Reviews*

Isidore Diala, *The Truce*
Isidore Diala, Krafts Books Limited, Ibadan, Oyo State, Nigeria. 2003, 109 pages, ISBN: 978-978-918-782-9.

The Truce is a 2023-published dramatic text written by Isidore Dial,a who is a well-known name in Nigeria's literary sphere. The play is published by Kraft Books Limited, Ibadan, Nigeria, and it is set in South East Nigeria. *The Truce*, written in three parts, portrays the life of Alozie, a cobbler with a haunting past. The narrative unfolds in his shop, 'The Foot Artist At Work', where three apprentices: Ajuzie, Iheme, and Eke work with him. Alozie shares his reason for hiring them, including Eke's ambition to create powerful football boots. As the story progresses, a play within a play evolves to enhance its narrative flow and creativity, focusing on Alozie's life and his connection with George, a student who becomes a son-like figure. The play mirrors Alozie's tragedy, with themes of lost love, betrayal, and the scars of war. Alozie's emotional journey culminates in a tragic ending, symbolizing the weight of his past. *The Truce* is an emotionally powerful play, a thought-provoking, striking and effective work.

From a synoptic presentation, it is easy to gloss over the significance of the play, especially in the context of Nigeria's twisted matrix and chequered historicity. However, an X-ray of the style, themes, subtext, and symbolism arouses curiosity with the discourse of the consequences of war and post-war violence. In terms of style, the play is written from the African total theatre form parading a rich display of indigenous songs, dance, nuances and play-within-a-play. In a sense his style is similar to that of Esiaba Irobi, winner of the 2010 NNLG Prize for Drama. In fact, the style of *The Truce* resonates with Irobi's plays such as *Hangmen also Die*, *Nwokedi*, and even *Cemetery Road,* In addition, the form of tragedy in *The Truce* is underpinned not necessarily by the mere fact that the play ends on a tragic note; rather, the tragedy is deepened by the messianic intimations, the anguish and the sense of loss and pain that the tragic hero Alozie evinces.

One of the themes in the play includes scars of war: The impact of war always manifests in one way or another. In the play the scars of war/postwar are evident through Alozie's limp and emotional thorns. *The Truce* also represents a fleeting respite from conflict, highlighting the fragile nature of peace. Ironically, as Alozie puts it, '…The foot injury was sustained when it was said the war has ended' (p.19). Loss and grief is another theme in the play. Alozie's mourning for his wife, Ekemma, and later, the loss of George, reflects the profound grief that can shape a person's life. Alozie's simile description of his affinity with George indi-

Reviews **215**

cates the extent of his grief: 'Maybe you are right about cultists. But you are wrong in this case. I knew the young man, George, well enough. He was like a son to me. He just took to me one of those mysterious experiences you can't for your life find sufficient explanation for.' (p.47). And about his wife, he laments that '… I returned home with the burden that my wife was dead. Ekemma was dead…' (p.19).

The theme of betrayal stands out as key in the play, especially in the manner in which it instigates the subplot. Betrayal is ubiquitous and has dominated human society and relationships from prehistorical times to the present. Alozie's friend Arugo's betrayal and subsequent guilt underscore the complexities of human relationships and the bleak potential for redemption. Arugo's weak explanation only adds salt to the injury: 'Her death was completely an accident. I couldn't possibly raise a hand against a woman I could have given my life for…' (p.97).

Another theme worth mentioning is symbolism. Here two elements stand out: the shoe and the sun. In the case of the shoe, the meaning stems from how Alozie describes it: 'The human feet are the pedestal of human dignity and cannot be trifled with. You are either born to this art or you find your true calling… our feet are sovereign by their willingness to bear the burden meant for the fore limbs' (p.25). Alozie also attaches some sort of messianic powers to the shoe when he compares the washing of his clients' feet to that of Jesus washing his disciples feet in the Bible – 'if I can't intervene in the matters of the soul, at least I can strive to tend to soles. Beside, I like to feel the contours of the feet I make shoes for in order to anticipate the pinch the foot feels – and eliminate it' (p.31). In addition, the shoe could also symbolise Abia state in Nigeria, which is known for making shoes, popularly called 'Aba shoes'. But even more poignant is the idea, as suggested in the blurb by Dan Izevbaye, that these images could well be a reference to soldiers and the Nigerian civil war.

The other element of symbolism is the sun. Here it could be a symbol of Biafra in the south-eastern part of Nigeria, since Biafra's logo is the image of a rising sun. In the play, Eke, who wants to learn the ritual incantation of shoe making, asks Alozie to teach him because he remembered Toronto, for whom Alozie made a football boot with the symbol of the sun on it: 'those who know about such things say you made his boots when the sun shone brightest and tidies it up under the full moon… But the same symbol has been seen on the pair of shoes Honourable Kaduru wore on the day he won the election into the senate. It is equally on the pair of shoes pastor Kamalu wears during his monthly anointing service.' (pp. 34–35). The sun is said to have mighty powers that brings victory to whoever has it on their shoes.

216   *Reviews*

At the level of subtext, the meaning of the play is multidimensional. Although the playwright has advised that there is no need to pay attention to his notes, it is worthy to observe here that an author's note points to his/her authorial ideology, which, as Terry Eagleton argues, can sometimes go against the general and or regional ideology of the state. Diala alludes to the civil war or 'genocide'. As he puts it: 'The *Truce* could be easily set in any human society where the survivors of a holocaust are compelled to relive daily the injustices that culminated in the initial genocidal war.' This is a clear reference to the Nigerian civil war, which has been described by many as genocide. Coming out in 2023, the meaning of the play cannot be lost on anyone who is aware of the siege on South East Nigeria before, during and even after the 2023 general elections, especially the 'Operation Python Dance', which prompted the attacks by some regiments of Nigerian soldiers on the compound of Nnamdi Kalu, the acclaimed leader of 'Independent People of Biafra' (IPOB) So, in the end, the play begs the question: what and whose truce is the playwright after? Is it that of the South East zone, Igbos or Nigeria?

As for the significance of the play in this perspective, there are few gaps that stare one in the face, and they are worth mentioning. First is the mere fact that the play is lacking in ethnic diversity. All the characters in the play are Igbos. Is the playwright saying that only Igbos live in South East Nigeria? Second is the fact that women play an insignificant role in the play. Is the playwright implying that women are not relevant in the scheme of events in South East Nigeria? Third is the death of Ekemma, which raises a lot of questions that are never resolved. However, *The Truce* is a brilliant text, blunt, clear and compelling; it captures the challenges of South East Nigeria in turbulent historical moments with lingering issues.

IRENE ISOKEN AGUNLOYE
University of Jos
Nigeria

Reviews **217**

Irene Isoken Agunloye, *Disposable Womb*
Kraft Books Limited, Ibadan, Nigeria, 2022, 80 pages, ISBN: 978-978-918-799-7

Disposable Womb is a play that unfolds fundamental twists in the lives of two prominent female characters who are bonded to each other by a fate that could easily be inverted. Zona is Yuwa's niece. Their lives begin with bright prospects: Yuwa is married to her loving husband, Robosa, and Zona is the second daughter of Idah, a professor, and Mina, a gynaecologist. She is very delightful and promising and a source of pride for her parents. Shortly after her international passport is received with the visa for her to leave for tertiary education outside Nigeria, events turn around, and it is discovered that she is pregnant. That could be a watershed in her life, but the complications that emerge from that development give credence to the currency of the major concerns of the play. She had a casual intimate time with a young man, Nosa, whom she hardly knew. Unfortunately, Nosa is deeply involved in the baby-production/sale business, which operates in a remote forest. On the other hand, Yuwa is childless, even after 12 years of marriage.

Evidently, the life trajectory for both Zona and Yuwa has gone against their expectations as well as the expectations of their families. Yuwa is resented by her mother-in-law, Iro, because Yuwa is attempting to make 'the blood of… [Robosa's] ancestors to clot in his veins' (21). That's a metaphor for Yuwa's attempt at terminating the lineage due to childlessness. Incidentally, Robosa has never subjected himself to any medical examination through all the years that Yuwa has not got pregnant. As Sede, Robosa's sister, indicts both Robosa and their mother, Iro, for their resentful and callous treatment of Yuwa and is also the subject of their ire. Both mother and son throw out Yuwa's possessions from her marital home, and she inevitably leaves in shame.

Unfortunately for Yuwa, the time of her marital cataclysm is when her brother and family are also dealing with Zona's pregnancy debacle. The most harrowing aspect of the discovery of Zona's pregnancy is her disappearance. Apparently, from the family doctor's office, where her pregnant is confirmed, she goes to inform Nosa, and he abducts her, taking her to the baby factory in the thick forest. All the intensive efforts set up by Zona's parents with law enforcement agencies to find her are not yielding results as quickly as desired. Zona is among many other young pregnant girls who were abducted and brought to the forest. Her first attempt to escape fails, but the second attempt, along with Ede, another pregnant girl, succeeds. Incidentally, Zona goes into labour while navigating the forest for an exit, and Ede assists

218 *Reviews*

her to deliver the baby. Zona loses consciousness due to the stress of childbirth and trekking the long distance in tortuous terrains, and Nosa intercepts them, collects the baby, and returns to the baby factory location in the forest. However, the forest is quickly invaded by the police, who recover Zona's baby from Nosa. While chasing after Nosa, he begins to shoot at the policemen, and in a gun duel between the two parties, Nosa is shot dead. The police are able to convey Zona to the hospital for urgent medical attention.

During Yuwa's absence, Robosa has had the opportunity to undergo medical examinations and has realized that he is responsible for his and Yuwa's childlessness. Yet, his mother, Iro, continues to heap all the blame for her son's childless marriage on the wife, Yuwa.

Essentially, as Zona is revived and is reunited with her baby, who was recovered from Nosa, in a very emotionally fraught scenario, she hands over the baby to her aunt, Yuwa, and her husband 'to have and to keep' (74). The irony here is that Zona has a baby that she does not need, while her aunt, who desperately needs one, has none. Zona's parents are reunited with Zona, and Yuwa's husband and mother-in-law reunite with Yuwa, and all ends well.

It is interesting that Irene Agunloye recreates the themes of childlessness and procreation, while also introducing the contemporary menace of child trafficking, teenage pregnancies, illegitimate deals, etc. that have been plaguing the Nigerian socio-cultural space. The story of *Disposable Womb* is a prototype of the story of Nigeria. Nosa is a notoriously randy guy who deliberately gets young girls pregnant to initiate them into the baby factory to bear the babies to be sold off for high sums. He and his cohorts that get the girls pregnant, then abduct and keep them in seclusion and under strict control, are emblematic of the two major categories of youths in Nigeria: first, those who acquire a reasonable education but cannot find any employment and consequently turn to criminality as an act of revolt against the Nigerian system; second, those that are compelled into the business as a survival strategy and a *modus vivendi*.

Prominently, this play expounds on the motif of parallel plots as the stories of Zona and Yuwa run together. One of them records a major loss that leads up to the enormous gain of the other: because of Zona's untimely pregnancy, she loses the treasured opportunity of going abroad to study medicine. After the police rescue her from her abductors, and she regains consciousness in the hospital, she hands over her baby to Aunty Yuwa. This is significant because, though she has the possibility of continuing her studies, her aunt Yuwa does not have the prospect of getting pregnant when she is reconciled with Robosa, her

Reviews **219**

husband. The concept of parallel plots as handled by Ogunloye in *Disposable Womb* is creatively applied to show the travails of the two female characters, Zona and Yuwa, whose misfortunes are intertwined until the *dénouement* where their issues are carefully resolved.

Ogunloye meticulously deploys Pidgin English and slang expressions, which provide local colour to the play. The expressions used are consistent with the characters in the play. Odeh, Idah's family driver as well as Ivie, the widow in the play who owns the baby factory, speak Pidgin English, implying that while the former has had a limited education, the latter is a guileful woman who can do anything to get rich, and stay rich.

The 28 constituent sections of the play are described as Movements, and none depends on or is a sequel to the other. The Movements relate different aspects of the actions from Idah's house, to Robosa's house, to Dr Tosa's clinic, to Nosa's house, to Ivie's house, to the forest and the baby factory, to the hospital, and others. Importantly, Movement 1 comprises a detailed scene description of the theme of childlessness, or the elusive desire for and pursuit of procreation, thereby introducing the reader to the major concern of the play. It describes a scene in the forest where a newborn baby is wrapped in an old, threadbare covering; the baby is crying, and a man, a woman, and a nineteen-year-old girl from different ends of the forest emerge with outstretched hands to snatch the baby, all in vain. This Movement offers a graphic portrayal of the thrust of the actions in the play: the desire to pursue an elusive item, but none of the pursuers succeeds because of a specific personal flaw: Zona cannot leave for her studies abroad because of the unwanted pregnancy, and then her abduction; Robosa cannot get his wife, Yuwa, pregnant because of his infertility; and Yuwa cannot get pregnant because Robosa, her husband is infertile. The playwright resolves these complexities through Zona's gift of her baby to Yuwa and her husband. This is a unique method of resolving the convolution in the play.

The play has a Glossary in which the playwright lists all the Pidgin English and slang expressions, onomatopoeic expressions, mother-tongue expressions, etc., and scrupulously explains their meanings and contexts of usage. She interprets *waka waka* as a 'perambulator'; *ode* as 'fool'; *abi* as 'is that not so?'; *iye* as 'mother', and *ya tota!* as 'go and sit down!', etc.

However, Ogunloye's *Disposable Womb* suffers a lot of infelicities and editing challenges. A major one is the omission of Sede, Robosa's sister and Iro's daughter, from the cast list on page 5. Others are as presented below, with the correct item in square brackets beside the error:

220 *Reviews*

Page	Source	Speech
9	ROBOSA	Where is the barren women [woman]?
10	Scene description	...Iro begging them, robbing [rubbing] her palms together.
14	Character's name	MINAL [MINA]
19	MINA	No, not his [this] time dear.
32	Scene description	Uyi leaves. As IDAH and MINA prepares [prepare] to...
35	Scene description	Each of the men carry [carries] one of the girls.
35	Scene description	TAMA set [sets] herself loose...
39	IVIE	They all sat... ordered me to park [pack] out my things...
40	IVIE	No, you go upstairs... to park [pack] your things.
41	Scene description	She jumps up ...wailing and rolling on the ground [floor].
42	UYI	Daddy, please, go and find Zona.
46	EDE	Zona shouted... and that is [was] how that girl was rescued.
50	ZONA	Lets [Let's] take one step at a time.
52	POLICEMAN	...you should know his whereabout [whereabouts].
57	Scene description	She turns... and let [lets] out an offended cry.
60	Scene description	IDAH and YUWA leaves [leave].
66	Scene description	EDE occasionally sit [sits] on the ground.
68	ROBOSA	I don't care what your tradition say [says]...
68	Scene description	Mama tries... but SEDE put [puts] forward her hand...
69	Scene description	Slowly, he begin [begins] to speak.
70	ROBOSA	Her jaws goes [go] slack...

The above template indicates the enormity of slips in the play. That the slips pervade the whole of the play raises a lot of queries about the effective editing of the manuscript of this play. The errors not only impinge on the quality of the book, but can also mislead young, immature readers and performers. Obviously, this implies that there is an urgent need for a revision of this book as soon as possible so that the slips may be checked and corrected.

Finally, *Disposable Womb* is an essential read because of the currency of its themes and the style used by the playwright. In a subtle way, this play indicts the African culture that regards childlessness as a sin and an offence by the woman. The reversal in the play is typified by the fact that Robosa takes full blame for the childlessness of his marriage to Yuwa. It is important to note the symbolism in the title *Disposable Womb*. The content, being the baby, of the womb of each of the young pregnant girls is usually disposed of, and the young mother misses the benefits that should accrue to her from the discomfort of pregnancy, the truncation of her education, as in Zona's case, as well as the pains of pregnancy and childbirth, etc. That the babies the girls deliver are taken by Nosa and his associates for sale, demonstrates the girls' losses and the futility of all their efforts. Herein lies the signification of disposable womb.

INIOBONG UKO
University of Uyo
Nigeria

Iquo Diana-Abasi, *Coming Undone as Stiches Tighten*
Sevhage, Makurdi, Benue State. 2021, 131 pages, ISBN: 978-978-562656-8

Becoming Undone as Stiches Tighten (Becoming Undone) is a collection of 71 poems that are classified into four groups. The first group of poems is called The Staccato Verses, with 25 poems. The second group is titled A Necessary Word, with 12 poems; the third set of poems is called Love Amidst the Staccato, with 25 poems; and the last section is titled In Memoriam, with nine poems. Though each of the sections of this collection treats a distinct set of themes, it is evident that the dominant motif in the poems largely reflects the Nigerian situation: its values, travails, prevailing phenomena, and prospects. Diana-Abasi explores issues of insecurity in the poems in The Staccato Verses. In fact, the staccato symbolizes the sound of bullets, which is parodied by New Year's Day fireworks. This is significant because within that context,

222   *Reviews*

the focus of the poems moves from the micro to macro dimensions of insecurity. In the micro framework, the speaker undertakes a poignant depiction of the different traumatic consequences of the activities of Boko Haram. Boko Haram literally refers to the prohibition of Western education. The terror that its adherents unleash on persons and groups constitute statements of their dissatisfaction with the specific trend in both the society and government. They set out as clandestine groups, but have now assumed prominence and audacity in their heinous activities, which include rape, arson, truncation of education, dislocation, homelessness, reckless killings of innocent people, kidnapping, and deliberate destruction of the spirit.

The poems in this section of Diana-Abasi's *Becoming Undone* reflect intense pains – physical, psychological, emotional, and spiritual. The imagery of 'staccato' coheres with gunshots, which truncate education and interrupt learning, and cause children to be orphaned, and hundreds of school girls to be kidnapped; others are raped, and unwanted pregnancies become a plague among the people, babies are born with Boko Haram gene. For the lead poem to be titled 'The Staccato was no Gunshot', Diana-Abasi makes a subtle distinction between the gunshots of fireworks, which are for aesthetics, creativity and entertainment, on one side, and those that are for destruction, on the other side. This dissimilarity sets the tone for the appreciation of the poems in this collection.

The poems also refer to the #End SARS movement, which was a decentralized concept that arose in 2020 when Nigerian youths protested the indiscriminate shootings/killings, assaults and harassments by personnel of SARS (Special Anti-Robbery Squad), a detachment of the Nigeria Police. The protests sought an end to police brutality and extrajudicial killings that were (and still are) prevalent in Nigeria. The gunshot motif is perceived in the poems from the activities of members of atrocious Boko Haram, the personnel of Nigeria Police, as well as the pain, trauma, and hopelessness that are outcomes of the staccato. These are encapsulated in the poems, typified by the one titled, 'Pain Fingers my Inside'. The personification aptly captures the reality where pain has assumed control of the persona's viscera, and that spells doom. That is actually what Nigeria represents.

The second section, titled *A Necessary Word*, comprises 12 poems that portray hope. It is interesting to note the shift of focus from the trauma that the poems in the first section of the collection generated to the spirit of expectancy and optimism. Significantly, many of the poems

Reviews **223**

in this section treat the female question. The lead poem, 'Calabash' is a symbol of African/Nigerian womanhood. It has undertones of female violation, sexual assault, and destructive female stereotypes. Within the context of hopefulness, the poet refers to credible and identifiable female legends as a way of motivating contemporary girls/women to aspire to make positive impact on their societies. They female legends include Moremi, Amina of Zazau, Margaret Ekpo, Funmilayo Ransom Kuti and Dora Akunyili. She also urges contemporary female Nigerians to strive to be self-sustaining, and surmount the limitations of traditions and patriarchy. The poems also address the theme of procreation, and highlight the central relevance of childbearing in African cosmology. The poem 'That Bottle of Water' is about a mother's interactions with her newly married daughter. It reveals the values that the mother wishes to inculcate in the daughter as the latter goes into marriage. The place of women in the family and society is given prominence in this section, and Diana-Abasi demonstrates her perception of the contemporary African/Nigerian women, their roles, the societal expectations, the common female stereotypes and how the women can get to transcend them, etc.

The third section, titled Love Amidst the Staccato comprises 25 poems, which treat natural circumstances vis-à-vis Nigerian peculiarities. The issues addressed in the poems deploy symbols to make the point about the uncertainties in life, the failure of Nigerian infrastructure, the culture of wastage, the value and disvalue of human life, the essence of contentment, sincere love and affection, reunion, companionship, the evil of betrayal, the inevitability of the natural cycle of sleep-and-wake, as well as the unreliability of human nature. Other concerns that the poems address are fraud and poor leadership in Nigeria.

Specifically, in 'Answers that will not be Swallowed', the poet reflects with scorn on the 2018 scandalous incident of a sales clerk in the office of the tertiary institutions' admission agency in Nigeria, the Joint Admissions and Matriculation Board (JAMB), Benue State, who told auditors that a snake swallowed up 36 million naira (₦36,000,000) that was missing from the agency's coffers! In 'Ephemeral star', the speaker derides the agency that provides public power in Nigeria called the Power Holding Company of Nigeria (PHCN). Comparing PHCN with a star that is described as ephemeral, the speaker notes that even the star with its ephemeral nature, is far more reliable than PHCN. This is a clear pointer to the ineptitude of the service providers,

224 *Reviews*

the insensitivity of the government, as well as the disappointment and hopelessness of the people.

The last section of the collection, titled In Memoriam, is composed of nine poems. As the title indicates, the poems are in honour of deceased persons who must have been of significance to the poet. She celebrates the lives of persons who were special to her. There are two poems in honour of Pius Adesanmi, viz., 'When an Iroko falls', (which she describes as '…in lieu of a wreath' for him), and 'You lived'. 'Metaphor woman' aims to celebrate Nike Adesuyi-Ojeikere; 'Our conversation has been silenced' immortalizes Austyn Njoku; and there are a few anonymous ones, including 'Upon encountering a mob', which captures the murder that results from a mob attack, a scenario of lynching that takes place because of misplaced identification, with no verification of the subject that is accused. Essentially, for the renowned personalities that the poet highlights – Pius Adesanmi, Austyn Njoku, and Nike Adesuyi-Ojeikere – it may be relevant to briefly introduce them. Adesanmi was a cerebral Nigerian-Canadian scholar, who died on 10 March2019, aboard an Ethiopian Airlines flight 302 that crashed after take-off from Addis Ababa heading to Nairobi. Adesuyi-Ojeikere was a Nigerian poet. She died in 2016. And Austyn Njoku (Augustine Njoku Obi) was a Nigerian Professor of Virology and former President of the Nigerian Academy of Science. Born in 1930, Professor Njoku was renowned for developing a cholera vaccine that was endorsed in 1971 by the World Health Organization as efficacious. He died in 2003.

In spite of all the above, it is pertinent to highlight some improprieties in the book. The initial pages – from the Dedication through Acknowledgements to Contents – should bear Roman numerals rather than having no pagination. There should also be a glossary to explain non-English words and terminologies. Generally, non-English words and terminologies, like 'Nwa m nọ Amerịka' should be in italics. There are several concepts that are typically Nigerian in the poems, and require some background information for non-Nigerians to fully comprehend the import of the message in each of the poems. Those include the reference to #EndSARS, Odi emergency, 36 million, Boko Haram, the snake's loot, etc. in 'Answers that will not be swallowed' on page 10; Chibok (girls and kidnapping) in 'Full frontal' on page 27, and 'SM withdrawal' on page 72; the stigmas on Yoruba and Igbo people of Nigeria in 'Love wears many faces' on pages 30 and 31; 'Beef boycott' on page 36; Oloibiri and Ogoni on page 47 in 'We did not inherit her'; PHCN in 'Ephemeral star' on page 80; local spices –

Reviews   **225**

adusa, uyayak, ntung and the local fish Inagha (should all be in italics) in 'In the absence of Inagha' on page 110; Pius Adesanmi in 'When an Iroko falls' on page 115; as well as ojuju in 'Farewell' on page 118.

In conclusion, in spite of the deep sense of loss in the poems in In Memoriam, and the annihilation and ruination that are constituting motifs in The Staccato Verses, A Necessary Word, and Love Amidst the Staccato, Iquo DianaAbasi's Coming Undone expounds values of intrinsic hope. The poet portrays hope as an integral aspect of the negative and largely irremediable experiences of the Nigerian masses, who have been reduced to pauperization especially due to sequential defective leadership, and a proliferation of reprobate and unscrupulous politicians. There is a dominance of familiarity of context and setting in the poems, and these make contributions to meaning, and subsequently, on nation-building. Recognizing the multiplicity of ethnic groups, languages, religious inclinations, etc. in Nigeria, DianaAbasi expresses the exegesis of the didactic significance of the issues in the poems, and their implications for national unity, reconciliation, and social cohesion. In the contextual delineation of landscape, concepts and personalities, the poet is audacious to deploy real names of persons and locations, as she makes references to actual events as they occurred in different locations and times in Nigeria.

In many of the poems, the poet subtly laments the ironic reality of Nigeria that is enormously blessed by Providence with natural resources, but which have not been harnessed for the benefit of the masses. She indicates that this is why the bane of Nigeria's economic recession, inflation, insecurity, and weak and deficient infrastructure is successive warped government. Here in lies the essence of the title of the collection, Coming Undone as Stitches Tighten.

INIOBONG UKO
University of Uyo
Nigeria

Printed in the United States
by Baker & Taylor Publisher Services